the newly qualified teacher's *handbook*

Elizabeth Holmes

**KOGAN
PAGE**

For my parents, Dorothy and Tony

First published in Great Britain and the United States in 2003 by Kogan Page Limited

Apart from any fair dealing for the purposes of research or private study, or criticism or review, as permitted under the Copyright, Designs and Patents Act 1988, this publication may only be reproduced, stored or transmitted, in any form or by any means, with the prior permission in writing of the publishers, or in the case of reprographic reproduction in accordance with the terms and licences issued by the CLA. Enquiries concerning reproduction outside these terms should be sent to the publishers at the undermentioned addresses:

120 Pentonville Road
London N1 9JN
UK
www.kogan-page.co.uk

22883 Quicksilver Drive
Sterling VA 20166–2012
USA

© Elizabeth Holmes, 2003

The right of Elizabeth Holmes to be identified as the author of this work has been asserted by her in accordance with the Copyright, Designs and Patents Act 1988.

British Library Cataloguing in Publication Data

A CIP record for this book is available from the British Library.

ISBN 0 7494 3857 6

Typeset by JS Typesetting Ltd, Wellingborough, Northants
Printed and bound in Great Britain by Clays Ltd, St Ives plc

Contents

Acknowledgements

This book could not have been written without the input of the many people who freely offered time, ideas, support and encouragement. In particular, I would like to thank:

- Charlotte Howard of Fox and Howard Literary Agency;
- Jonathan Simpson and the Kogan Page team;
- Emma Martin and The Stationery Office team involved with the first two editions of this book;
- all those at the Teacher Training Agency past and present who responded to my many enquiries, especially Martin Dore, Gordon Griffiths and Andy Bate;
- the staff of the Department for Education and Skills, especially Darren Davison;
- Annabelle Chalker and her colleagues at the General Teaching Council for England;
- Jo Kenny at HMSO Licensing and Permissions;
- the ever-growing group of NQTs, teachers and induction tutors who contribute ideas and respond to my questions;
- the teaching unions and professional associations, all of which contributed information;
- the many education authority staff who offered insights into local practice;
- my parents and David, Carolyn, Kevin and Maisie.

Introduction

Rewarding and stimulating as it can be, teaching is an extremely complex career requiring high-level expertise in many skills areas. It is also a profession in which the nation is permanently interested, and of which seemingly increasing levels of accountability are demanded. You only have to glance at a newspaper or listen to the news to see how frequently education issues are, sometimes inaccurately, discussed. Add to this the pace of change in education, and you could easily find yourself confused, however satisfying your job is.

The purpose of *The Newly Qualified Teacher's Handbook* is to provide newly qualified teachers (NQTs) in primary and secondary schools, as well as those considering a return to teaching and supply teachers, with a valuable resource for their first few years in the profession. It includes ideas on easing your way into your new career and draws from the Standards for the Award of Qualified Teacher Status, the Induction Standards and OFSTED guidance, as well as dealing with the other needs of new teachers, such as finding a job, how to deal with work-related stress and union membership, to name a few.

Keeping up with the latest developments in a profession such as teaching can be a challenge. Working as a teacher requires that you be familiar with a wide variety of laws, circulars and guidance, strategies and initiatives, not to mention the latest curriculum and requirements of Qualified Teacher Status (QTS). All of these aspects of teaching in England necessarily develop as time passes and, for this reason, *The Newly Qualified Teacher's Handbook* has been thoroughly updated since the first two editions were published by The Stationery Office in 1999 and 2000 respectively.

Some teachers experience teaching as a relatively lonely career, with many NQTs feeling that they must cope with the job alone. This book is designed to help you accept that you don't have to muddle through – that there are lines of support that you can follow and lean on. Your first few years of teaching should not be about 'getting through' induction and surviving the profession; surviving is only a marginal improvement on barely existing, and no one can teach effectively under those circumstances. Your induction year is about building on your sense of security in your job, as well as developing and encouraging enjoyment of it.

The Newly Qualified Teacher's Handbook is not an academic textbook, relying heavily on teaching and learning theory. It doesn't attempt to tell you how to teach – a skill that you will continue to perfect throughout your career – and neither is it a digest of academic papers and texts. It does, however, seek to draw together good practice and a heavy dose of common sense in an easily accessed way. It is a practical, functional guide for everyday use – for you to reach for and dip into whenever you need an idea, support or inspiration. It seeks to enable rather than preach, to help you guard against misinformation and dogma and to encourage you to develop your own ideas about the best way of managing your job with integrity.

The following features have been used in the book:

- *Checklists.* For ease of information retrieval, many hints have been organized into lists. It is not intended that you should follow each list slavishly; rather use them as a springboard for your own ideas. They are designed to be a time-saving device for you. Simply dip in, select the information you need, and go.
- *Action features.* These have not been written around hypothetical issues, requiring you to spend time on hypothetical answers. Rather, they are intended to draw from your own wealth of resources for problem solving. Again, there is no need to work through them systematically.
- *Example features.* All of the examples have been drawn from the real experiences of teachers, although some of the names have been changed. They have been included to illustrate points in the text, and some deal with relatively unusual situations.
- *About boxes.* These boxes contain succinct information covering the many issues and situations that face new teachers.

No book is perfect, and there are bound to be comments and ideas that you, as an NQT, would wish to make about the material presented here. If you would like to make your thoughts known, then you can e-mail me at: eh@elizabethholmes.co.uk. Feedback from trainees, trainers, induction tutors, headteachers, returners and NQTs themselves inspired many of the improvements that have been made in this edition and there is no doubt that this has contributed to the evolutionary nature of this book.

Should any of the information presented here become obsolete during the life of this book, updates will be posted at www.elizabethholmes.co.uk.

Finally, I offer my good wishes to all of you working through your induction and your first few years of teaching, and sincerely hope that *The Newly Qualified Teacher's Handbook* will be an important companion, helping you to find your job valuable, rewarding, exciting and, at times, exhilarating.

PART I

Getting a job

CHAPTER I

Location, location, location – where do you want to teach?

Completing your initial teacher-training (ITT) course leaves you with many decisions to make. You have to decide not only whether you would like to continue your teaching career in education but, also, in which type of school you would like to work – independent or state, community or voluntary-aided, mixed or single-sex, inner-city or rural. You may even decide you would prefer to work in a profession related to teaching.

Rather than falling into the first vacancy that comes your way, it is worth considering all the options available to you. What kinds of experience do you want to gain? Do you want to consolidate your training in a school similar to, or the same as, your teaching practice school? Are you eager for a complete change?

JOINING THE MAINSTREAM

By far the largest percentage of all schools falls into the category of mainstream education, including state and independent schools, voluntary-aided schools and colleges of further education.

The independents

Independent schools vary in size and ethos just as much as maintained schools do. There are currently 2,400 independent schools in the UK, with 600,000 pupils between them. They invariably involve the payment of fees, although the parental burden can vary tremendously as some children will be eligible for bursaries, scholarships and sponsorships. They do not come under the guidance of a local education authority (LEA) and are free to develop the curriculum and teaching styles as they see fit. That said, most do use the National Curriculum as a framework and offer the opportunity for pupils to prepare for and take national qualifications. In direct contrast to the state system, the headteacher of an independent school usually has the final say over the way in which the school is run, with a board of governors adopting an advisory and ratifying role.

ABOUT THE INDEPENDENT SCHOOLS COUNCIL

The Independent Schools Council (ISC) brings together the eight independent schools' associations in a single unified organization. It serves to promote independent schools' common interests as well as having overall responsibility for the Independent Schools Inspectorate (ISI), which works under a framework agreed with the Office for Standards in Education (OFSTED). ISC schools undergo inspection every six years, and the ISI also ensures that the legal standards required to remain registered with the Department for Education and Skills (DfES) are met. (See Appendix 8 for contact details.)

For the teacher, working in an independent school is a different experience from working in a maintained school. Although, in both kinds of establishment, an educational package is being offered to parents and pupils, in the independent sector market forces do seem to play a more central role. Naturally, when parents are choosing which product to buy, they are going to be conscious of the quality of education on offer. This can create a culture of exceptionally high expectations being placed on teachers by:

- the school management (wanting to keep the standards high enough to attract more clients);
- the parents (who are aware of value for their money);
- the pupils (who often understand their relatively powerful position at the centre of these dynamics).

Interestingly, the ISC reports that more than half of children now entering independent schools have parents who were educated in maintained schools. The ISC also reports that mobility between independent and maintained schools is very common among teachers.

If you do decide to apply for a job in the independent sector, be aware that pay and conditions of service vary throughout the sector. You may be eligible for additional pay as a member of house or pastoral staff in a boarding school, for example.

Seek answers to these questions before accepting an offer of a teaching post at an independent school:

- Will you be able to serve a statutory induction period at this school?
- Does the school adopt the same pay spine as the maintained sector?
- Is your contract comparable to one you would receive in the maintained sector?
- Under what circumstances could your contract be terminated?
- What are the arrangements for your pension?
- What expectations will be made of you in terms of extra-curricular activities?

ABOUT SERVING AN INDUCTION PERIOD IN AN INDEPENDENT SCHOOL

It is possible to serve an induction period in an independent school, but only under the following conditions:

- if there are primary pupils at the school, the primary curriculum meets National Curriculum requirements;
- if you are employed to teach pupils at key stages 3 and 4, the curriculum must include all the core and foundation subjects that you are employed to teach;
- there must be an agreement between the school and either the LEA or the Independent Schools Council Teacher Induction Panel (ISCTIP) that they will act as the appropriate body (see Chapter 5) before the start of your induction period).

It is not a requirement of law that NQTs in independent schools serve an induction period, but the ISC strongly recommends that new teachers complete their induction so that they may have the opportunity to work in maintained schools and register with the General Teaching Council in the future.

If you are employed by an independent school and will be serving an induction period, be sure that your school registers you with the ISCTIP as soon as you take up your appointment. You can get further information on serving your induction period in an independent school from the ISCTIP on 020 8886 4369.

Teaching in independent schools

Pros are:

- Misbehaviour is generally less common.
- Class sizes are considerably smaller than in most maintained schools.
- Parental support for the school can be greater.
- Independent schools can sometimes offer a wider variety of subjects, which may suit your interests.
- An anti-staff subculture is relatively uncommon.
- Holidays are longer in an independent school.

Cons are:

- You may not be able to serve an induction period.
- Teachers can be expected to perform duties outside the teaching day, eg sports training, clubs etc.
- Independent schools are exclusive on the grounds of the fees payable.
- You may not be paid on the same scale as your maintained colleagues.
- The pension arrangements may be down to you.
- It can prove difficult to move from the independent sector into the state sector.

ABOUT WORKING IN A BOARDING SCHOOL

Boarding schools are unique educational establishments in that all staff can find themselves playing the roles of mother, father, teacher and guardian. Certainly during term-time, teachers at boarding schools are fully immersed in the life of the school (which extends way beyond the usual teaching day) and may even be required to live on site. Working in a well-run boarding school can be like working within a commune, the intensity of which may be balanced by the unusually long holidays.

Vacancies for jobs in independent schools are advertised in the educational press and on Internet recruitment sites. Gabbitas Educational Consultants (see Appendix 8 for contact details) recruits at all levels on behalf of independent schools both at home and abroad.

Maintained schools

As an NQT, you need to be aware of which institutions can provide an induction period (see Chapter 5). It is also important to be aware of whether the school you join is maintained by the LEA, or is a voluntary-aided/foundation school (with the governing body as the employer).

ABOUT WHERE YOU CAN COMPLETE AN INDUCTION PERIOD

You can complete your induction period in the following:

- maintained schools;
- non-maintained special schools;
- sixth form colleges where the LEA acts as the appropriate body;
- independent schools (under certain circumstances).

These schools cannot provide induction:

- pupil referral units;
- schools requiring special measures (unless certain circumstances apply);
- independent schools that do not meet the relevant conditions.

Community schools
These are state schools maintained by the LEA, which is also the employer of the teachers. There are community special schools.

Voluntary-aided schools
These are state schools maintained by the LEA and aided by another body, usually a church or diocese. A foundation (often religious) appoints most of the governing body, which is responsible for all aspects of the working of the school, including the appointment of staff and dealing with complaints and grievances; it is the contractual employer.

Voluntary-controlled schools
These are state schools that are funded by another body such as a church or diocese and aided by the LEA. In reality, the LEA often has very little input in these schools.

Foundation schools

Some of the schools that were previously grant-maintained are now run as foundation schools. This is very close to the way in which voluntary-aided schools are run now. The governing body is the contractual employer and control is held by the governors and not by the LEA. There are also foundation special schools.

City technology colleges

City technology colleges are specialist colleges that receive extra funding from the state.

Community special schools

Community special schools are state schools for pupils with special educational needs (SEN).

Non-maintained special schools

Non-maintained special schools are state SEN schools where funding comes from somewhere other than the LEA.

Pupil referral units

Pupil referral units are established for pupils who have been excluded from mainstream schools.

Considerations

Faith schools

While all schools have to have an element of spiritual teaching, joining a faith school carries specific obligations on the part of the teacher. You will usually be expected to at least respect, if not live according to, the doctrines and tenets that the school represents and, as with most religions, degrees of tolerance vary.

According to the Schools Register, there are currently faith schools in England of the following denominations:

- Church of England;
- Roman Catholic;
- Methodist;
- Jewish;
- Muslim;
- Seventh Day Adventist;

- United Reformed Church;
- Quaker;
- Congregational Church;
- Free Church;
- Sikh;
- Greek.

Special schools

It is possible to gain employment in a special school for your first post, and if you are sure that this type of teaching is for you then all is well. However, it is often a good idea to consolidate your experience in mainstream-ability ranges first, before specializing. You can use this time to become involved in SEN at your school and gather skills and experience.

Post-16 colleges

These are very tempting for those with a real love of their subject. However, do think about how committed you are to this age range, because it could be difficult to adjust to secondary level once you have worked with the 16–19s, should you subsequently decide to work in a school. Another consideration is that post-16 colleges receive their funding from the Further Education Funding Council and are totally independent of the LEA. Many require staff members to teach evening classes as well and the salary you can expect may be slightly lower than that of an NQT teaching in a school.

Single-sex schools

Opinion about single-sex education seems to change with great frequency, as do ideas on the merits of working in such a school. Girls' schools are very different places from boys' schools and it would be worth spending a few days observing in each to assess whether single-sex teaching is for you. You may also like to consider the fact that you are likely to be in the minority if you teach in a single-sex school of the opposite sex to your own.

Specialist schools

These are schools offering particular expertise in one of four areas: technology, languages, sports or the arts. They receive extra funding and some offer special classes to challenge the brightest pupils. If your particular interest falls under one of the above headings, it could be rewarding working in a specialist school.

ABOUT INVESTORS IN PEOPLE

Some schools are Investors in People (IiP) schools, meaning that they use the IiP framework to meet national standards. This framework helps schools to manage all they must do and achieve as well as any additional activities they choose to do. The core purpose of the IiP Standard is to support the development of staff so that the performance of the school improves.

The IiP Standard has four principles:

- Commitment – an Investor in People is fully committed to developing its people in order to achieve its aims and objectives.
- Planning – an Investor in People is clear about its aims and its objectives and what its people need to do to achieve them.
- Action – an Investor in People develops its people effectively in order to improve performance.
- Evaluation – an Investor in People understands the impact of its investment in people on its performance.

These principles are supported by indicators and examples of evidence that would show that they are being met.

ALTERNATIVE AND PROGRESSIVE EDUCATION

This is your opportunity to choose not only the type of school in which you want to work but the philosophy of teaching you want to pursue. Progressive education is almost exclusively offered by 'small schools'. These are schools in which the learning environment specifically aims to allow for the creative, spiritual, psychological, intellectual and physical aspects of each child to be nurtured. Unlike the USA and the rest of Europe, where progressive education is part of the package of choice on offer to pupils, parents and teachers, in the UK it is almost entirely in the private sector and parents are usually required to contribute to the costs of providing such education.

ABOUT HUMAN SCALE EDUCATION

Human Scale Education (HSE) is an educational charity set up to promote the education being offered by small schools and small classes, 'because of the many educational benefits which small size can bring'. Its main belief is that teachers, pupils and society all benefit from the opportunities that small classes, small schools and large schools restructured into smaller units offer children for active, participatory learning in groups small enough for solid interpersonal relationships to be built. Human Scale Education wants children to be educated to develop purpose, imagination and a sense of truth, and for personal development skills to be nurtured.

For further information, visit www.hse.org.uk.

At the heart of progressive education lies the teacher/pupil relationship, which is based on mutual trust and respect. Pupils are usually instrumental in decision making in these schools, made possible because of the relatively low pupil populations and high teacher/pupil ratios. Some small schools offer their pupils the National Curriculum; others select from it what is most appropriate for their students, as learning intentions can be influenced by both the curriculum and the other needs of each child.

The ideas of the small school movement are filtering into mainstream schools, with some reorganizing themselves into a collection of mini-schools. Flexi-schooling has also been adopted in some areas, which allows for pupils to be educated at school and in the community as appropriate.

Small schools offer new teachers some distinct advantages:

- It is believed that, if children can make decisions about their education on some level, they are more motivated academically.
- Teaching groups are often very small - about 10 pupils or fewer.
- Such small groups allow teaching skills to be developed and confidence gained.
- Fewer curriculum constraints allow for more creative teaching and the easy dissemination of good practice.

However:

- In Britain progressive education is almost entirely in the private sector, so the same considerations need to be made when accepting a job in a small school as in any other independent school.

ABOUT USING PROGRESSIVE IDEAS

You don't have to work in a small school to use progressive ideas in your teaching and develop your own philosophies as an educator. There is no reason why you cannot pull threads of progressive education through to the mainstream setting in which you work. The organization Re:membering Education promotes the teaching of awe and wonder at the world and the ability to reflect on events and raise self-esteem. It suggests that teachers look at relationships on all levels: between learner and subject, between learner and teacher, and between subjects. Educating about and through the emotions is something that all teachers can attempt. Aim to visit small schools in your area.

For further information, these sites may be of interest:

- The National Association of Small Schools: www.smallschools.org.uk;
- Council for Environmental Education: www.cee.org.uk;
- Campaign for Learning: www.campaign-for-learning.org.uk;
- Steiner Waldorf Fellowship: www.steinerwaldorf.org.uk;
- Schumacher Society: www.schumacher.org.uk.

- Teachers attempting to move from the private sector to the state sector may have to contend with negative discrimination.
- Salaries are usually lower than those in the state sector.

ACTION Spend at least a day when you actively implement some of the ideas of progressive education. Perhaps set aside some time in a lesson for pupils to decide on their own targets for learning or focus on how emotional intelligence/literacy may affect the absorption of the subject(s) you teach.

Emotional intelligence/literacy

We are being judged by a new yardstick: not just how smart we are, but also by how well we handle ourselves and each other.

(Daniel Goleman, 1998)

Emotional intelligence (sometimes known as emotional literacy) is fast becoming a priority in many LEAs, with some, like Southampton City Council, identifying it as a specific goal for its pupils alongside the more traditional goals of literacy and numeracy. There is a vast amount of literature available now on this most crucial aspect of teaching, with organizations such as Heartskills, Re:membering Education and Antidote producing particularly relevant and useful information for teachers.

Emotional intelligence has many definitions, but can broadly be taken to mean the ability to recognize the role that our feelings have in the way we live our lives and interact with others. It is thought that there are emotional intelligence competencies. These comprise:

- self-awareness:
  - emotional self-awareness;
  - accurate self-assessment;
  - self-confidence;
- self-management:
  - self-control;
  - trustworthiness;
  - conscientiousness;
  - achievement orientation;
  - initiative;
- social awareness:
  - empathy;
  - organizational awareness;
  - service orientation;
- social skills:
  - developing others;
  - leadership;
  - influence;
  - communication;
  - change catalyst;
  - conflict management;
  - building bonds;
  - teamwork and collaboration.

Web sites worth browsing for ideas on how emotional intelligence/literacy can be incorporated into your teaching include:

- www.remember.mcmail.com (Re:membering Education);
- www.heartskills.com (Heartskills);
- www.antidote.org.uk (Antidote);
- www.nelig.com (National Emotional Literacy Interest Group – NELIG);
- www.eiconsortium.org (Consortium for Research on Emotional Intelligence in Organizations);
- www.eqi.org (an extensive source of information grouped into scientific and academic research into the field of emotions and emotional intelligence/literacy);
- www.casel.org (the Collaborative for the Advancement of Social and Emotional Learning);
- www.esrnational.org (Educators for Social Responsibility).

Daniel Goleman's books are also well worth the read. *Emotional Intelligence* and *Working with Emotional Intelligence* are both published by Bloomsbury.

TEMPORARY CONTRACTS

A verbal contract isn't worth the paper it's written on.

(Sam Goldwyn – a phrase of caution to be heeded, although verbal contracts may not be as ineffective in law as is generally believed)

The type of contract you have been offered may not seem important when you have just secured your first teaching job, but it is important to be circumspect when accepting anything other than a permanent contract. That said, a contract is only as permanent as the notice period!

The main two temporary contracts concerning NQTs are: 1) *fixed-term contracts*, which allow schools to plan for falling rolls or other foreseeable situations that will result in fewer teachers being required, and which specify an end date; 2) *specific-task contracts*, which are typically used by schools to cover maternity leave or long-term sick leave, and last until the job is completed, so don't specify a termination date.

Such contracts should never be, but sometimes are, used by a school as insurance against a new teacher who may turn out to be unsuitable. It is sometimes believed that it is easier not to renew the contract of a 'weak' teacher than provide the necessary professional support.

However, a temporary contract can be appropriate in certain circumstances. You may want to gain experience in a variety of settings before committing to one particular type of school, or you may need to move your home mid-year, making a permanent contract less important.

The references you can pick up from your employment on a temporary contract are far more detailed regarding your skills once in post than anything your tutors are in a position to write. In that respect they add greatly to the value of your CV. Don't forget, there really is no such thing as a job for life!

If you do accept a temporary contract, keep these points in mind:

- Regardless of the type of contract you accept, as an NQT you are entitled to an induction programme and should be offered the same opportunities as NQTs on permanent contracts. Don't miss out. You need to find out when you will be deemed to have completed your induction period if you take a temporary contract.
- Taking over from another teacher mid-year can be difficult, especially if the pupils know that you are not a permanent member of staff. Support from your school at this stage is crucial. Make your mark on each class you teach; you are not simply a babysitter, and can do things 'your way'.
- Make sure you know the termination date of your contact, its type and the reason why it is temporary.
- 'Fixed-term' contracts carry more employment protection than 'specific-task' contracts. If you are employed on a series of fixed-term contracts, your employment rights regarding unfair dismissal and redundancy accrue after one year and two years respectively. Seek advice from your union if you feel you have been treated unfairly.
- If your post will be open beyond your termination date, you should be offered a renewal of contract without the post being re-advertised. However, if you have not been employed for one year, the law does not protect you if your employer chooses to re-advertise your post.
- Make sure you will be receiving the correct remuneration – some schools calculate bizarre combinations of salary and supply rates in order to save money, especially if your contract takes you over a long holiday.

PART-TIME TEACHING

Current legislation means that there are few, if any, differences between full- and part-time employees apart from hours worked. All employees are equal. This means that part-timers have the same holiday and sick pay entitlements (pro rata) as full-time employees. For this reason, part-time teaching can be attractive to some teachers, providing you can afford to accept the necessary reduction in salary! It also offers these benefits:

- It gives you the chance to pursue other career options.
- It can allow you to continue your career at a time when you have domestic pressures such as child rearing or caring for a relative.
- It frees time to concentrate on further professional development such as obtaining additional qualifications.
- There is usually flexibility to increase your working hours, often through covering for absent staff.

ABOUT TAKING CARE OVER CONTRACTS

It can feel as though you are being unnecessarily meticulous if you question the finer details of your contract, but it is important to protect yourself against possible future disputes, which can drain your energy and place a negative focus on your career. There is no reason why a contract that is fair to you and the school cannot be negotiated. Your union and LEA education personnel office are able to offer contract advice and some lawyers will also do this free of charge. Make sure you clearly understand your contractual obligations, so that you are free to commence your career from a position of knowledge and security. Above all, do not sign or agree to anything unless you are happy with the implications – if not, your first job could be your worst job.

Disputes over contracts seem to be common, and for this reason some unions are fighting for national standards.

However, even if it has been possible to negotiate part-time hours at your school, there are always disadvantages that should be considered:

- It can feel as though you are not fully involved in the life of the school when you only attend at certain times.
- Liaising with colleagues can become difficult because of your work patterns.
- Part-time teachers invariably spend more time than their pay suggests preparing for lessons and marking/assessing.
- Career progression can become difficult (and in some schools impossible).

- Depending on how efficient your school is at disseminating information, it can be very difficult to stay fully informed of the latest changes.
- You will probably spend a disproportionate amount of time travelling to and from school if you do not work full days.

Job sharing

As the work profile of the nation changes and increasing numbers of people are looking for more flexibility in their work, job sharing seems to have become an interesting option. Many schools have job-sharing schemes in place, which can offer all the advantages (and disadvantages) of part-time teaching, as well as the added bonus of having ready-made cover should you need time off for any reason. You should, however, be aware of these factors:

- Job sharing can be an extremely good deal for the school – the sum of two half-teachers is often greater than one!
- Time must be spent liaising with your colleague for the purposes of planning, marking and assessment.
- Difficulties can arise if one side of the partnership leaves and good working dynamics have to be established quickly with a newcomer.
- As with any job, full-time, part-time or shared, always check the finer details of your contract, and consider the implications for your pension.

CAREERS RELATED TO TEACHING

Receiving QTS does not mean that you are obliged or committed to take a job as a teacher, or to teaching in this country. There are many opportunities for qualified teachers – in fact, people with teaching qualifications are often sought by industry because of the transferable skills they possess. These include skills such as the ability to multi-task, to work to extremely tight deadlines, to relate to a variety of different people within each working day and to adjust the time spent working each day as appropriate.

Here are just some ideas you may like to consider.

Choices within teaching

You may not want to take a permanent job in a British school, but there are many other ways of earning money from teaching.

Teaching English as a foreign language

Teaching English as a foreign language (TEFL) can offer excellent opportunities to work with students of all ages and even travel around the world. Some language schools insist on specific TEFL qualifications, which can be gained by attending various courses, either full- or part-time. Training is advisable, as it will enhance employment opportunities, particularly if you go through the British Council (see www.britishcouncil.org, or e-mail elt.group@britishcouncil.org for further information). There will always be a world market of people keen to learn English, as either a second or a third language, or for specific purposes such as business.

ABOUT SEEKING CAREERS ADVICE

Most institutes of higher education offer students and ex-students careers advice free of charge, specifically for people with higher-education qualifications. This is probably the best place to start. An agreement of 'mutual aid' means that you may be able to get careers advice from the university/college in your home area as well as the university/college you attended. You may, however, have to wait for an appointment, as university careers services will put their own students first.

You can also get advice from independent careers offices but it is a good idea to use a county service that employs trained careers advisers. There is usually a charge for the advice they give, but the time, resources and follow-up care you are given can be worth the investment.

Other sources of careers advice for teachers are the Teacher Training Agency (www.canteach.gov.uk) and the Internet (in particular, the National Grid for Learning, http://careers.ngfl.gov.uk).

Teaching in developing countries

Voluntary Service Overseas (VSO) can offer opportunities for graduate teachers to teach overseas, normally for at least two years. Payment is at local rates. Some aid agencies and religious organizations also employ teachers to work abroad. Embassies and the educational press often have details of overseas teaching opportunities.

Other work abroad

Opportunities in the USA, Canada, Australia, New Zealand and non-European Union countries are relatively limited, but European Union (EU) countries offer some possibilities. Again, the relevant embassies or high commissions will be able to advise as to how to obtain employment. Also, the careers section of your local library will have information on job opportunities in EU countries.

ABOUT RETURNING AFTER WORKING ABROAD

If you spend time in your career teaching abroad, there will inevitably be some employers who do not value the extra experience you will have gained. In order to capitalize on your breadth of experience, carefully select elements of your work abroad that have specific application to teaching in this country. Find ways of working this information into any interviews that you have on your return. Unfortunately, some schools may not recognize work abroad as a justification for an additional point on the salary scale.

It is worth noting that you will have to complete an induction period if you have not already done so in order to be eligible to teach in a maintained school or a non-maintained special school.

For information on taking a gap year, take a look at www.yearoutgroup.org and www.thegapyear.co.uk.

Private tutoring

There are often advertisements for teachers to work as private tutors in families, both in this country and abroad, in the educational press. Some teaching agencies maintain registers of private tutors, although obtaining work through such agencies can result in having to pay a fee for the introduction, or a percentage of any earnings you receive from work through the agency.

For this reason it can be more lucrative to advertise your teaching services in your local press. Such advertisements usually cost less than £20. If timed well, for example around Easter time to catch the exam crammers and the beginning of September for those students whose parents want them to improve on their performance in the previous year, you can quickly recoup your expenses. Do remember that any earnings from private tutoring form part of your taxable income!

Many teachers find private tutoring extremely rewarding, as it allows an opportunity to focus on teaching and interacting without the need to consider the dynamics of a large group. Your union will be able to advise on what is the current rate for private tutoring.

Supply teaching

Supply teaching is quite a tough route to take as a newly qualified teacher. As you move from school to school covering for absent staff, your abilities to adapt to different institutions, subjects and age groups will need to be well honed. However, there seem to be increasing opportunities whereby supply teaching leads to a temporary contract, which could in turn become a permanent one.

Supply teaching makes it virtually impossible to gain a valuable induction into the teaching profession if you are not based in one school for a term or more, and this has grave implications for your chances of satisfying the requirements of what should be your first year of teaching. Professional support is likely to be patchy too, at a time when behaviour management will be most challenging. For this reason, supply teaching should only really be considered in extreme circumstances.

The best way into supply teaching is through your own contacts. If you have connections with a particular school, ask the headteacher for an informal interview with a view to being added to the school's list of supply teachers. Alternatively, if there is a school you would like to work in, doing some voluntary work as a precursor to paid employment is a great way of convincing the powers that be of your skills and abilities.

All LEAs maintain a list of teachers available for supply work that is distributed to schools within its remit. Contact the appropriate LEA's education personnel office for details.

If you decide to work through a supply agency, you should be aware that your rate of pay will not necessarily be according to the latest *Pay and Conditions Document*. Pension contributions may not be made either. Teaching service completed through an LEA or arranged directly with a school can count for incremental purposes. A future employer may not count supply work through an agency as worthy of an increment point.

Do not enter the world of supply teaching as a newly qualified teacher without first seeking the advice of your union. Your local representative should be in a position to tell you how the system works best in your area. If in any doubt, apply first to your LEA.

Choices outside teaching

You're not selling your soul if you decide to go for work outside teaching. There is tremendous scope for using your qualifications, and the profession will invariably welcome any experience you gain should you decide to return to teaching at a later date.

Project work
Look in the education press for advertisements for trained teachers to take part in projects. These are usually research-based, fixed-term contracts, which offer the chance to become involved in a specialist area of education.

Resource development
Most teachers write their own materials on occasion (if not all the time) and there are opportunities within publishing to become involved in book and resource package projects. Either approach suitable publishers directly with a brief synopsis of your idea (the *Writers' and Artists' Yearbook*, published by A & C Black, is invaluable for information on publishing companies) or look out for 'creative' and 'media' advertisements in the quality press.

Multi-media educational-resource development is another growth area and one in which it could be wise for teachers to become involved.

Education administration
There are opportunities at many levels in local education administration from planning and budgeting to policy implementation and problem solving. Vacancies will usually be advertised in the local press, but it is also worth arranging some work experience or talking to key personnel in your LEA. Many local government education administration jobs still allow for close contact with schools.

Education officer posts
Most museums, heritage and conservation sites, large companies and major charities have education officers whose job it is to liaise with visitors and generally inform the public of the work of the organization. This may be through writing worksheets and newsletters or organizing exhibitions and fund-raising.

Often, such jobs are advertised in the education press but, again, if there is a particular organization you would like to work for, make your own introductions through speculative applications, work experience and voluntary work.

Training in industry and commerce

The training department of any company performs a vital role, especially now that the pace of change within the workplace is so rapid. The skills you need for a job in training are very similar to those needed in the teaching profession, ie good communication, motivation, organization, analysis and problem solving.

As training departments in companies are often part of the human resources services, you may need to do some further study to acquire the relevant professional qualifications.

Caring work

This general term covers all jobs involving caring for others, such as social work, youth and community work, educational welfare and residential care. Caring work often allows you to develop solid relationships with those you are working with over a long period of time and will demand many skills.

Jobs in other areas

These job areas are also worth considering:

- retail management;
- public relations;
- marketing;
- librarianship;
- broadcasting;
- research;
- leisure;
- careers advising;
- counselling;
- writing;
- journalism.

RETURNING TO THE TEACHING PROFESSION

Returning to the teaching profession after a career break can be a daunting challenge. The pace of change in education remains fairly rapid, and concerns about how you would compare with the competition in terms of current knowledge and appropriateness for the job can prevail. This reduced confidence seems to be a common experience amongst those who are contemplating a return to the profession, which is a great pity, as the pool of out-of-service teachers is a resource that the government and LEAs are keen to tap.

If you are a potential returner to the profession, be sure to contact the Teacher Training Agency's (TTA's) Keeping In Touch (KIT) Programme. You will receive a newsletter that will keep you up to date with all the latest developments in the world of education as well as details of returner courses. These courses are run by colleges, higher-education institutions and LEAs, can be part-time, full-time or distance learning, and are an extremely cost-effective way of gaining, and brushing up on, vital skills such as behaviour management and ICT (see contact details below).

The following points may also be of interest:

- As long as you have QTS and a DfES number you are able to return to teaching. Your qualification does not 'expire' after a certain period.
- Training bursaries exist for participants of TTA-funded returners' courses.
- Volunteering in a local school can be a great way of deciding whether a return to the profession would be good for you. You could either speak directly to local schools or try the TTA's Open Schools Programme. This initiative gives potential trainees the opportunity to visit schools, but would also be open to returners. Contact the Teaching Information Line on 0845 600 0991 for further details.
- Other ways to keep in touch include the DfES's termly magazine, *Teachers* (available free of charge on 0845 602 2260).

These Web sites may also be useful:

- the Open University, www.open.ac.uk (tel: 01908 653231), for educational materials and study packs;
- the Qualifications and Curriculum Authority, www.qca.ac.uk (tel: 020 8867 3333), for literature on the National Curriculum among others;
- the General Teaching Council, www.gtce.org.uk (tel: 0870 001 0308), for information on registration, professional conduct and professional development among others;
- Career Development Loans, www.lifelonglearning.co.uk (tel: 0800 585 505), for information on development loans that are paid back once in employment;

● Childcare Link, www.childcarelink.gov.uk (tel: 0800 096 0296), www.
  inlandrevenue.gov.uk (tel: 0800 597 5976), www.newdeal.gov.uk (tel: 0845
  606 2626), for information on assistance with childcare.

The address for the TTA KIT Programme is PO Box 3049, Chelmsford CM1
3YT (tel: 0845 600 0993; e-mail: helpline@kit-tta.co.uk).

CHAPTER 2

Making your application

Unless you fall into the relatively small category of trainee teachers who are offered a job in their teaching practice school and want to accept that job, you will have to apply to an unfamiliar school for a teaching post at some stage. Although this may seem daunting, when you view the challenge as a project that can easily be broken down into stages you could not only be successful in receiving a job offer but also in ensuring that it is suitable.

ABOUT WHERE YOU CAN TEACH

The law relating to education differs between all the countries of the United Kingdom. However, if you have completed your ITT in the UK you can teach in England, Wales or Northern Ireland. If you would like to teach in Scotland, but did not train there, you will need to seek the advice of the General Teaching Council for Scotland (www.gtcs.org.uk; tel: 0131 314 6000).

TUNING YOUR VACANCY RADAR

Somewhere, your ideal job will be advertised and, if you are not looking in the likely places, it will be offered to someone else. The best way to start the great hunt is to decide on the geographical area in which you are prepared to work. Obviously, the smaller your chosen area the more limited your search, but that is no reason to force yourself into applying for jobs in areas about which you have doubts. Once you have a list of places in which you would be happy to work, pursue every lead in the hunt for the ideal vacancy.

Covering every option

Resignations of teaching posts are made to three deadlines throughout the year – 31 October, 28 February and 31 May – although these deadlines may be waived if both parties agree. Naturally the few weeks following these deadlines are particularly good times to search for job advertisements.

The national press

Many vacancies in the teaching profession are advertised in *The Times Educational Supplement*, which comes out on Fridays. Other newspapers to scour are the *Guardian*, the *Daily Telegraph* and the *Independent*, all of which have interesting education sections usually including several pages of vacancies. Those advertised in the *Independent* can also be found on the teacher recruitment Web site, www.eteach.com.

   If you are looking for a post in a denominational school you may also want to look out for:

- *Church Times* (Church of England);
- *Universe* and *Catholic Teachers Gazette* (Roman Catholic);
- *Jewish Chronicle*;
- *Daily Jang*.

The local press

As only vacancies for heads and deputies have to be advertised nationally, it is well worth scrutinizing the local press. If you are not living where you would eventually like to be working, contact the appropriate local paper and they will arrange to send you the copies you require.

LEA bulletins

These are invaluable to the job-searching NQT, as vacancies will often be advertised here before they go into the national press. Arrange with relevant LEAs to have newsletters posted to you. Contacting the appropriate education personnel department is usually enough to get this set up.

The Internet

Many LEAs (or equivalent) have channelled resources into creating sophisticated Web sites (see Appendix 4 – Appendix 7) where current vacancies, amongst other things, may be posted. These are worth browsing regularly to see what you can find.

ABOUT RECRUITMENT STRATEGY MANAGERS

Specialist Recruitment Managers (SRMs) and Recruitment Strategy Managers (RSMs) play important roles in local recruitment. There are three SRMs and they support headteachers of schools in challenging circumstances, working to develop recruitment and retention strategies. Most LEAs have an RSM now. They are funded by the TTA and employed by LEAs to draw up recruitment strategies for the area. RSMs and SRMs have the very latest information on local recruitment needs at their fingertips, which is a great benefit to the NQT, as there are certainly regional variations in recruitment needs. RSMs can be contacted through your LEA.

Another 'must see' Web site is www.eteach.com, which is the largest fully interactive database of teaching jobs in the UK. It is free to join and not only has sophisticated job search tools, but will also send you job alerts by e-mail. The lively staffroom forum is great for advice to do with your career and teaching in general, and for making useful contacts.

It is worth scanning the education newsgroups, as they are a good source of contacts and you may pick up advance information on interesting vacancies. Some union Web sites have job-search links too.

ABOUT WHAT TO LOOK FOR IN A VACANCY

Although it is important to be enthusiastic and have high aspirations, you should never accept extra responsibility points in your first year of teaching. Leave the promotions until you have completed your induction period.

Go for vacancies that either specifically refer to NQTs or are advertised as being on the main scale. A school that is prepared to offer an NQT extra responsibilities is probably thinking more of the budget than of your abilities to cope, and the additional support you will need is unlikely to be forthcoming.

If you are returning to the profession, your new post should be a supportive one that will enable you to settle into teaching at a reasonable pace. If this means taking a 'backward step', do it; this approach will almost certainly gain you time in the long run. If you need advice on what salary to expect, get in touch with your union, which should be able to give you a salary assessment.

Contacts made during teaching practice

Don't underestimate how valuable networking can be when you have the opportunity during training to visit a variety of schools. Utilize any contacts you have made and you may be privy to information about a vacancy before it is advertised to the general public. Such contacts could be mentors, heads and deputies, course tutors (who invariably retain close links with local schools) and any inspectors and advisers you may have come across in the course of your studies. A phone call or letter could provide you with a specific piece of information that puts you at an advantage.

DECIDING TO APPLY

Actually deciding to apply for a teaching vacancy is a commitment to a fair amount of work and, therefore, not to be undertaken lightly. Minimize the possibility of pulling out at any stage by finding out as much as you can about the school.

The job advertisement will give limited information and, if this sounds tempting, request an application form and job description. You can do this by telephone, e-mail or post, although some schools may request that you send in a stamped, addressed envelope. It is essential not to apply for a job unless you have been sent the application form and job description.

The job description should contain at the very least the following information:

- the title of the post (eg class teacher, history teacher etc);
- the salary;
- details of the person to whom the post is responsible (eg head of department);
- what the responsibilities are;
- any extra duties;
- an indication of the timetable;
- an applicant profile.

Vacancies can be advertised on the basis of a verbal resignation. Whilst retraction of the resignation is extremely unlikely, do bear in mind that this could, in theory, happen right up to the interview stage. Before sitting down to complete the necessary forms, do some mental questioning to establish whether, based on the information available to you at this stage, you would accept the job if offered. It will be helpful to consider these questions:

- Is it an NQT post?
- Would you be able to complete your induction period there?
- Would the job allow you to live in an area in which you want to live?
- Is it in the type of school of which you would like to be a part?
- Would you be teaching subjects you have specialized in?
- Would you be teaching an age group you have specialized in?
- Is the school in an Education Action Zone (EAZ) (see Chapter 3)?

ABOUT COMPETITION

Some NQTs develop unshakeable ideas about the sort of school that they are prepared to work in, and this can deteriorate into a 'whose school is most challenging' contest. Don't get involved. Apply to the schools with a job description and ethos most suited to you, your skills and experiences. Only challenge yourself deliberately if you genuinely want to, and try not to limit yourself to a particular type of school. A wish list of an inner-city, single-sex, 11–16, church-aided school will be much harder to find than something a little more flexible, and such rigidity may block opportunities.

ACTION What are your unique selling points? This can be hard to think about without some feedback from other people. Talk to at least two trusted friends (preferably with whom you have worked). Ask them what your outstanding skills are and you should end up with a list that will get you started.

COMPLETING THE NECESSARY FORMS

The method of application varies among schools and LEAs, so it is essential to follow any guidance given carefully, especially if you are making applications in different authorities. The minimum you will have to do is fill in an application form including a supporting statement in which you have the opportunity honestly to sell your skills. Most schools require a medical form as well.

It is a good idea to have a current CV printed and ready to send at short notice. Your training institution will be able to offer advice on how it should be set out, and the careers portal of the National Grid for Learning (NGfL) is also a source of advice. However, even if you are employed on the basis of your

CV, most personnel departments still require a completed application form for their records. Before you put your mark on the form, take a photocopy so that you can have a dry run.

ABOUT SPECULATIVE APPLICATIONS

If you have set your heart on a particular school but have not seen an advertisement for a vacancy, send in a speculative application.

Points to remember

- Plan your letter carefully, being sure to include any achievements and outstanding skills. Keep it punchy and use bullet points as appropriate. One side of A4 paper should be ample, as you will be sending a current CV with the letter. Remember, don't plead; the idea is for the school to feel that they can't function without you!
- Write or type on good-quality paper.
- First state what kind of vacancy you are interested in.
- Match your skills and experience to what you know of the school.
- State some attributes that you can bring to the school.
- Ask for an interview – offer broad suggestions for possible dates.
- End with the expectation of a reply, eg 'I look forward to hearing from you', and include an SAE.
- If you don't hear within a week, make a follow-up call – ask to speak to the person to whom you wrote.

EXAMPLE

John has extensive experience working to support lesbian and gay people in the community. As a gay man, he describes himself as 'out and proud', but he has concerns about how he should include this experience on his application forms for teaching posts.

There is no right and wrong answer here. The best thing to do, in such a situation, is to trust your instincts when debating how much information to reveal about yourself on an application form. One way to view such a dilemma is that, if a potential employer creates difficulties because of your sexual orientation, the school would almost certainly be one in which no one could truly thrive. You can only do what feels most supportive to you, and if you feel at any stage that you are being unfairly discriminated against, contact your union as soon as possible.

Selling your skills

The application form is designed to elicit basic information about you, your education and employment history. This alone will not make you stand out from the crowd, but your real opportunity to shine is in the supporting statement.

Your main goals when writing your supporting statement must be to match your skills to the job description and to include your unique selling points. Don't simply write about the experiences you have had. There are many experienced teachers, but are they necessarily skilled? Inform your future employers of your achievements. Your leading sentence must engage the reader immediately, giving a sense of your personality. Always optimize your positive aspects and end with something memorable.

Although the supporting statement is by far the most trying part of the application process, don't be tempted to reproduce it for all your applications, without relating it directly to respective job descriptions.

ABOUT YOUR MEDICAL FITNESS FOR EMPLOYMENT AS A TEACHER

It has long been accepted that a career in the teaching profession demands a high level of physical and mental fitness. Teachers act *in loco parentis* for their pupils and this is paramount in the decision over who is considered fit for the classroom.

Circular 4/99 (*Physical and Mental Fitness to Teach of Teachers and of Entrants to Initial Teacher Training*) states:

> For newly qualified teachers, the prospective employer's medical adviser should obtain details of the applicant's medical history from the medical adviser to the training provider with the written consent of the teacher… Possession of qualified teacher status (QTS) does not indicate the Secretary of State has been satisfied that a teacher is medically fit to teach.
>
> The employer's medical adviser may, in the light of local factors, recommend routine health screening or other requirements for teachers and teacher trainees on first appointment. Trainees and serving teachers should keep their immunisations up to date… The need for any other immunisation, e.g. against hepatitis A or B or further BCG should be assessed on the basis of advice from the medical adviser and the local consultant in Communicable disease control.

Immunization is *not* mandatory and new teachers should never feel compelled to agree to a vaccine if they have any objections, whether philosophical or otherwise. The concept of vaccination is increasingly contentious and it is vitally important for teachers to make their decisions based on information from the full spectrum of research available.

Checklist for writing a supporting statement

- Before starting, write a list of key points from the job description (eg year 3 class teacher, class contains pupils with special needs, high display standards, strong singing tradition in the school etc).
- Write a list of your unique selling points, ensuring that they relate directly to your first list (see above).
- Begin with impact and end unforgettably!
- Convey a sense of your personality.
- Fill the main body of the statement with your skills and achievements, always optimizing the positive. Include an explanation of your motivation to teach.
- Use impeccable grammar throughout, avoiding lengthy sentences and aimless paragraphs. Brevity is the key. Use so-called 'action' words to avoid overuse of 'I did'. The following may be helpful:

accomplished	conducted
achieved	consolidated
acquired	counselled
addressed	created
advised	cultivated
analysed	defined
arranged	delivered
assessed	demonstrated
assimilated	designed
averted	developed
collaborated	devised
compiled	diversified
composed	documented
conceived	effected
concluded	eliminated

enacted

engaged

established

evaluated

expanded

formulated

generated

implemented

improved

improvised

incorporated

initiated

inspired

instigated

instructed

integrated

intervened

introduced

invented

launched

led

maintained

managed

modernized

monitored

observed

organized

originated

performed

pioneered

predicted

prevented

produced

promoted

proposed

provided

recommended

redesigned

reduced

regulated

renegotiated

reorganized

resolved

reviewed

revised

revitalized

shaped

simplified

specified

standardized

streamlined

strengthened

structured

supported

tightened

uncovered

unified

unravelled

utilized

visualized

vitalized

vivified

volunteered

- Express what your teaching practice has taught you, and convey an idea of your philosophy of teaching.
- Include information on any travel, hobbies and voluntary work that you have done, and how this equips you for the job.
- If possible, or unless requested otherwise, type your statement.

ABOUT REFEREES

Think carefully about whom you appoint as referees. Employers will look closely at their status and how recent your contact was, so your favourite primary teacher or best mate from the pub are probably bad choices! Choose referees who will be in a position to match your qualities and capabilities to the job's requirements and be as supportive as possible. Perhaps a past employer and your tutor from your ITT institution would be good choices. Make sure you have their permission before appointing them as referees.

ABOUT APPLYING TO A POOL

Some LEAs operate a pool system whereby applicants apply to work in the LEA rather than in a particular school. Successful applicants are then matched as closely as possible with suitable schools. The application form for a pool job will be very similar to the forms used by individual schools, and the supporting statement will still be an important section. Interviews for pool jobs are usually conducted in a central location in the LEA and you should expect to be interviewed by a panel consisting of representatives from the LEA and local teachers and headteachers. Questions won't be specific to a school or post, but will be based in generic aspects of teaching such as behaviour management, learning styles, underachievement, the literacy and numeracy strategies and so on. Interviews for pools are usually around 20 minutes long.

By applying to a pool you are declaring your desire to work in a particular authority so it is a good idea to express clearly why you want to work there. Be sure to get your application in on time, as it will almost certainly not be looked at if it arrives during the short-listing stage.

SENDING IN YOUR APPLICATION

Always use an A4 (preferably cardboard-backed) envelope for your application so that it does not have to be folded. Write down a checklist of items that need to be included, for example the application form, CV and medical form, and tick them off as you put them in the envelope. Send in the originals, but keep a photocopy of everything so you can refer to them before an interview.

If at all possible, deliver your application to the school. If you do have to post it, include a stamped, self-addressed postcard that can be sent to you as acknowledgement of receipt. Schools rarely do this unless you provide the stamp. Now all you have to do is sit back and wait for an invitation to an interview!

ABOUT NOT BEING INVITED FOR AN INTERVIEW

If you are not asked to attend for an interview, try not to think about it as a disaster. It is certainly frustrating that your hard work has not apparently paid off, but there are always positive aspects in any situation. Cultivate the attitude that perhaps the job was not as suited to you as you first thought, and that the experience has been a valuable one. Think how much easier future applications will be now that you have gone this far. Do, however, take the opportunity to reassess your application to see if there are any obvious weaknesses that can be tightened up in future.

If you suspect ageism may be the problem, contact your union. Statistics show that those over 45 are twice as likely to be unemployed six months after training as those in their 20s (*Independent*, London, 25 February 1999). The reason for this is almost certainly financial, with younger NQTs being cheaper to employ than those with significant experience outside the profession (providing this experience is rewarded).

ATTENDING FOR AN INTERVIEW

If you think you can or you think you can't you're right.

(Henry Ford)

Failure to prepare is preparing to fail.

(John Wooden)

The interview is an opportunity for both sides to gather the additional information needed before a commitment to employment can be made. At this stage, a positive attitude is at least as important as any other factor in securing a job offer.

Preparing for the day

While it is important to be prepared for an interview in terms of physical appearance, knowledge of the job and of the school etc, there is something to be said for maintaining a balance. Over-rigorous preparation can lead to excessive anxiety that will inevitably limit your chances of success.

As soon as possible after receiving your invitation to an interview, send a reply confirming the arrangements. At this stage you can ask if the school will be paying your interview expenses and, if so, at what rate. Only in extreme circumstances would you be justified in attempting to change the arrangements suggested by the school.

You should have been sent a map and advice on accommodation if you will be travelling a long distance, together with additional information about the school, such as a description of the surrounding area, site and buildings, an outline of the staffing structure and details of the governing body, along with the interview format.

What are the interviewers looking for?

They are looking for:

- the person who matches the job criteria most closely;
- the person who will fit in with the existing staff;
- the person who will be able to make a valuable contribution to the work of the school;
- your attitudes to management and governors;
- your personal philosophy of teaching;
- your motivations, satisfactions and dissatisfactions;
- your ability to assert yourself.

That said, the success of the interview in terms of extracting this information depends on the skills of those asking the questions.

Dressing to win

Nothing succeeds like the appearance of success.

(Christopher Lasch)

It sounds totally irrational, but instant judgements will be made of you based on your appearance. For this reason, there are some basic ground rules to follow when deciding what to wear on the big day.

ABOUT PORTFOLIOS

There is an unwritten expectation now that NQTs will take a portfolio of examples of work to interviews. You will probably have received guidance from your training institution on how best to build a portfolio but, if not, the ideas below will help:

- An A3 folder is the ideal size. Portfolio folders are readily available in good-quality stationery shops. Avoid the folders with plastic inner pockets so that you can easily retrieve contents.
- Include items that show the breadth of experience you have. For example:
  - samples of planning (if possible, short-term and long-term planning, although you may not have had the opportunity to do long-term planning on teaching practice);
  - photographs of displays or special events that you have been involved in;
  - examples of your assessment of pupils' work;
  - samples of work that, if possible, show an idea of your teaching philosophy or, at least, your understanding of current priorities in education.
- Don't shy away from including examples of work that did not go down well. This will give you the opportunity to demonstrate the fact that you are a reflective practitioner and to explain how you dealt with the situation.
- Before each interview, select for your portfolio only those items that will enable you to link specifically to the job in question.
- Organize the contents of your portfolio so that you can retrieve items in the order in which you will discuss them. This will avoid having to fumble around pulling out samples of work at random!

By offering your interviewers a portfolio of your best work to peruse, you are handing them a positive focus for questioning. That has to be a good thing!

Schools vary tremendously in their dress codes. From jeans and T-shirts to suits and ties, there is a school at every point on the spectrum. As far as is possible, try to find out what the dress code is for your school. If it is local, catching a glimpse of staff is useful, or arranging an informal visit will settle the matter. Otherwise, ring the headteacher and ask if there is a dress code. This enables you to establish whether you need to wear a suit, or toning separates. Feeling inappropriately dressed, be it too formally or otherwise, will not boost your confidence on the day.

Use these guidelines:

- Darker, coordinated colours are most appropriate.
- Avoid extremes in style, eg nothing too short, baggy, striped or patterned.
- Go for comfort. Your clothes should be an extension of your body, ie you shouldn't have to think about them.
- If you will be wearing tights or stockings, take a spare pair with you.
- Get your hair trimmed and wear it in a style that won't need constant adjustment.
- Be moderate in your use of jewellery, make-up and perfume or aftershave.

Before the big day

It is so easy to get anxious about events like job interviews, especially if your heart is set on a positive outcome. Yet this anxiety can rapidly backfire and severely affect performance on the day if you don't actively strive for balance. For this reason, physical and mental preparation needs to begin a few days in advance.

Here are some ideas on maximizing your chances:

- Do eat sensibly. A diet high in fresh fruits and vegetables will provide you with the extra energy you need to sail through the interview.
- Do focus on your breathing. Slow, deep breaths are instantly calming in stressful situations.
- Do plan your route to the interview and aim to arrive about 30 minutes early. This will give you not only extra time in case you are delayed but also the chance to freshen up when you arrive, familiarize yourself with your surroundings and practise some deep breathing if you are nervous.
- Do read the education press or visit education-based Web sites to ensure that you are familiar with current developments and popular jargon.
- Don't let negative thinking spoil your day. Say to yourself that the interview will be a success and the outcome will be the best possible one.

ABOUT OPTIMISM

The optimist sees the doughnut; the pessimist sees the hole.

(Anonymous)

According to *The New Oxford Dictionary of English*, the noun 'optimism' means: 'hopefulness and confidence about the future or the successful outcome of something'. The extent to which we are in control of our levels of optimism has been fiercely debated and, no doubt, will continue to be, but the fact that we can have at least some influence over the way we think about a future event is certain.

Nurturing optimism can be the difference between success and failure, winning and losing. Most sportsmen and women, and death-defying adventurers such as those who summit Everest cultivate utterly positive outlooks; after all, climbing through the 'death zone' while muttering under your oxygen-starved breath that you will probably not make it safely down to base camp could well become a self-fulfilling prophecy. Likewise, attending an interview with a pessimistic attitude is sure to produce the very outcome you are drawing towards you.

There are many books on optimism, and the Internet is a fine source of information on this topic. Take a look at: www.psych.upenn.edu/seligman/ (the site of a not-for-profit organization at the University of Pennsylvania that researches learnt helplessness, depression, optimism and pessimism); and www.queendom.com/tests/personality/optimism_pessimism_r_access.html (a bit of light relief – how optimistic are you?).

If low self-esteem is preventing you from making the conscious decision to be optimistic, there are many good exercises in Dr David Burns's book, *Ten Days to Great Self-Esteem*, published by Vermilion.

- Don't smoke anywhere near your interview clothes.
- Don't drink alcohol for 24 hours before the interview. It affects physical appearance, not to mention wits!
- Don't worry about potential problem areas in your application such as gaps in employment or a long period of illness. Work out ways of expressing this in positive terms, eg what adversity taught you.

ACTION If anxiety can be a problem, you need to be able to control it with your breathing. This can be done surreptitiously. Relax your jaw by unclenching your teeth, placing your lips lightly together and teeth slightly apart. It is virtually impossible to retain tension in your face in this position. Then start 4-2-4-2 breathing, ie breathe in to a count of four, hold for two, breathe out to a count of four, pause for two. Keep going until you feel noticeably better.

Interview scenarios

Interviews for teaching jobs generally involve a tour of the school, possibly some food or a drink and questioning by a panel, usually comprising the headteacher, a deputy, head of department or year and at least one governor. Each member of the panel should be introduced to you and his or her position in the school made clear. If not, you are justified in tactfully asking. Although the governors of a school hold a good deal of power, they will draw heavily on the expertise of the senior management team. There are distinct advantages in panel interviews, as personal biases are less likely to be strong deciding factors.

The practice of asking interviewees to perform a task or teach a sample lesson has become the norm in most schools. This can be of limited value in terms of determining which candidate will be most suitable in the long run unless your interviewers are highly skilled in their interpretation of the results.

If you are asked to perform in your interview you should have been given plenty of advance warning. Anything sprung on you unexpectedly, besides the usual panel questioning, is not acceptable practice and you may even consider the implications for your possible employment at the school. Do you want to work for this type of management team?

Assuming you have been given prior warning of anything you might have to do, you owe it to yourself to prepare thoroughly, asking advice from tutors and mentors and gathering resources where appropriate. View it as an exciting challenge.

Remember, if you feel that to continue with the interview would weaken your confidence thus jeopardizing future interviews, or you simply don't want to work at the school, you may politely withdraw from the proceedings at any stage.

EXAMPLE Some NQTs have had bizarre interview experiences. From being asked to write an unseen lesson plan in 30 minutes, to being asked to teach a group of pupils a lesson that the same group had been taught by three other candidates that day, there are clearly some strange views prevailing on how best to judge interviewees! One NQT was even asked to give a presentation on the role of middle management; this is of dubious relevance to a first position.

Another complaint that has been raised by NQTs is the rather unsubtle way in which some schools distinguish between those candidates whom they are genuinely interested in and those who are simply making up the numbers. It has even been reported by some that they were not interviewed by the full interview panel whereas other interviewees were. If anything like this happens to you, there are two ways of looking at it. You could feel satisfied that you have had a close escape. This is an underhand way of approaching interviewing and there are grave implications for the way the school is run and the general treatment of staff. Or you could raise the issue with your union, which may want to investigate what is going on at the school and perhaps lodge a complaint. Whatever you decide to do, remember that not all schools are the same and the chances are that your next interview will be a much more positive experience.

Seating arrangements

Be prepared for a wide variety of creative seating plans. Ideas on the optimum arrangement are changing all the time and you could find yourself:

- facing the panel across a desk;
- sitting around a table with the panel;
- in comfortable chairs around a coffee table;
- in comfortable chairs with no table;
- most oddly, sitting in front of a panel, the members of which are seated in a row with no desk – formal informality!

EXAMPLE Armena was surprised to get all the way through her interview to the stage of being offered the job without being introduced to her future head of department. Be extremely suspicious if you are not given the opportunity to meet the key personnel with whom you would be working. Ask yourself (and your interviewers) why you have not been introduced and draw your own conclusions.

Questions to answer and questions to ask

Every interview offers the opportunity to show your appropriateness for the job through the answers you give and the questions you ask. However, there are two golden rules that should always be remembered: 1) listen carefully to every question and answer so you don't misinterpret what is being said; 2) never begin your answer until you know how you intend to end.

If you do find you have not understood a question or have allowed your mind temporarily to wander, there is no harm in asking for it to be repeated. Likewise, if you begin an answer and lose your thread, own up as soon as possible to avoid an embarrassing ramble.

When putting your answers together, try not to use vague, tentative, colloquial language like 'sort of' or 'You know what I mean, right?' At the same time, avoid appearing to be dogmatically fixed in your beliefs to the point of becoming argumentative with questioners. If you're flappable with adults, what is going to happen in the classroom? A balance must be struck through the use of appropriate language delivered at a steady pace and moderate pitch and volume.

Be yourself and be honest. Don't say anything that can be challenged or contradicted (worst of all by you!) at a later date. Cut the blather – if you get the job you're going to have to live with your words!

You will be asked two different kinds of questions. The key is to know the difference.

Types of questions

Open questions
Example: 'You had the opportunity to teach A level during your initial teacher training. Was that something you enjoyed?' These require more than short, factual answers.

Advantages of open questions are: they give the opportunity to add depth to your answers and to expand on ideas; and they offer the chance to reveal aspects of your character.

Disadvantages are: they can trip you up if you have misunderstood the question and lead you to 'waffle'; and they could show that you can be side-tracked off the key issues and that you haven't thought your answer through.

Closed questions
Example: 'How long have you lived in Sussex?' These require short, factual answers. They are not trick questions!

ABOUT BODY LANGUAGE

Mortals can keep no secret. If their lips are silent, they gossip with their fingertips; betrayal forces its way through every pore.

(Sigmund Freud)

Body language can shout louder than any other form of communication, so utilize it and make it work for you. Without being aware of it, we are all experts at reading body language, but often allow it to give away our innermost thoughts. When greeting your interviewers, use a firm grip for handshakes, and smile. This indicates cooperation and friendliness. Be aware of your posture when walking and, when invited to sit, keep your back straight. Avoid crossing your legs.

Eye contact is essential. Maintain it without letting it deteriorate into a staring contest! A calm, steady gaze that follows the speaker's hands when a point is being made will be read as confident. If you need glasses or contact lenses, wear them.

Other positive signals are to lean forward slightly and smile or nod in agreement. Aim to keep your hands lower than your elbows and limit your movements. This will give you at least the appearance of calm serenity.

Negative signals to be avoided are folding your arms or holding something in front of your body, clasping your hands behind your head, putting your hands in your pockets, fidgeting with fingers or things (holding your fingers in a 'steeple' can control active digits), adjusting hair or clothing and slouching.

Advantages of closed questions are: they don't demand creativity or the ability to 'think on your feet'; and they allow the interview to move on at a pace.

Disadvantages are: they don't allow you to expand and justify answers you give; and they can make you feel as though you are on a programme like *University Challenge*!

Although you will be expected to do most of the talking in an interview, apparently the more your questioners talk, the more likely it is that they are impressed with you. So if you can't get a word in, you're doing well!

The following lists of general questions and questions for recent graduates contain some of those that are being asked in teaching interviews today. A list of tricky questions has also been included, with some suggestions on how to tackle them.

Expect to be asked a variety of questions. You will also be asked specifically about your year or subject specialisms so be up to date with recent developments. Tutors and mentors will be invaluable here.

ABOUT REVEALING PERSONAL AND PROFESSIONAL SKILLS

There are key skills that employers want to see in applicants and these fall into two broad categories: personal and professional. Under the heading 'personal skills', expect to find drive, motivation, communication abilities, energy, determination and confidence. Under 'professional skills' fall reliability, honesty and integrity, loyalty, pride and skills of analysis and listening. Formulate your answers to reveal these characteristics.

General questions you may be asked

- 'Give examples of methods of teaching you have used.'
- 'How would you deal with potential problems, like difficult parents or troublesome pupils?'
- 'What are your major accomplishments?'
- 'What are your career aspirations?'
- 'Describe your worst experience on teaching practice.'
- 'What interests you most about this job?'
- 'How do you handle stress?'
- 'What do you feel about taking work home?'
- 'Are you a team player?'
- 'What is your greatest strength?'
- 'What can you offer outside your subject/age specialism?'
- 'What are your views on school uniform?'

And even:

- 'What was the last book you read?'
- 'What film did you last see?'

Questions for recent graduates

- 'Why do you want to be a teacher?'
- 'So many teachers leave the profession; what makes you think you'll stay?'
- 'Tell me about your dissertation work.'
- 'What issues in education interest you?'
- 'What are you looking for in your career?'

- 'What direction do you think your career will take?'
- 'What have you done that shows initiative?'
- 'What motivates you?'

Tough questions you may be asked

- 'Tell me about yourself.' This is a tricky question. 'How long have you got?' might be on the tip of your tongue. Rather than begin a soliloquy on your best characteristics, it might be better to ask, 'Is there a particular aspect that interests you?'
- 'What did you dislike about the last school you taught in?' This is the one situation when honesty may not be the best policy. 'I hated the head – he was amoral' is probably not going to win you favours. Even if your experience of the school showed it to be run by mavericks and attended by thugs, say something tactful about what you learnt there and express your desire to expand your horizons.
- 'Why did you take a job strawberry picking?' Every job, no matter how apparently menial, has given you experience and taught you some skills. Formulate an answer that reflects this and shows that you can extract positive benefits from every situation. If you can possibly relate it to teaching, then do so.
- 'Why did you choose to train at… institution?' Avoid answers like 'Because my Dad went there', 'Because it was the only one that would have me' or 'It meant that I didn't have to leave home.' You have spent at least a year there so speak about its strong points and how much you enjoyed being a part of the institution.
- 'Why do you think you would like this post?' Regardless of the truth, you must relate your answer to the job specification. Tell the panel what they want to hear. When you have done that, there is no harm in injecting a little humour into the proceedings and admitting, for example, that it would allow you to live on the doorstep of your favourite football team. At this stage they will have made a decision and you can afford to reveal more aspects of your character.
- 'What do you know about this school?' Be honest about what you know. Do not be tempted to bluff. If you have to think on your feet, mention aspects you have learnt since being at the school for the interview. Outsiders' perceptions are always very helpful for a school to understand how it is viewed by the world. The key points here are honesty, tact and diplomacy. There is also a great amount you can find out from a school's Web site. (Even if they don't have one, that tells you something!) Also look up their

OFSTED report on the Internet, available through the OFSTED site, www.ofsted.gov.uk.

- 'What aspects of the job are most crucial?' Do not focus on the parts you would most like to do. They are looking for tendencies towards task avoidance and your abilities to prioritize.

- 'What are your energy levels like?' Everyone goes through periods when their energy levels are low; it is in our nature to experience these fluctuations. However, prospective employers, some of whom think that because you are (probably) young you will be able to keep a consistent pace indefinitely, do not always understand this. Rather than speak about how you have a tendency to get tired if you work too hard, focus on what you do to maintain good health, such as eating sensibly, taking regular exercise, going to a relaxation class etc.

- 'How long do you think you would stay in the job if we offered it to you today?' This is a really difficult one! How could you possibly know or answer with any accuracy? You could say something like 'I intend to commit to this job and work conscientiously. I would be delighted if it was offered to me and do not envisage any need to move jobs in the foreseeable future.'

ABOUT UNFAIR DISCRIMINATION

Interviewers have a moral and legal duty to avoid unfair discrimination on the grounds of disability, race, ethnic background, religion (with the exception of church-aided schools), marital status, political preferences (including trade union membership), sexual orientation and gender. While it is not illegal for you to be questioned on any of these areas, it is generally considered to be bad practice, and any questions asked of you must also be asked of all the other candidates if unfair discrimination is to be avoided. However, many candidates are asked such questions and are happy to answer.

The best policy if you are asked such a question is to take one of two options. Either answer it, taking care to remember the context in which the question was asked for future reference, or politely explain that you would rather not answer that question. Only if your interviewers persist should you offer further explanation of your decision.

Interview questions should be based on the person specification for the job, rather than the private life of the individual. If a school goes beyond this boundary, ask yourself, why do they want this information, and what are they going to do with it?

Questions you may like to ask

At some stage in the interview you should be offered the opportunity to ask some questions. It is wise to have some ready to show how well you have prepared and your interest in the school and the job. Alternatively, if absolutely everything has been discussed and you can think of no further comments to make, say that you are happy that all of your questions have been covered. This implies that you had thought of some in advance!

The following should give you some ideas:

- Has the school had an OFSTED inspection? What was the outcome?
- Who would be your employers, the governing body or the LEA?
- Will you be a form tutor? What pastoral support will there be for you as a tutor?
- Will you have to teach personal and social education, or does a specialist teach that?
- Will you be offered the chance to come into school before starting work if you are successful?

EXAMPLE One of the reasons for the smooth progress of my first few days at Stafford was the knowledge that I had gained during a number of visits to the school before the summer holiday. These proved to be invaluable, particularly as they allowed me to familiarize myself with the basic layout of the school, its routines and its policies and schemes of work. I was particularly pleased to have the opportunity to meet my future class and to discuss their progress with their present teacher. It was extremely reassuring to discover that they were not the class of horrors that I had dreamt of over the past few nights.

(Lee, NQT, East Sussex)

- What would your starting salary be (if this has not been made clear)?
- Would any pre-qualification employment be taken into consideration when you are placed on the salary scale?
- Does this school have plans to become part of an Education Action Zone? If so, what would be the implications for you as a teacher?
- Does this school have plans to become a Beacon school?
- Is there an active parent–staff association?
- Do parents come into the school to help?

- Does the school put on any drama or music productions during the year?
- Is there information and communications technology (ICT) support for staff?
- What outings do pupils go on?
- Have there been any other NQTs at this school recently? Did they successfully complete their induction periods?
- What are the main strengths of the induction programme here?
- Will there be consortium arrangements for the induction of NQTs (eg clusters of schools getting together to deliver support)?

It is always better to ask one utterly appropriate question than a flurry of non-specific ones.

Out-of-school-hours learning activities are big now. Over two-thirds of schools have increased their provision of these activities in recent years to the extent that a typical primary pupil is now spending nearly two hours a week on out-of-school-hours activities and a typical secondary pupil three hours a week. It would be shrewd to find out what activities are offered by the school so that you can determine whether or not you can offer an activity that has not been available at the school before.

ABOUT DELIBERATIONS

When all the candidates have been interviewed, you will have to wait for the panel to reach a decision on whom they want to employ. This decision is usually reached on the same day and you will probably be informed of the outcome before you leave the building.

While the panel is deliberating, use the opportunity to make some judgements of your own. Listen to your gut reactions when you consider the school's ethos, size, physical environment, discipline and style of management. If offered the job, would you be happy? Can you visualize your first day?

POSSIBLE OUTCOMES

- You are offered the job. Congratulations! Make sure the offer is unambiguous – 'Are you in a position to accept this job?' does not constitute an offer. Providing you are happy to accept, some schools may want you to start before the end of term, even if only as a classroom assistant. If this offer is made, you would be wise to accept. It will make the start of term far less daunting. When your offer letter arrives, write a brief letter of thanks, confirming arrangements for your first day if appropriate.

- You are unsuccessful. Although this is disappointing, it can be a blessing in disguise. You should be offered a debriefing that will be invaluable for future interviews. If you are turned down but desperately want to work there, it is worth sending a letter saying how much you enjoyed the interview, how impressed you were with the school and that you would like to be considered for future vacancies.

- You are offered the job, but are not sure if you want to accept. One reason for this could be that you have another interview lined up in a school that you feel you would prefer. If this is the case, be honest with the panel and ask for 24 hours in which to make your decision. This should be granted, but any longer and the school may want to offer the job to the second choice. Difficult as it may seem, you may find yourself having to take a leap of faith in either rejecting the job in the hope of being offered the one that you would prefer, or accepting and resolving to make a go of it. Do not accept the job with the intention of pulling out should you be offered another in the future as you may find yourself in breach of contract, for which you could be sued, even if you only accept a verbal offer. Seek union advice urgently if you find yourself in this predicament.

If you verbally accept a job, make sure that it is subject to your acceptance of the written terms and conditions of the position. If you decide to pull out before accepting the post in writing, you may still be in breach of contract, but it would be unusual for this to be pursued by the school. Once you have accepted the job in writing, to withdraw may see you facing legal action. Don't do anything without seeking the advice of your union.

MOVING TO A NEW AREA

Any home move involves a tremendous amount of organization, and sometimes important tasks such as registering with a dentist and doctor are left until you are forced to act.

Registering with practitioners

Aim to get this sorted out before you start your first term at your new school. This will avoid any unnecessary delay in getting treatment when you need it.

ABOUT THE CRIMINAL RECORDS BUREAU (CRB) CHECK

All teachers have to be checked by the Criminal Records Bureau (CRB) for previous convictions. This check can only be done after selection, not on all of the candidates for a job; therefore all verbal job offers are subject to this check. The purpose of this exercise is to protect children as far as possible from those unsuitable for the job.

It is vitally important to declare all convictions, cautions or bind-overs that you may have incurred, including any that would normally be regarded as 'spent'. Failure to do so could be interpreted as falsifying your application and could be grounds for instant dismissal. This is because being employed in a school when you have contact with pupils under the age of 18 exempts you from the conditions of the Rehabilitation of Offenders Act 1974. Therefore convictions may not be considered spent.

There is a Disclosure Service helpline number if you are in any doubt about this criminal record check: 0870 90 90 811, www.disclosure.gov.uk.

Your application will also be checked against List 99. This List contains details of people who are barred or restricted from working in schools by the secretary of state.

ACTION Regardless of the outcome of your interview, take some time to evaluate what happened and your interview strengths and weaknesses. This will be useful to review before future interviews.

Getting a GP

Every public library carries a list of GPs in the area. Use it to identify the practice nearest your new home. When you make an appointment to register with a new doctor, take into account any preferences you may have for either a male doctor or a female one, and any specialisms the GPs at the practice may have.

Most GPs carry out a mini-medical as part of the registration process, including weight and blood-pressure checks and blood and urine tests, so be prepared for a slightly longer initial consultation.

Finding a dentist

Don't leave it until crippling toothache forces you into a dentist's chair before registering. Although few and far between, there are still some dentists taking on NHS dental work, which is by far the cheapest option for newly qualified teachers. Your GP's surgery should maintain a list of NHS dentists in your area, as should your local library.

Other healthcare providers

Many people now combine conventional medical treatment with complementary therapies. The availability of such therapies on the NHS is increasing rapidly as the medical profession starts to embrace their success in treating many of today's common ailments. Ask your GP what complementary therapies are available on the NHS. Otherwise, your local health-food store or *Yellow Pages* will be sources of information on private practitioners. The professional body of a particular therapy can put you in touch with local practitioners and, as ever, personal recommendations are always valuable.

Arranging childcare

Arranging suitable childcare can be particularly difficult if you move to a new area. In the absence of personal recommendation, the Children's Information Services Development Project (CISDP), which supports the National Childcare Strategy, may be a good start. For information and factsheets, call Childcare-Link on 0800 096 0296 or e-mail childcarelink@opp-links.org.uk. For a local childcare register, visit their Web site, www.childcarelink.gov.uk. You can also get information on childcare issues from the Inland Revenue (www.inland revenue.gov.uk; tel: 0800 597 5976).

PART II

Joining a school

CHAPTER 3

Your responsibilities and rights – maintaining the balance

BECOMING A PROFESSIONAL

Once you have gained QTS, you are no longer a student, and doing the job for real can be a frightening prospect.

ABOUT ACKNOWLEDGING YOUR NEW STATUS

You are now a qualified teacher, but don't expect too much of yourself. David Berliner has identified four stages of teacher development: novice; advanced beginner; competent; proficient. It can be easy to expect yourself to sail from novice to proficient in the summer months between qualifying and starting your first job, but this would be an unrealistic pressure. That said, your rate of growth throughout your first year of teaching will probably be rapid.

The Standards for the Award of Qualified Teacher Status (see Appendix 1) clearly define what is expected of you and the way you should work within the wider context of the school community.

ESTABLISHING YOUR POSITION IN THE SCHOOL

If you have joined a new school, you will have to start from scratch as far as establishing your position with staff and pupils is concerned. They will expect you to fit in and work with shared values and a corporate purpose, and may even look to you to convince them you should be respected. You will have to set up your own routines and expectations and, above all, be consistent at a time when many of your pupils will be more familiar with the working of the school than you are:

- Make sure you have read and absorbed the appropriate staff handbooks so you know the professional procedures of the school, including information on special educational needs, sport and discipline. Also read other documentation relating to health and safety, resources, harassment, equal opportunities, child protection, first aid, emergency procedures, security (eg in the event of an assault or intruder), accident reporting and school visits.
- Make learning names (of both pupils and colleagues) a priority. Employ techniques such as making seating plans, spending time on name games and introductory sessions, handing out books yourself or taking pictures of your pupils to display on the wall of your classroom. Relating a piece of work to the image of a pupil is also effective.

EXAMPLE NQT Richard knew how effective it had been to learn the names of his pupils on teaching practice and decided to ease this task once in post by taking a photograph of each pupil he taught. He asked three students to sit together for each photograph to reduce costs and once the film had been developed he cut the photographs up, stuck them to a piece of card and put the name of the child under each picture. He then had an excellent resource to use when marking work, allowing him to make direct connections with each child.

- Do all you can to become familiar with your pupils' personalities. Their abilities will flourish (and sometimes fester) throughout the school year, so it is a good idea to avoid making rash judgements that pupils then have to live up (or down) to.
- Aim to build on what you have achieved in your training in the first crucial weeks. Do not try to 'build Rome in a day'.
- Be aware of your levels of self-confidence and how others might see you. Do not neglect your relationships with other members of staff. If you consider yourself to be fully immersed into the team so will they.

ABOUT VIEWING YOURSELF THROUGH THE EYES OF YOUR PUPILS AND COLLEAGUES

Everyone you meet, from pupils to fellow teachers to parents, will be aware of the fact that you are new. They will wonder what you are like. Are you strict or soft, funny or 'boring', better or worse than your predecessor? Most people will assess you in your first meeting and these impressions are hard to change. Bear this in mind as you meet new people, and try to view your classes and colleagues as groups of individuals that you will enjoy getting to know.

You should also consider that some members of the profession view NQTs with a sense of caution. The training you have undergone and professional expectations that are made of NQTs are now very different from previous years. It is worth being aware that some colleagues may not be familiar with current terminology relating to new teachers and induction.

- Take opportunities to become involved in the whole of school life. For example, attend school concerts and plays, PTA fund-raisers and staff social events. If time permits, there are usually extra-curricular activities that you can contribute to.
- Be aware of the areas of school life where you will have to make your presence known. You will need to interact with many groups of people so aim to build solid working relationships with each group.
- Aim to keep links with your ITT institution.

ABOUT BEING IN THE MINORITY

It is possible that you may experience additional difficulties settling in if the majority of staff members are of the opposite sex. This can happen to males particularly in the primary sector, and both males and females in single-sex schools.

While what sex you are may not seem relevant when it is equally represented on the staff, if you are the only male or only female gender identity can suddenly take on new significance. Try these tips to prevent loneliness:

- Establish a class link with a teacher of the same sex from another school.
- Create friendships and links when on INSET courses.

- Encourage speakers of the same sex as you to visit your school. The pupils will also benefit from the attempt at gender balance.
- Keep discussions with colleagues open about the issues you face as a member of a gender minority. This may encourage sensitivity on the part of your co-workers.
- If you find yourself in a minority for another reason and you are not happy in your situation, talk to your induction tutor/mentor. Your union may also be able to offer support, and Internet newsgroups and staffroom forums on education Web sites can be good ways of making links with other teachers in the same position as you.

But it's only me

Many new teachers go through a confidence crisis as they make the transition from student to qualified teacher. It is common to wonder why classes *should* listen to you and pupils respect you. Never forget that there is a whole culture and tradition of education and teaching of which you are about to become a part and, to a certain extent, you can lean on that as you start your career.

When you take your first class as a qualified teacher, it is not 'only you'. It is you, the teacher, in whom many people – not least your tutors and the team of professionals who employed you – have a tremendous amount of faith.

EXAMPLE In my first few weeks of term I couldn't get over what a fine line there is between anarchy and order in schools. I felt that things could really get out of hand very easily and having sole responsibility for my classes suddenly felt like a massive challenge. It took me time to realize that what I felt inside wasn't how the kids saw me and that, even if I felt unsure about my place in the profession, to them I was a fully fledged teacher.

(Becky, languages teacher)

ACTION Think about the reasons why you became a teacher. Now think about how you can incorporate those ideals into your new post, using the opportunities that your job will give you. Allow yourself to indulge in a little positive thinking on how eminently suitable you are for the task that lies ahead of you.

Becoming part of a team

None of us is as smart as all of us.

(Japanese proverb)

As an NQT, you will be part of several teams, not least the team that makes up the staff at your school. Within the team(s) of which you are a part, it is essential that good relationships are created so that work can be completed, values shared and progress made. Good staff relations also have a knock-on effect throughout the school – a cohesive team will be less open to pupil manipulation ('I didn't do my homework because Miss Jones told me that if it was too difficult I should leave it') and more receptive to the dissemination of good practice. They also allow a sense of collective worth and direction to be felt by all staff members.

Ask yourself how effective you are as a team member:

- Do you listen well to others?
- Do you contribute your ideas in good time?
- Do you fulfil your share of the tasks?
- Are you aware of the balance of the distribution of tasks?
- Do you accept assistance from other members of the team?
- Do you offer assistance when you can?
- Are you able to assert your own needs as an NQT? For example, you may have a slightly reduced burden of work within the team because of your other commitments.

Too often, teachers are working hard at creating resources that may be improved by a little collective creativity. There is no doubt that this is the most effective way of coping with the rapidly shifting ground on which teachers work.

Effective teams don't carry dead weight in the form of teachers who are not willing to share.

ABOUT OWNING YOUR PROFESSION

'What do I say when people ask me what I do?' is a question that some NQTs have asked. The assumption is that people will view your profession with a sense of ridicule. Not only that, but the question implies that some NQTs themselves have doubts over the validity of their chosen career. The only answer is to be honest. Explain what kind of teacher you are (eg history teacher, primary teacher etc) and follow up your answer with something positive, eg 'I really enjoy working with teenagers' or 'I'm lucky to have a job that offers such variety.' Be proud!

YOUR RESPONSIBILITIES AND RIGHTS

Any form of employment involves obligations and duties on the side of both employer and employee. The difficulties related to understanding this in the teaching profession are that a teacher's responsibilities are outlined in several separate documents. This means that you will have to read around to ensure you know the particular responsibilities and rights associated with your post. It is worth remembering that the Standards for the Award of Qualified Teacher Status state that new teachers should be 'aware of, and work within, the statutory frameworks relating to teachers' responsibilities'.

The following documents will be invaluable:

- your contract and job description, which may not be given to you before you begin work;
- the TTA document, *Qualifying to Teach: Professional standards for Qualified Teacher Status and requirements for Initial Teacher Training* (available from the TTA publication line: 0845 606 0323);
- the Induction Standards (Annex A of DfES Guidance, reference 582/2001, available on the DfES Web site: www.dfes.gov.uk);
- the Teachers' Pay and Conditions Act 1991, and the current Teachers' Pay and Conditions Document (known as the Blue Book, issued under the Teachers' Pay and Conditions Act 1991, available from the DfES Publication Centre or to download from the DfES Web site, and your school's office for reference);

- the *Conditions of Service for School Teachers in England and Wales* (known as the Burgundy Book), available for reference from your school's office, which sets out non-statutory conditions of employment. It is not a legal document, but a set of collective agreements, which can of course be overridden under certain circumstances;
- the Sex Discrimination Act 1975;
- the Race Relations (Amendment) Act 2000;
- Special Educational Needs and Disability Act 2001;
- DfEE Guidance 10/98: *The Use of Reasonable Force to Control or Restrain Pupils*;
- DfEE Guidance 10/99: *Social Inclusion: Pupil support*;
- DfEE Guidance 9/94: *The Education of Children with Emotional and Behavioural Difficulties*;
- any documentation from your union regarding your professional duties.

The TTA also suggests that the following documents may be useful for reference purposes (there is no expectation that new teachers should have read these documents):

- Education Act 1996;
- the Children Act 1989, section 3 (5), Safeguarding and promoting children's welfare;
- National Curriculum (2000) Inclusion Statement;
- OFSTED (2000) *Evaluating Educational Inclusion*;
- OFSTED (1999) *Raising the Attainment of Ethnic Minority Pupils*;
- NGfL Inclusion Web site: www.inclusion.ngfl.gov.uk;
- DfEE 0064/2000: *Bullying – Don't Suffer in Silence: An anti-bullying pack for schools*;
- DfEE (2001) *Raising the Achievement of Children in Public Care*;
- DfEE (1994) *Code of Practice on the Identification and Assessment of Special Educational Needs*;
- DfES Guidance 0732/2001: *Access to Education for Children and Young People with Medical Needs*;
- DfEE (1996) *Supporting Pupils with Medical Needs*;
- Commission for Racial Equality (CRE), *Code of Practice for the Elimination of Racial Discrimination in Education*, CRE Web site (www.cre.gov.uk/pubs);
- Safety at Work Act 1974, sections 7 and 8;
- DfEE Research Report 90: *EBD in Mainstream Schools*;
- Education Act 1997, section 5, Detention of pupils on disciplinary grounds;

- DfEE Guidance 10/95: *The Role of the Education Service in Protecting Children from Abuse*;
- Home Office/DfEE/Department of Health (January 2000) Guidance: *Working Together to Safeguard Children*;
- Department of Health: Framework for the Assessment of Children in Need and their Families (March 2000);
- Sexual Offences (Amendment) Act 2000, section 3.

ABOUT UNDERSTANDING YOUR RESPONSIBILITIES AND RIGHTS

It may seem as though you are wasting valuable time by even thinking about your legal liabilities, and a chat with a fellow teacher may reveal that he/she has never bothered looking into this area of employment. However, knowing what you are obliged to do gives you an understanding of what you should *not* be doing, and will minimize the chances of you becoming involved in a dispute related to your employment. It is also a requirement of having QTS that you know what your responsibilities are. Spend a little time now browsing some of the relevant documents for added peace of mind in the classroom.

The information that follows is designed to explain *generally* what the responsibilities and rights of teachers are. It should not be considered to be a definitive guide in the event of a dispute or contractual issue. In fact, no document should, unless it is a complete and authoritative statement of the law. Even then, you should also seek advice from your union on any aspect of your employment that concerns you.

YOUR RESPONSIBILITIES

Before you were awarded QTS, certain standards were satisfied. Those standards have been reproduced in Appendix 1. All the sections of the Standards for the Award of Qualified Teacher Status are equally important, but it is essential that the implications of Section 1, 'Professional values and practice', are fully understood.

Teachers' professional duties

A new teacher's professional duties can be summarized as follows, drawing on the Standards for QTS. These lists are not intended to be exhaustive, but to illustrate broadly the range of professional duties that teachers have.

For teaching, duties include:

- having the knowledge to teach the age range and subjects for which teachers are qualified;
- having high expectations of pupils;
- building purposeful relationships with pupils based on 'teaching and learning';
- preparing courses and lessons that are clearly structured and motivating, taking account of the interests and experiences of pupils, with evident learning objectives;
- using appropriate teaching methods and differentiating work where necessary;
- organizing teaching and learning space and time efficiently;
- managing pupil behaviour;
- using ICT effectively;
- encouraging independent learning through out-of-class work;
- collaborating with others in the profession to enhance learning;
- preparing and selecting appropriate resources;
- understanding the impact of the physical, emotional, linguistic, social, cultural and intellectual development of pupils;
- monitoring, assessing, recording and reporting on the development, attainment and progress of pupils.

For professional practice, duties include:

- demonstrating the values and behaviour expected of pupils;
- contributing to the school's corporate life;
- working within the relevant statutory frameworks;
- improving teaching through self-evaluation and professional development;
- communicating when necessary with bodies outside the school;
- participating in relevant meetings;
- safeguarding the health and safety of pupils both on school premises and when taking part in out-of-school activities;
- participating in arrangements for preparing pupils for public examinations;
- participating in the necessary administration required of the post;

- supervising and 'so far as is practicable' teaching any pupils whose teacher is not available.

An individual teacher is not required to provide cover after the colleague who is absent has been so for three or more consecutive working days unless the relevant authority has 'exhausted all reasonable means of providing supply cover without success'. (This also applies if the fact that such absence would occur was known to the relevant authority two or more working days before it commenced.)

The DfEE Guidance (Circular 0105/2000) makes the point that some teacher absence is inevitable and therefore the relevant authorities 'should have regard to the need for the efficient organisation of supply cover'. In particular, they should give priority to providing sufficient resources within school budgets for the estimated levels of supply cover likely to be needed during the school year.

ABOUT WORKING TIME

If you are employed as a full-time teacher, you are required to work on 195 days of a year, on 190 of which you may be required to teach. Over those 195 days you will be required to work at least 1,265 hours (called 'directed time') – although the burden of your workload should be reasonably distributed. Your headteacher is at liberty to determine how much directed time is spent on teaching and how much is spent on other duties. In addition to the 1,265 hours of directed time, you are obliged to work the extra hours needed to perform your duties. For example, you will have to spend additional time on marking, preparation, planning, training and report writing. You should be allowed a break 'of reasonable length' between the hours of 12 noon and 2 pm, or between school sessions.

The European Working Time Directive, which came into force in October 1998, limits the working week to a maximum of 48 hours, averaged over 17 weeks. Because of this 'averaging' it is unlikely that teachers in general will benefit from this part of the legislation. However, this does not mean that you should ever agree to be excluded from the working-time limit. There are grave concerns about the effectiveness of people who work consistently long hours as well as the implications for health and safety issues. This is an extremely difficult area for teachers, many of whom, when faced with the choice of going over the 48-hour limit in order to be prepared, or staying under the limit but teaching 'cold', would opt for the former. Seek advice from your union if working-time issues are affecting you.

Staff conduct

The conduct expected of you should have been made clear when you were employed by your school. It is the governing body of maintained schools that has overall responsibility for regulating teachers' conduct and there should be reasonable and non-discriminatory disciplinary rules and procedures made known to all staff. Grievance procedures should also be made known to staff.

ABOUT 'DISOBEDIENCE'

Your conditions of service will oblige you to obey the 'reasonable directions of the head', be they spoken or written in the various policies of the school. In extreme cases, 'disobedience' could be interpreted as a breach of contract, whether or not you verbally express, or simply demonstrate through your actions, your 'disobedience'. As disciplinary action and, worse, dismissal can follow, it is always essential to discuss with your headteacher any legitimate reasons you may have for not being willing to carry out his/her instructions.

Discrimination on the grounds of sex and race

In areas of both sex and race discrimination, you should be aware of the direct and indirect ways in which teachers can (sometimes inadvertently) act in a discriminatory way.

Direct negative discrimination involves treating one particular sex or race in a deliberately unfavourable way. Indirect negative discrimination refers to any discrimination that takes place as an effect of apparently fair and equal treatment.

There are certain situations in which it is illegal to discriminate against a pupil, for example when allocating resources to pupils, when deciding which subjects pupils should be taught (for example, offering ICT to boys and not to girls) and when making decisions on exclusions.

A paper by the Equal Opportunities Commission and OFSTED (1996), entitled *The Gender Divide*, reported that:

About one secondary school in five is weak in meeting the particular needs of one or other sex. In these, some or all of the following characteristics obtain: one sex might be seriously under-performing in lessons or in examinations; the books and resources used might not take appropriate account of gender issues; pupils might not be being prepared well for opportunities in working life.

The paper suggests that the following issues (among others) be considered to help improve the quality of learning in both sexes. It would be worth bearing them in mind as you prepare and deliver your lessons:

● To what extent are pupils' attitudes to learning, their confidence in particular subjects and their eventual success affected by their gender? Is it possible to establish meaningful generalizations without constructing stereotypes?
● How do pupils' gender-related attitudes change as they mature and why are some more influenced by their gender than others? Why do some pupils put barriers to progress in front of themselves? What role is played by social class, culture and geographic location?
● It appears that one reason why girls often achieve more than boys in school is that they more often demonstrate diligence, good behaviour and enthusiasm for learning. If this is so, how can schools encourage boys to acquire these qualities?

Do remember that when OFSTED visits, inspectors will be looking at all equal opportunities issues in the school. It is worth thinking about how your personal prejudices (and everyone has them) may affect your teaching. Are equal opportunities at the forefront of your mind when you speak, present information and organize the class? An open focus on equal opportunities helps to encourage acceptance of others and tolerance.

ACTION Write down at least three ways in which you can introduce an awareness of equal opportunities to your pupils, whatever the age group you teach. This may be through a discussion, illustrated examples, or a question and answer session. This will help you to get in the habit of focusing on equal opportunities in your teaching; you may even want to jot down in your planner when and how equal opportunities are met in your lessons.

Common-law duty of care

All teachers have what is called a 'common-law duty of care', although precisely what this means is not properly defined. Consequently any judgements made regarding the duty of care are based on case law.

As an NQT, you should understand the 'common-law duty of care' to mean that you will do 'what is reasonably practicable' when caring for pupils. This means that carrying out ongoing risk assessment is probably wise so as to minimize the number of potential hazards. Teachers should bear these factors (at least) in mind when assessing risk:

- the hazards and who would be affected by them;
- the safety measures needed to ensure an acceptable level of risk;
- the cognitive development and skill acquisition of pupils (including motor skills);
- pupils' physical strength, size or shape;
- the school environment.

As long as you demonstrate reasonably careful standards while at work, you should not bear any liability for accidents.

Safeguarding or promoting children's welfare

Every child has the right to protection from abuse and exploitation, and to have enquiries made to safeguard his or her welfare, as enshrined in the Children Act 1989. Although responsibility for investigating child abuse rests outside schools, there may be occasions when you and members of the pastoral team in your school will have to liaise with social services departments over the possible abuse that one of your pupils may be suffering. This is an extremely problematic area for teachers and, as an NQT, you should always talk to the member of the pastoral team who has been designated as the receiver of information about possible abuse *as soon as you suspect neglect or any form of abuse*. Under no circumstances should you wait to gather more evidence, or talk to the child about your suspicions, before voicing your concerns to the appropriate person.

Child abuse has been organized into the following categories for the purposes of the child protection register, as defined in Circular 10/95:

- *neglect*: persistent or severe neglect, or the failure to protect a child from exposure to any kind of danger, including cold or starvation, or extreme failure to carry out important aspects of care, resulting in the significant impairment of the child's health or development, including non-organic failure to thrive;

- *physical injury*: actual or likely physical injury to a child, or failure to prevent physical injury (or suffering) to a child including deliberate poisoning, suffocation and Munchausen's syndrome by proxy;
- *sexual abuse*: actual or likely sexual exploitation of a child or adolescent; the child may be dependent and/or developmentally immature;
- *emotional abuse*: actual or likely severe adverse effect on the emotional and behavioural development of a child caused by persistent or severe emotional ill-treatment or rejection.

Your school will have set procedures for dealing with suspected abuse and will pass any information on to the social services department. Only then can investigations begin, which will probably require the cooperation of the school. For this reason, it is vital that you keep a record of every conversation you have regarding the possible abuse of a child, including details of whom you spoke to, what was said, what was decided and the date/time.

ABOUT RECORDING YOUR CONCERNS

Protecting children from abuse is a teacher's legal obligation and part of that duty must be to protect yourself from allegations of negligence in the future. Always document every conversation you have about suspected abuse. You could also keep a diary in which you keep track of the development of your concerns. Such information can be invaluable at a later stage, especially if there are court proceedings. Remember, record:

- whom you spoke to;
- what was said;
- what was decided;
- the date and time.

Above all, make sure anything you commit to paper is strictly confidential and cannot be accessed by any child or adult other than the person in your school designated to deal with suspected abuse.

Appropriate physical contact with pupils

A common misconception is that teachers can have no physical contact with pupils in their care. Pupils (and employers) have sometimes exploited this belief so it is important to know the legal situation. Physical contact can be appropriate under several circumstances, mostly dictated by common sense, for example to prevent an accident, to stop a criminal offence being committed, to avoid damage to property or to prevent physical harm being done to a child.

Circular 10/95, *The Role of the Education Service in Protecting Children from Abuse*, is clear in the understanding that there are situations in which teachers will need to have physical contact with pupils, offering this advice:

> It is unnecessary and unrealistic to suggest that teachers should touch pupils only in emergencies. Particularly with younger pupils, touching them is inevitable and can give welcome reassurance to the child. However, teachers must bear in mind that even perfectly innocent actions can sometimes be misconstrued. Children may find being touched uncomfortable or distressing for a variety of reasons. It is important for teachers to be sensitive to a child's reaction to physical contact and to act appropriately. It is also important not to touch pupils, however casually, in ways or on parts of the body that might be considered indecent.

If there is ever a need to have physical contact with a pupil, keep in mind at all times that this contact must be *appropriate* to the situation and to the child concerned (some will be, perhaps for religious or social reasons, particularly sensitive to touch). It is always possible for perfectly innocent actions to be misconstrued, leading to the possibility of devastating accusations of misconduct or abuse.

Your school should have developed clear guidelines on what constitutes appropriate behaviour when it comes to physical contact with pupils. Make sure that you know the details of this policy.

The physical restraint of pupils

There are situations when it would be perfectly appropriate for you reasonably to restrain a pupil, although you should always be aware of your own safety. However, the word 'reasonably' is again open to interpretation in the absence of a clear definition. Many considerations need to be made, such as the age and size of the child, how serious the situation is (for example, is a vicious fight going on, or is it simply a case of rudeness or insolence?) and what could happen without intervention (might someone get badly hurt?). Of course, the use of corporal punishment is not legal under any circumstances in maintained schools or for publicly funded pupils in independent schools. 'For those pupils the law forbids a teacher to use any degree of physical contact which is deliberately intended to punish a pupil, or which is primarily intended to cause pain or injury or humiliation' (DfEE, 1998).

It is up to individual schools to draw up clear policies on the restraint of pupils so make sure you know exactly what you can do and under what circumstances in your particular school. Circular 10/98, *Section 550A of the Education Act 1996: The use of force to control or restrain pupils*, will offer additional information and advice, and your LEA may well have drawn up guidelines for schools to follow.

ABOUT RESTRAINING A CHILD

Circular 10/98 states that the law:

allows teachers, and other persons who are authorised by the Head-teacher to have control or charge of pupils to use such force as is reasonable in all the circumstances to prevent a pupil from doing, or continuing to do, any of the following:

- committing a criminal offence (including behaving in a way that would be an offence if the pupil were not under the age of criminal responsibility);
- injuring themselves or others;
- causing damage to property (including the pupil's own property);
- engaging in any behaviour prejudicial to maintaining good order and discipline at the school or among any of its pupils, whether that behaviour occurs in a classroom during a teaching session or elsewhere.

There are, according to Circular 10/98, three broad categories of situations in which physical intervention might be necessary:

- where action is necessary in self-defence or because there is an imminent risk of injury;
- where there is a developing risk of injury, or significant damage to property;

- where a pupil is behaving in a way that is compromising good order and discipline.

It goes without saying that a calm approach is more effective than anger or frustration. At all times you should think of your own safety and, immediately after the event, record exactly what happened with a senior member of staff. Describe who was involved (including pupils, staff and witnesses), what action you took to end the situation without restraint, how the pupil responded and why you took the action you did. Try to remember as accurately as possible exactly what every party said. Keep your own copies of any reports that are written.

If at all possible, do not attempt to restrain a pupil physically without the assistance of a colleague. Circular 10/98 states that physical intervention might involve staff:

- physically interposing between pupils;
- blocking a pupil's path;
- holding;
- pushing;
- pulling;
- leading a pupil by the hand or arm;
- shepherding a pupil away by placing a hand in the centre of the back; or
- (in extreme circumstances) using more restrictive holds.

Circular 10/98 also states that teachers should not:

act in a way that might reasonably be expected to cause injury, for example by:

- holding a pupil around the neck, or by the collar, or in any other way that might restrict the pupil's ability to breathe;
- slapping, punching or kicking a pupil;
- twisting or forcing limbs against a joint;
- tripping up a pupil;
- holding or pulling a pupil by the hair or ear;
- holding a pupil face down on the ground.

Personal property

Opportunity makes a thief.

(Francis Bacon)

All teachers take personal property to school with them, which may or may not be valuable. An item such as a handbag, containing money and credit/debit cards as well as keys etc, will be extremely tempting to some pupils. To a certain extent, you should consider that it is your responsibility to avoid placing pupils in positions of temptation, however much you feel you can trust them. This approach usually guards against potentially unpleasant situations arising. For this reason, schools should ensure that teachers have somewhere to secure valuables, such as a lockable desk drawer or a locker. Some teachers prefer to keep valuables on them all the time.

- Find out what insurance cover you have for loss of, or damage to, personal items. Check your own home contents insurance and any cover your union may provide. It may seem unfair, but your school and LEA have no legal obligation to protect your property.
- In the event of loss or damage, report the incident to your headteacher and ask what may be done about it. You could also approach your LEA's education personnel department and your union, depending on the seriousness of the loss.
- If ever you suspect that something has been stolen, don't deal with the situation alone. Ask for assistance from your line manager. Never accuse a pupil, however sure you may be; for many people, a false accusation will seem a worse crime than the theft itself.
- If you are asked to look after a pupil's personal property for any reason, do so as though it was your own – lock it away. Always return the property personally. Don't give it to another child to pass on, or give your keys to the child so they may help themselves. However, children should be discouraged from bringing valuables of any kind to school.
- Be sensitive about what you ask pupils to bring in for lessons. It may seem perfectly fair to ask year 10 to bring their own cricket bats in for PE, but do think about the implications of this for your colleagues!

YOUR RIGHTS

This is a far more difficult area to quantify. It's not that you do not have any rights as an NQT, far from it, but the rights you have are, in the main, moral rights, such as the right to dignity at work, which is open to varied interpretations.

Education law is incredibly complicated and can change at a fast pace. Do not assume, therefore, that your rights are being deliberately flouted if you are not granted the rights discussed below. It could be that your school has acted inadvertently. Seek advice from your union, Redress (see Appendix 8) and the documents mentioned above if you feel you have been treated unfairly at any time.

What follows is what NQTs can consider to be the minimum in terms of rights at work. It is not intended to be definitive and you should refer to your own conditions of employment documents and local practices for more details of your specific situation. Rights associated with induction and professional advice from outside your school are dealt with elsewhere in this book.

The right to correct pay

The governing body of a school commonly has the responsibility for developing a school pay policy and reviewing teachers' salaries annually. The LEA then has the duty to act on the decisions made by the governing body and arrange for payments to be made to the teachers of the school.

The main pay scale that was introduced in September 2002 has six points, from M1 to M6. There is no longer a distinction for newly qualified entrants to teaching between those with and those without a second-class honours degree or better. The minimum starting point for NQTs is M1.

Classroom teachers can also be awarded additional allowances for the following:

- management responsibilities – there are five levels, and the award of these should be linked to a clearly defined job description;
- recruitment and retention – there are five levels, which can be paid wholly or in part as a lump sum;
- teaching wholly or mainly children with special educational needs (not simply having SEN pupils in your class) – there are two levels.

If you work in the London area you are entitled to an additional allowance. At the time of writing, there are three areas of London for which different rates apply. They are:

- Inner London;
- Outer London;
- Fringes of London.

Check with your union and LEA education personnel office that you have been placed on the correct point with the appropriate allowances. From that starting position, every teacher must have an annual salary assessment by the school's governing body and be given a formal statement explaining what his/her salary is and how it has been arrived at. Salary assessments should also be made whenever the need arises throughout the year, for example if you take on an additional responsibility mid-year.

Unless your LEA or governing body decides that your teaching experience has been insufficient, or you have been employed for fewer than 26 weeks in any one year (not necessarily in the same school or consecutively), you are entitled to an additional full point every year, up to a total of eight points (including the point received for a good honours degree or equivalent). The 26 weeks do not have to run consecutively, nor do they have to be served in the same school. Holidays and periods of sick, maternity and paternity leave count as time in service for the purposes of the 26-week rule.

If your performance has been unsatisfactory for any reason, you must be told in good time (in writing) if one of these experience points is going to be withheld. It would be most unusual for a point to be withheld without incompetency procedures being followed. You must also be given suitable help and additional training to help improve performance and, as soon as it is deemed to be adequate, the additional point should be awarded, regardless of when this is in the school year.

Not only are you entitled to correct pay, but also to being paid on time. This is usually the responsibility of your LEA's payroll department. Do be aware that the day you receive your payslip may not be the day you can start to draw on the money. Some LEAs issue payslips the day before.

ABOUT PAY FOR PART-TIME AND SUPPLY
TEACHERS

If you are teaching on a part-time contract, you are eligible for the same main scale points and relevant allowances as full-time teachers. Your pay should be on a pro rata basis. If you complete service during any 26 weeks of a year, you are entitled to a point on the main scale for experience.

If you are employed on a day-to-day basis, commonly as a supply teacher, your pay should be calculated on the basis that a full year consists of 195 days. Some unions have evidence that a divisor of 365 days has been used in some areas so, if this type of contract applies to you, be sure that you are being paid the correct amount. Your union will be able to assist you if you have any doubts or concerns about the way in which you are being paid.

It is a little-known fact that governing bodies also have the discretion to make additional payments to teachers who undertake voluntary continuing professional development (CPD) at the weekends or during the school holidays (ie outside the directed time of 1,265 hours). The reason behind these payments is to help reduce the number of school days that teachers may miss through attending training courses. You should not be required to undertake CPD outside your directed time, and heads should respect the fact that weekends and holidays may be sacred times for you!

Governing bodies can also decide whether to make payments to teachers who are involved in out-of-school-hours learning activities, for example breakfast clubs, homework clubs, summer schools, outdoor activities and so on. There is, however, the proviso that involvement in out-of-school-hours learning activity 'is entirely voluntary and payments can only be made for substantial and, where appropriate, regular commitment outside a teacher's 1,265 hours of directed time' (DfES, 2001a). Part-time teachers are not eligible for such payments.

The right to equal opportunities

While issues relating to equal opportunities will need to be addressed in your teaching, you also have entitlements as an employee. Most LEAs have their own equal opportunities statements. These will aim to ensure equality of opportunity for all employees on the grounds of:

- gender;
- race;
- religion or creed;
- colour;
- disabilities and medical conditions;
- nationality;
- ethnic origin;
- marital status;
- sexual orientation;
- social class;
- living with HIV and AIDS;
- political belief;
- age;
- dependants;
- trade union membership and affiliation.

This usually entails a commitment on the part of employers to review selection criteria and procedures so that those who can best perform the duties of the job fill vacancies. That way, the focus can remain on abilities and merits as opposed to anything else. This could mean that, in order to remain true to an equal opportunities policy, you may be entitled to extra training so that professional progress can be made.

ABOUT AFFIRMING YOUR RIGHTS TO EQUAL OPPORTUNITIES

Part of an effective equal opportunities policy must be the provision of facilities for complaint and appeal for all employees who feel they have been treated without due regard for the policy. Make sure you know what the procedures are for lodging a complaint about unfair treatment under your school's equal opportunities policy. To ease the process, document any situations that you feel flout the standards set out in the policy, and talk to a trusted colleague or mentor and a representative from your union about your experiences before making a complaint. Input from others helps you to retain perspective.

The right to take leave

There could be many situations when you may need to take leave. The most common reason is for ill health, but you may also need maternity/paternity or compassionate leave. The exact arrangements and entitlements for leave vary from LEA to LEA, but there are some minimum standards that you can expect.

Sick leave

As an NQT you are entitled to a minimum of 25 working days of sick leave on full pay, followed by 50 working days on half-pay, on completion of four months of service. Your sick leave entitlements increase with years in service to 50 working days on full pay and 50 working days on half-pay in your second year, 75 working days on full pay and 75 working days on half-pay in your third year and the maximum of 100 working days on full pay and 100 working days on half-pay in your fourth and successive years. Working days are the 190/5 days (190 days with pupils in attendance and 5 days without pupils) that your school is open.

Any sick leave you take that occurs in holidays is not counted as part of the number of days available to you. For example, if your GP signs you off work for two weeks, one week of which is a half-term holiday, you will use just five days of your sick leave entitlement and not 10.

You are entitled to self-certificate for seven calendar days of absence due to ill health. This means that you can return to school on the eighth calendar day after the start of your absence and not have to produce a certificate from your GP. You will have to complete a self-certification form on your return to school. However, if it is necessary for your absence to go beyond about four days, you should consult your doctor or other healthcare provider anyway.

Keep copies of any letters and certificates that your doctor gives you for your employers. After 28 weeks of sick leave, during which time you will have been receiving Statutory Sick Pay as part of your salary, you will have to start claiming State Incapacity Benefit. Your employer will send the necessary forms to you.

It goes without saying that you should keep your school informed at every stage of your illness.

Maternity/paternity leave

If your school has adopted the agreements in the Burgundy Book, you are entitled to at least 18 weeks of *maternity* leave regardless of whether you are a full-time or part-time teacher or how long you have been in service.

After one year's continuous service you will be entitled to be paid for the first 18 weeks of maternity absence at the following rate:

- full pay for the first four weeks;
- 90 per cent of a week's salary for each of the next two weeks;
- for the next 12 weeks, half-pay in addition to statutory maternity pay.

In addition you will be entitled to be absent for a further period of up to 29 weeks counting from the beginning of the week of childbirth.

- There may also be additional entitlements based on local arrangements.
- If maternity leave is an issue for you, contact your union as early as possible for the latest information on your entitlements.
- Regarding paternity leave, this again is decided locally, although employees have a statutory right to 13 weeks of unpaid parental leave (conditions apply, see below). Again, as soon as you know you will need paternity leave contact your union for details of local arrangements. You may find that this is where the time you invested in building good working relationships comes to fruition. Do sort things out as early as possible so you are not trying to negotiate time off at the last minute.

EXAMPLE Andrew's wife was expecting their baby any day when he was called in to speak to his headteacher. He was told that it would be convenient for the school if she gave birth on the Friday evening, as that would allow Andrew to spend two full days with her without needing to take time off!

- If, during your pregnancy, you need time off for illness, you are entitled to take sick leave under the normal arrangements for your school. Your maternity leave will automatically kick in if your illness is deemed to be related to your pregnancy and it occurs during the six weeks before your baby is due.
- When you return from maternity leave, you should be offered 'no less favourable' terms and conditions than you had before taking leave.
- If you have any concerns about the terms of your maternity leave, contact your union.

Parental leave

Teachers who are parents of children born after 15 December 1994, and who have one year's continuous service, are entitled to 13 weeks' unpaid leave for the purposes of caring for a child, as enshrined in the Fairness at Work legislation. In order to qualify for this leave you need to have responsibility for a child.

According to the Employers' Organisation for local government, employees may only take four weeks' parental leave for each child during a particular year, beginning on the date upon which the employee becomes entitled to leave. Employees may take this in blocks of four weeks for four years and in the fifth year for one week only or in multiples of a week with the agreement of the employer (this is the so-called default scheme). The default scheme exists where there is no collective agreement on a different scheme of parental leave between management and trade unions.

There is a potential difficulty in this legislation for teachers, however. It is not yet clear how easily teachers will be able to take advantage of this right, as employers can defer the absence if it is expected to be 'unduly disruptive'. Your union and LEA will be able to offer advice if you decide to pursue your right to parental leave.

Compassionate/emergency leave

- You do not have an automatic right to paid compassionate leave, but, on the whole, employers understand the occasional need of employees to take compassionate leave in the event of the death of a close family member or friend. You do, however, have a statutory right to unpaid compassionate leave. Your employer will be able to advise you.
- You will need to keep your school informed of your requirements at such a time, and under no circumstances should you feel guilty about taking time off.
- Your GP will be able to sign you off if you both decide you should have some more time. As soon as your compassionate leave turns into sick leave, your sick leave entitlements kick in.
- Compassionate leave is extended in some areas to allow for a day for moving house. Obviously, at such a stressful and busy time you need to be aware of easing your situation. Moving on a Friday or even in the holidays would be the ideal, but clearly this is not always possible.
- Other reasons for taking leave may include weddings, christenings, funerals etc. There will be local arrangements, which your union and LEA can

inform you of. Such rites of passage can be incredibly important, so don't assume that you won't be able to take time off. It could be that you only need a half-day, which may well be accommodated, but may not be paid.

- If you need advice on any of the agreements set out in the Burgundy Book, contact your union or the Employers' Organisation for local government.

The right to knowledge of agreed duties and codes of conduct

You have a right to be fully informed of your duties before you begin work at a school. This should include *every* aspect of the expectations that will be made of you, including such things as break duties etc. If you have not been told fully what your duties and obligations entail, you cannot be held responsible for their non-fulfilment.

You also are entitled to be told of the individual codes of conduct at your school, so that you do not have to suffer embarrassment when you inadvertently break one. Such codes of conduct are often unwritten rules such as standing up with your class when the headteacher enters your room, or wearing a tie etc.

The right to be treated in accordance with education law

Although this should be assumed, it is surprising how often teachers find themselves victims of treatment that is either not in accordance with education law or only just within the legal framework when interpreted literally. Advice from your union, Redress and your LEA will be useful here.

The right to knowledge of a clear line of authority

You have entitlement to guidance on the power structure in your school and your position therein. This should include information on which personnel you should consult under which circumstances, for example in the event of discipline problems. Much of this will be covered in the early days of induction. Without such knowledge, you may be in danger of ignoring the lines of authority that are already established in your school.

The right to knowledge of disciplinary and appeal procedures

Before any disciplinary action needs to be taken, you should be informed as to where you can find details of disciplinary and appeal procedures. The chances are you will never need to refer to such information, but you do need to be in a position of knowledge.

Such procedures are usually a matter of local agreements, and your governing body or LEA should give you a copy of the procedures. If ever you are involved in a disciplinary matter, it is essential that you consult Redress and your union. There are usually informal and formal ways of addressing disciplinary matters. If formal procedures are invoked, you have the right to representation, full information as to the timing and schedule of the process and protection from unnecessary delays.

ABOUT REDUNDANCY

If there is a need to make you redundant on the grounds that your post will cease or significantly diminish, the DfES advises governors that they must:

- give as much warning as possible;
- consult your unions to seek agreement on the criteria for selection of staff for redundancy;
- ensure that the criteria are reasonably objective;
- consider any representations by union reps;
- consider whether alternative work can be offered.

If ever you are told that there is a possibility that you will be made redundant, or even if rumours start to circulate about imminent redundancies, be sure to consult your union at the earliest stage.

The right to dignity at work

Dignity at work covers many different areas, but holds equal importance to other rights you have. Some of these rights to dignity at work stem from written laws; others are moral rights that you are entitled to assert in a civilized society, for example:

- the right to work in a safe environment with due recognition of health and safety legislation – this includes all safety at work issues and the right to appropriate medical assistance if/when needed;
- the right to work in a clean environment – this especially covers the state of your immediate workspace as well as staff kitchen areas and toilets;
- the right to appropriate treatment from peers and superiors without harassment or bullying.

EXAMPLE Ann was suffering from a mild kidney infection, which her doctor had advised her to treat by drinking glasses of water throughout the day. When her headteacher visited her classroom and saw her take a sip of water in front of the pupils, he announced, loud enough for the class to hear, 'We don't drink in front of the class, do we, Miss Smith?', an example of a headteacher not granting a member of staff dignity at work and undermining her authority in the class by publicly reprimanding her. That said, Ann could have prevented this from happening by explaining the situation to her headteacher in advance.

ABOUT ACCOUNTABILITY

Questions about whom teachers are accountable to have been asked since the start of formal education in this country, and will, no doubt, continue to be asked. It is an inherently-complicated issue. There is a temptation to assume that, because of the extent to which the work of a teacher is directed externally, personal accountability and responsibility cannot be equated with public accountability.

When thinking about your accountability as a teacher, consider your pupils, their parents, society generally, the teaching profession as a whole (including the General Teaching Councils), your managers, the governors of your school, your LEA and other stakeholders. Above all, though, be aware of the extent to which your own reflections on your work affect your feelings of accountability. As Professor John Tomlinson, former vice-chair of the General Teaching Council for England, said, 'teaching is about conscience'.

Although the above list seems all-encompassing, the multiplicity of both external and internal accountabilities is a positive thing. There are elements of accountability in all aspects of business and industry, and knowing you are accountable can certainly help to maintain high professional standards.

THE EDUCATION POWER STRUCTURE

As a teacher, you are part of the whole structure of education, not simply of your school. It is useful to appreciate this, not only to gain an idea of your place in the grand scheme of things but also to gain awareness of the roles of the many tiers within your LEA and your school's power structure. There are interactions and interdependencies with which to become familiar. With a little skill, you will be able to turn this knowledge to your advantage.

The LEA

The LEA is essentially the county or borough council. Rather than try to deal with such a large area of the council's responsibilities *en masse*, the council usually organizes its responsibility for the education provision in the county or borough through the LEA.

The LEA has responsibilities to provide for all maintained schools (for example, community and community special schools) as far as running costs and buildings are concerned. The arrangements for voluntary and foundation schools are slightly different, as their governing bodies hold more responsibilities. While schools themselves have the responsibility for raising standards, LEAs have the task of supporting and challenging schools so that improvements are as continuous as possible. They also have a role in implementing national initiatives such as the numeracy and literacy strategies.

The government holds the view that there are certain functions of LEAs that should not be discharged by schools themselves. These have the headings:

- special educational needs;
- access and school transport;
- school improvement and tackling failure;
- educating excluded pupils;
- pupil welfare.

LEAs are expected to delegate both funding and responsibility to schools so that they can be genuinely self-managing.

The following model is not the rule, but is often the case:

- The LEA is led by a director of education (sometimes called a chief education officer or county education officer) who is usually assisted by a deputy and assistant directors. These positions are non-elected and non-political.

- The assistant directors usually share the responsibilities of all the different aspects of the education service on offer in the county including pupil services, buildings and the advisory and inspection service.
- Senior education officers then look after matters delegated to them by the assistant directors. In turn, assistant education officers help the senior education officers.
- There is then a tier of administration staff to support all of the above.
- Depending on the geographical size of the LEA, there may also be area education officers working in local offices (often where teachers' professional centres are based), but reporting to the main LEA office (usually County Hall).

The school organization committee

The school organization committee is central to local education decision making in England, as it must approve the school organization plan for the area and take decisions on proposals to change individual schools. Education is invariably the largest local government responsibility and it often accounts for over half of an authority's total budget. It is the LEA's responsibility to form a school organization committee for its area and to appoint members.

This committee is a specific statutory entity and is separate from the LEA and any education committees that it may run. The aim is that it brings together all the key partners in education provision at local level and that each has an equal voice. By making decisions that were previously made by the secretary of state for education, it strengthens local decision-making abilities. It convenes to vote on the school organization plan and to vote on statutory proposals.

The committee is organized in a maximum of six groups with no more than seven members in each group. Each group has a single vote, regardless of how many members it has. The groups will represent:

- the LEA (elected members who are appointed in proportion to the balance of political power within the authority);
- the Church of England (nominated by the diocese(s) covering the local authority area);
- the Roman Catholic Church (nominated by the diocese(s) covering the local authority area);
- the Further Education Funding Council;
- schools (members drawn from serving school governors);
- an optional extra group appointed at the discretion of the LEA – possibly representative of an ethnic minority in the area.

The LEA's education personnel/human resources department

While each education personnel/human resources office is set up differently across the country, there are basic services that they all provide. The function of the education personnel/human resources department is like that of any other personnel department, apart from the fact that teachers also have staff in the school where they work who will be able to advise on personnel issues as well.

Most education personnel departments would like to think that they offer a friendly, supportive service. They also offer the advantage of being open for advice at times when schools are not, such as in the holidays. Here are some examples of the services you can expect from your education personnel department as an NQT:

- in some cases, a free, confidential helpline for teachers and other council employees covering issues such as HIV and AIDS, stress and anxiety, personal finances, drugs and alcohol abuse and relationship problems;
- vacancy lists for jobs in the area;
- county housing for short-term letting (in some areas), or help securing appropriate accommodation if you are moving to a new area;
- advice on salaries, contracts and some legal issues;
- references for banks and letting purposes;
- advice and support through sick leave – some even offer home visits.

The advisory and inspection service

Each LEA has an advisory and inspection service (AIS, sometimes called an advisory, inspection and training service – AITS). As the name implies, this team of people advises and inspects teachers in the LEA (see Chapter 10 on inspection). There will probably be an adviser with responsibilities for NQTs, and you will meet advisers and inspectors when you take part in your school and county induction programme. Your school will have to buy the services of relevant advisers and you may well be invited to sit in with your head of year or department when they have an adviser in. If you are given this opportunity, take it.

The AIS offers support not only to teachers but also to headteachers, and again many advisers and inspectors used to be teachers. It also offers in-service training, which can cover general topics such as school improvement and the curriculum, or specific-focus courses such as behaviour management and, for example, teaching history to year 3. However, do not be surprised if the person delivering INSET and advice one week is the person inspecting you the next.

It would be a good idea to find out where the AIS in your LEA is based. It will not necessarily be in the main buildings of the LEA.

Your school personnel

> Always be nice to secretaries. They are the real gatekeepers in the world.
>
> (Anthony J D'Angelo)

Many of the personnel in your school will hold responsibilities above and beyond what their title suggests. For example, there will probably be someone with responsibilities for staff development, examinations, resources, ICT and assessment. There must also be:

- a special educational needs coordinator (SENCO);
- a head of careers and guidance;
- a named person to deal with child protection issues;
- a health and safety officer.

The management and teaching staff in your school are likely to include:

- the board of governors;
- a senior management/leadership team usually comprising headteacher and one or more deputies depending on the size of the school (responsible for formulating and implementing policies on the approval of the governing body, managing the school's work and administration and organizing the school's curriculum);
- heads of school or heads of year in the pastoral structure;
- faculty heads in the academic structure;
- heads of department and their assistants;
- classroom teachers;
- paid classroom assistants (some of whom may be given the opportunity to take on extra responsibilities and possibly train as teachers).

Non-teaching staff are by no means the least important members of your school's team. It simply could not function without these people:

- unpaid classroom helpers;
- secretaries;
- bursar;

- reprographic staff;
- technicians, eg science, ICT and art;
- midday meal supervisors;
- premises officer/caretaker/site manager;
- lollipop men and women;
- cleaners, caterers and gardeners.

The governing body

Every school has a governing body. In the maintained sector, these governing bodies have far-reaching powers and responsibilities, especially in aided and controlled schools. It is worth knowing that in these schools the only person to whom you can make a complaint about a governor is the Secretary of State for Education, although your union and LEA would want to know about the nature of the grievance, and would seek to resolve the situation before the need for a formal complaint arose.

The nature of governing bodies varies from school to school. Some governors are rarely seen in the building between meetings, yet others are fully integrated in the work of the school, often helping in classes and with school events. Most schools welcome the help and support that is freely given by those governors who have no personal ambitions and who are generous with their time and skills.

Governors are volunteers and are responsible for a school's budget. They are central to the running of your school, and must steer it through all eventualities in accordance with the law, the school's articles of government and the policies of the LEA (in community schools).

A school's governing body consists of appointed, elected and co-opted governors. There will be parent governors, teacher governors and partnership governors (in foundation schools), as well as representatives from the non-teaching staff. The size of a governing body is dependent on the size of the school it serves, and it runs on the basis of collective responsibility. There does not need to be a chair of governors.

The role of governing bodies

- The main role of governing bodies is to aid in the raising of standards in a school, including creating plans for the school's development. This entails ensuring that pupils at the school are offered the best education possible, through effective management and correct delivery of the National Curriculum and religious education, assessments and target setting.

- Governors must also ensure that the school has a character in line with its ethos and mission, particularly in voluntary-aided schools. To do this, they must determine the aims of the school as well as the conduct, and appoint, promote, support and discipline staff (including headteachers and deputies) as appropriate. They also set the times of the school day, and the governors in foundation and voluntary schools can set term dates as well.
- Governors have a role in deciding how best the school can promote the spiritual, moral and cultural development of pupils.
- Governors must manage the school's budget in accordance with current education law.

When these roles are considered, it is essential that the governing body and the senior management/leadership team have a good working relationship. The decisions that a governing body has to make are far-reaching but as long as they stay with education law they are protected from financial liability. The strength of a governing body comes from the ability of its members to work as a team using the resources and skills at their disposal.

EXAMPLE A teacher in her fourth year in the profession was staggered to realize the extent of the power that the chair of governors of her school had assumed, following the withholding of her salary. He denied access to minutes of meetings, offered no complaints procedure and blocked communication with other members of the governing body. This is an example of how damaging this power can be when misused by someone with personal agendas. This is by no means the norm, but has happened nonetheless. Always insist on your rights to correct procedure.

Key figures

In an ideal world, you would get on well with everyone. However, these people will be of particular use to you and all will support different aspects of your work:

- your headteacher;
- those governors who may be attached to your department or class;
- your induction tutor/mentor;
- your line managers;

- secretaries and bursars;
- library staff;
- cleaners and caretaker – don't underestimate how valuable these may be when it comes to staging displays, for they will know where unusual resources and props may be found;
- technicians and reprographic staff.

ABOUT WORKING WITH YOUR GOVERNORS

Your governing body must meet at least once a term. Between meetings, the headteacher of your school will keep governors informed of curriculum matters and anything else that is relevant, and there should always be a continuous dialogue between these two aspects of management. The agenda, minutes and related papers from governors' meetings must be available for staff to read. Teacher governors are usually the ones to ensure that this is done.

- Get to know the teacher governors in your school. They are the conduits of information between teachers and governors although they are not the delegates of the teaching body. You may pass on your views to teacher governors but they don't necessarily have to be represented at meetings.
- Find out who the parent governors are at your school. This is particularly important if you teach their children.
- Attend the annual meeting between parents and governors at your school.
- If a governor visits you, find the time to talk about the issues that are facing you in your classroom.
- Try to think of the governors at your school as 'critical friends' as well as nurturers and supporters of your work. Allow (or ask!) them to be motivational and inspirational.
- Use governors as a valuable resource.
- When a vacancy arises for a teacher governor in your school, consider applying (although ideally not in your first year in the profession).
- Governing bodies must establish a complaints procedure and make it public to all it concerns. If you have a grievance with your governing body you should seek advice from your headteacher, Redress, your union and (if you work in a faith school) your diocese. If you work in a community school you can also seek advice from your LEA. Governing bodies have a duty to deal with grievances fairly and promptly.

ABOUT GETTING ON WITH YOUR COLLEAGUES

It can be easy to forget what impact other people are making in order to ease your day when you are busy and rushed off your feet. However, it is important to recognize the efforts of others. It is also vital that you get to know the pressures that other people are under – you are not the only busy person. Positive comments about what other people have done for you will never go amiss. Perhaps a small gift for the secretary who prepared your worksheet at the last minute or the bursar who dealt with your muddle of monies for the school trip will nurture your relationships. You could also get to know your cleaners' working times and ask if there is anything you and your classes can do to help them.

The General Teaching Council for England (GTCE)

The General Teaching Council is the professional body for teachers in England. It was established on 1 September 2000 and the register of teachers was established on 1 June 2001. The GTCE is an independent body and is not answerable to government.

The Teaching and Higher Education Act 1998 set out the GTCE's main aims, which can be summarized as follows: to contribute to improving the standards of teaching and the quality of learning; and to maintain and improve standards of professional conduct among teachers.

It also has a statutory duty to provide advice to the government and other bodies on education policy, including the recruitment and supply of new teachers, ITT and induction, professional development, medical fitness to teach and professional conduct. Within these aims lie the priorities to listen to and work for teachers, to raise the status of the profession, to provide a professional voice for teachers and to guarantee high standards. The GTCE's Corporate Plan sets out the Council's work programme for the coming year. For the latest Plan, visit the Web site: www.gtce.org.uk.

The GTCE is not a union – it has no role to play in pay and conditions of employment – so it is advisable for all new teachers to join a union as well as registering with the GTCE (see the section on unions in Chapter 4).

The GTCE's register of teachers with QTS will record current employment, qualifications and entitlement to teach, as well as names and addresses. The law requires all qualified teachers currently teaching in maintained schools or non-maintained special schools to be registered. Potential employers and members of the public will be able to enquire whether or not a teacher is registered. The GTCE has the power to register and deregister individuals. Those in the independent sector and further education are encouraged, but not required, to register, as are all those with QTS, as holding a place on the register guarantees each teacher's qualifications and fitness to teach.

The GTCE has 64 members comprising:

- 25 teacher elected members (11 primary teachers, 11 secondary teachers, 1 primary headteacher, 1 secondary headteacher and 1 special school teacher);
- 9 nominees from the teacher unions and associations;
- 17 nominees from other interest groups mostly from within the education system (but not teachers);
- 13 nominees of the secretary of state, including teachers and parents.

Profiles of the Council members can be viewed on the GTCE Web site.

The GTCE will provide information, services and support for teachers as well as putting them in touch with professional networks and assessing professional development opportunities.

Through the GTCE, teachers are regulating their own profession, helping to safeguard its own standards. This is in line with other professions such as medicine, law and nursing. Council members will hear cases referred to them by employers of alleged unacceptable professional conduct or serious professional incompetence. Such hearings could ultimately mean removal from the register, although this would be a final resort.

To date, the GTCE has had a significant impact on entitlement to continuing professional development as well as influencing debate on accountability and inspection, and teacher qualifications.

For more information on the GTCE, take a look at www.gtce.org.uk or telephone 0870 001 0308. The online community on the Web site is one way of getting involved in the work of the GTCE. Publications from the Council offer feedback opportunities.

There are also General Teaching Councils for Wales, Scotland and Northern Ireland. Information on the General Teaching Council for Wales can be found at www.gtcw.org.uk, for Scotland at www.gtcs.org.uk and for Northern Ireland at www.deni.gov.uk/teachers/.

THE SCHOOL AND THE COMMUNITY

The school in which you teach is not isolated. It forms part of the complex structure of society in which many institutions are codependent. Schools are crucial in the preparation of the community's young for adult life, and the many institutions and organizations that will either employ them or educate them when they leave your school seem to be playing an increasing part in the education these children receive. For this reason, NQTs should look to the community in which they are working for ways of involving the many agencies that can add to the education they offer.

The quality of a school's links with the community and other schools is a focus of OFSTED inspections under the section of the evaluation schedule (the framework for inspection) that deals with the curricular and other opportunities offered to the pupils of a school. This is another reason to develop and nurture relationships within the community.

Utilizing connections

Your school may already have well-established links with schools and businesses in the community. Ask your induction tutor/mentor or headteacher for details of such links so that you may benefit from them. There is much to be gained here, such as:

- the possible sharing of resources between schools;
- cooperation on major projects such as school plays, concerts and sometimes even residential trips;
- input from specialists who may not be on the school's staff;
- support for the needs of the school – many businesses are happy to supply equipment if it means good publicity;
- opportunities for work experience for pupils, and for them to gain greater economic awareness;
- the chance for teachers to update their knowledge of the world outside education and what will be required of their pupils.

Links with other schools

This is where you can really benefit from sharing resources and ideas with colleagues from outside your own school. The value of developing strong working relationships with other schools cannot be overestimated. On a professional level, such links will ensure that your teaching and resources enjoy regular injections of added inspiration and, on a personal level, they put you in a better position for retaining your perspective.

ABOUT UTILIZING CONNECTIONS

If your school does have well-established links with other schools and businesses, aim to make use of them where possible. Think of ways in which you can supplement your lessons, thereby adding an extra dimension as well as easing your own pressures. Always explain to your classes the relevance of any visitors and try to devise follow-up work that will record the event in some way.

Ways of creating links with other schools

- Use INSET courses and other professional development opportunities to strike up friendships with your counterparts in other schools. With your headteacher's consent, liaise with another school over a particular project by way of experiment. If it works, the road is open for future collaboration.
- Ask any LEA advisers you meet if they can put you in touch with suitable colleagues in local schools. Advisers are in the position of knowing a wide selection of schools and the strengths and weaknesses of individual teachers. They also have an overall view of the work in progress in their subject area across a range of schools.

Links with businesses and public services

There is so much scope for combining education and the world of employment. It may take a little time to set up useful links, but you could find that it's time well spent. The choice of possible visitors is vast, from police, local religious groups, the medical profession and civil servants to all levels of business, retail and charity personnel. There is, therefore, bound to be someone who could add a dimension to a scheme of work in some way. It is also worth considering that it is generally lessons that outsiders have attended that pupils remember well.

Ways of creating links with businesses and public services

- Ask your headteacher about links that currently exist, and get permission to create your own as appropriate.
- Read the local press, flick through the *Yellow Pages* and listen to local commercial radio to gain ideas and information on businesses and public services in your area.
- Find out if there are any parents and governors at your school who might be useful to you. You could also involve any family and friends who may be able to contribute to a lesson.
- When contacting appropriate businesses, find out if there is an education officer. These people will be in the best position to arrange what you require.

Public relations

There are few professions so much in the public domain as teaching. It sometimes seems that the only qualification needed to pass judgement on the state of education today is attendance at school yourself! For this reason it is particularly important to appreciate that the extra roles related to teaching that you may not have been informed about include marketing and public relations for your school.

Before you open your classroom up to visitors, consider these points:

- Cast an eye over the appearance of pupils before they meet outsiders. Deal with any obvious grime and untidiness discreetly.
- Take a look at your own appearance. Is your clothing appropriate for your day and reflective of your professional status?
- Think about how your class will greet a visitor.
- Make sure your classroom is tidy and that wall displays look neat and up to date.
- Your headteacher may want to meet any visitors personally. Arrange beforehand the best time to do this so you don't have to drag your guest around the school on a hunt for him or her.
- Spend time creating a congenial atmosphere in the class before visitors arrive. Deal with questions such as 'What's this got to do with anything?' in good time.
- Encourage your pupils to interact freely with visitors and talk about the processes they have used in their work related to the visit.

- Plan questions in advance with your pupils that they may want to ask the guest. Prompt individuals if necessary.
- Take any opportunities to demonstrate good achievement and progress.
- Involve the local media (and national educational press if appropriate). Favourable reporting will undoubtedly impress the governors.

ABOUT INVOLVING OUTSIDERS

It seems today that it's not only teachers who are pushed for time. Many of the people you need to contact when creating and utilizing links with outsiders will be giving up time in order to help you out. Follow these points to help ensure everything goes smoothly:

- Think about what aspects of the curriculum you teach could benefit from outside input before contacting anyone. You will probably need to explain your ideas to your head of department and headteacher, so make sure they are relevant to the curriculum and make sure you have identified clear learning intentions that would not be possible without the input of the outsider.
- Decide what level of input you would like – information and free items such as posters etc, someone to visit the school or a chance to take your class out into the community.
- Follow your school's guidelines on visitors. It is extremely important that anyone you involve is suitable for the task, and under no circumstances should you leave your visitor alone with pupils.
- Try to greet your visitor personally and make him/her feel at ease. The last time he/she visited a school could have been as a pupil.
- Be respectful of your visitor's time. Tell your visitor exactly when he/she is needed.
- Arrange for your visitor to be offered at least a drink.
- Always involve the class in thanking outsiders, whether visitors or contributors, for their input. This will make the people more likely to help again in the future.
- Be aware of any biases that may be presented. These can then be discussed with your class as appropriate.
- Share your contacts with colleagues. You may want to invite other classes to listen to outside speakers.

> **ACTION** Make a list of any local businesses or services that may be able to support your teaching. Keep a keen eye on any organizations that are in the local news or that seem to be raising their public profile. Perhaps these are the ones to approach when you want to involve outsiders.

Education Action Zones

Education Action Zones (EAZs) aim to provide an opportunity for parents, businesses, LEAs and others in the community to work with schools (usually in clusters) to develop new approaches to improving learning and education in the area. These approaches must be eminently suitable for the locality and aim to help alleviate the deprivation that is experienced by the community. The idea of zones recognizes the fact that education alone cannot tackle the problems faced by the zone's community. Zones work towards improvements focused on four main themes:

- improving the quality of teaching and learning;
- social inclusion;
- family and pupil support;
- working with business and other organizations.

An EAZ can cover up to 20 primary and secondary schools, and receives additional funding to help enable it to reach the targets for learning that it has set itself. A forum of businesses, parents, schools, the LEA and community organizations run each zone, led by a project director.

It is hoped that EAZs will help by:

- increasing achievement, for example by improving pupils' results in literacy, numeracy and GCSE examinations
- increasing opportunities for pupils
- increasing the number of pupils entering further education
- improving pupil attendance
- reducing exclusions from schools
- providing a broader programme of out-of-school activities
- improving the coordination of services to the community
- reducing youth crime

(DfEE, 1999)

For further information on EAZs visit the Standards site at www.standards. dfes.gov.uk/eaz/.

Excellence in Cities

Excellence in Cities (EiC) is a programme specifically targeted at improving the education of children in core urban areas. The aim is to raise standards in city schools higher and faster to match the standards of excellence found in the best schools elsewhere.

There are seven main policy strands to the EiC programme:

- City Learning Centres;
- specialist schools;
- gifted and talented;
- Beacon schools (see below);
- learning mentors (each child in the EiC target area will have access to a mentor);
- Learning Support Units;
- small EAZs.

Take a look at www.standards.dfes.gov.uk/excellence/ for more information, or e-mail eic.contact@dfes.gsi.gov.uk with specific queries.

Beacon schools

Beacon schools are those schools that have been identified as being top performers in the country. The scheme aims to raise standards by encouraging schools to share good practice and build strong working partnerships. They receive additional funding of around £35,000 a year on average to assist them in performing their responsibilities (for example, presenting seminars for teachers and governors from other schools, releasing teachers to other schools to share good practice, preparing new curriculum materials and so on).

There has been much debate over the concept and success of Beacon schools. Some view them as elitist and even patronizing whereas for others they are nothing short of brilliant in the way they facilitate the sharing of ideas and the dissemination of good practice. Although there is plenty of information available on Beacon schools (just take a look at www.standards.dfes.gov.uk/ beaconschools/ for a start), the only way to find out just how useful and effective they can be is to be involved in direct collaboration. There may well be a Beacon school in your area (your LEA will have a current list, or take a look at the above Web site). If there is, talk to your headteacher and induction tutor/mentor about making a visit and how your time there might best be utilized (do remember that your induction period should offer you the opportunity to visit a Beacon school).

CHAPTER 4

Your refuge – the staffroom

STAFFROOM POLITICS AND ETIQUETTE

The best teachers are positive teachers.

(Robert Grice)

Is the staffroom a place of peaceful sanctuary or of frightening fiends waiting to devour the fresh NQT? Whatever the presumptions about teachers being nurturers, educators and balanced all-rounders, staffrooms across the country may appear to contradict this! Before you mutter, 'There but for the grace of God. . .', it is important to consider how you can ensure solid working relationships with all your colleagues. You may have to bite your tongue a few times as yet another old-timer mutters, 'Career Entry Profile – didn't have anything so flash in my day' or 'Why on earth did you choose a career in teaching?' Don't forget that the time spent in staffrooms can be all too short an opportunity to divest yourself of the frustrations of the day. These have to be stored until you have an adult audience and this is the same for all teachers, regardless of their age or experience.

The staffroom has often been described as the 'backstage' area of a school and this is quite a useful analogy. Just as the audience in a theatre rarely glimpses what happens behind the scenes, so too are pupils banished from this most sacred of safe havens while teachers 'rest' after their 'performance'.

Staffroom characters

In order to gain understanding of the dynamics of the staffroom it is necessary to look at some of the characters you are likely to meet. Always be aware that you are joining an establishment that probably has an extended history, and long-serving staff at the school will have distinct habits and traditions.

Don't be put off by what seem to be incorrigible moaners. Try to observe your fellow teachers rather than be drawn into another individual's perspective. It is sometimes possible for a dominant staff member to dictate the whole tone of the staffroom, spreading his or her mood like a virus, which is not at all constructive.

Find your place in the staffroom by following these tips:

- Don't be daunted by other teachers' approaches to their jobs. Some will be bursting with enthusiasm while others will be counting the days to the next holiday. Try to retain your own perspective.
- Don't judge your fellow teachers too harshly. Everyone has reasons for the way they are, and a little understanding can go a long way.
- Remove yourself from any situation or conversation that makes you feel uncomfortable. Teachers always have a plethora of excuses they can employ to excuse themselves, eg an arrangement to see a pupil, photocopying to do or books that urgently need marking. If you don't like the atmosphere, take a walk outside in the fresh air for a few minutes.
- Be yourself. The staffroom is your place to rest and recuperate in time for the next lesson.
- Be discreet when others confide in you. Staffrooms in any place of work can become hotbeds of gossip, but this serves little purpose. Also, take care over discussing confidential matters within earshot of colleagues, who may not be aware of the sensitive nature of the discussion.
- Try not to use the staffroom as an extension of your working space. Not only is it hard to concentrate in a room full of chattering people but your mess could annoy your colleagues. Clear your lunch things away too – you won't be popular with the cleaners if you leave it all to them!

The alternative power structure

The staffroom is the place where the real power structure of your school can be revealed. It is worth observing the reaction of certain members of staff to new ideals and innovations and seeing how influential they are on the mood of the staffroom. Understanding the dynamics of the staffroom in this way will help you to resist the flow of current staff thinking and make your own informed decisions over particular issues.

ABOUT STAFFROOM SEATING ARRANGEMENTS

It would be great to report that the days of military-style occupation of certain items of furniture located in optimum positions of the room are over! Sadly, according to many NQTs, they are not. However, you are unlikely to be told of the Law of Seating Arrangements in your school until you commit the ultimate offence. Observe your colleagues for a few days before attaching yourself to a particular area in the staffroom. After a few weeks you will appreciate your caution as you realize how hard it is to move from one group's area to another. Teachers are no different from any other profession in this respect. In fast-paced, demanding jobs, people can be forgiven for retaining some element of habit.

Staffroom bullying

It is not just in the playground that members of the school community can experience bullying. Sadly, the concept of bullying seems inextricably linked with educational establishments and while all respectable institutions will have a policy on how to deal with child victims and perpetrators it can take a long time for staffroom bullying to be identified and dealt with.

Research suggests that teachers form the largest occupational group to suffer from workplace bullying – it appears that schools can be hostile places for some teachers. For NQTs, being forewarned is being forearmed. Bullying and stress are closely linked and negative stress invariably leads to illness. Bullying amongst staff presents great complications, not least because there is no consensus of approach over how it should be dealt with. However, your school should have devised a specific policy, rather than squeezing it under the heading of 'harassment'.

Identifying what bullying is

It is important to establish a definition of bullying as opposed to a personality clash or difference of opinion. True bullying can involve:

- insidious, relentless criticism;
- fault finding;
- humiliation;
- excessive work expectations;
- abuse of discipline and competence procedures;

- inappropriate forms of communication (eg shouting, ordering or 'death by a thousand memos');
- inexcusable blocks to promotion and training;
- withholding of recognition for performance;
- manipulation;
- lack of compassion in difficult circumstances.

ABOUT PERSONALITY CLASHES

Personality clashes are almost inevitable, especially in large schools with huge numbers of staff. It could be that the person you are having difficulties with is someone that other teachers find hard to relate to as well. Some surreptitious observation may help you here.

Never write off a relationship as being beyond hope. It may be stretching your skills of compassion, but there is always a thread of empathy that can be built on. You don't always have to agree with the opinions of others, but you can try to understand why they hold their opinions and why they behave as they do. You may find that those with whom you initially clashed become your closest allies.

ABOUT ADULT BULLIES

An adult bully aims to exert power negatively and consistently over another person with the purpose of inciting fear and causing professional and emotional damage. The bully is inherently destructive, but his/her actions could result from feelings of inadequacy, which have been deflected on to another person, who may be accused of the very flaws the bully detects in him or herself.

How bullying can affect you

Victims of bullying often have to cope with a multitude of symptoms. Most victims of staffroom bullying find themselves dealing with some of these:

- reactive depression;
- hyper-vigilance;
- shattered confidence;

- anxiety;
- fatigue;
- negative stress;
- digestive disorders;
- menstrual disorders.

This is perfectly normal under the circumstances, and can be short-lived as long as the cause of the bullying is dealt with. Victims of bullying can also anguish over the question, 'Why me?' The answer is often the same as for a child who is bullied – peers may perceive the person as being too popular, too accomplished, incorruptible or highlighting incompetence through competence.

EXAMPLE As soon as she realized that one member of staff was responding to her negatively, NQT Nessa started to develop a selection of symptoms, most worrying of which was uncharacteristic introversion. She started to question every action she took, which had a negative effect on her work. It became a downward spiral with every criticism leading to a worsening of her performance and so attracting further criticism.

Strong management or bullying?

> Never pay attention to what critics say. . . A statue has never been set up in honour of a critic!
>
> (Jean Sibelius)

There is a clear difference between strong management and bullying. All managers have the facilities to correct the behaviour or work performance of an employee, but this must be done in accordance with proper procedure. A sign of good management is how nurtured and encouraged you feel after a 'pep talk'. If you are left feeling despondent or humiliated, it is likely that bullying tactics have been employed. Good managers will observe aspects of your work performance that might need correcting and advise you in good time. In fact, they are obliged to do so. Your side of the bargain is to take on board what has been said and act on improving the areas that need attention.

However, there are tell-tale signs of bully-tolerant institutions. High absenteeism and turnover of staff seem to indicate staffroom distress. This in turn reduces the morale of the staff and a subculture of disrespect towards the management quickly develops.

Workplace bullying is illegal on several grounds. The responsibility for its prevention lies firmly with your employers.

EXAMPLE I found my induction tutor and headteacher to be really unpleasant. I couldn't pick out anything positive about the way they treated me. My experiences at the school went from bad to worse and by the end of my first term I was really ill. I ended up leaving the school and the area and doing day-to-day supply to rebuild my confidence. It has interrupted my induction period but I knew I had to get out of that environment. I still feel confused about why I had to suffer such a high level of personal criticism.

(NQT)

Dealing with bullies

If you feel you are experiencing bullying at work, there are many things you can do to minimize its ill effects. Try following this action plan:

- Talk to a trusted friend about your experiences. A second opinion can really help to give you a sense of perspective about the situation and will help you to decide whether to take action.
- Reread your job description, the Standards for Qualified Teacher Status, the Induction Standards and any information on the responsibilities of teachers, including the Burgundy Book available for inspection from the school office. This will reaffirm what tasks you should and should not be performing in your job. It is also worth reading the latest version of the *Governors' Guide to the Law*, which will inform you of procedures relevant to your situation. Be sure to read the correct version, as they vary depending on the type of school. These guides can be downloaded from the DfES Web site.
- Attend an assertiveness course, or read about it. Your professionalism may be under question and you will need to be able to deal with it calmly and rationally. Confidential professional counselling would also be a good idea at this stage and may be on offer from your LEA. Again, retaining perspective is crucial to the way in which you approach your bully. Try to avoid allowing the situation to permeate every aspect of your life.
- Seek advice from your union and Redress: The Bullied Teachers' Support Network. Bullying destroys good teaching and you don't want to be facing

accusations of incompetence in addition to the bullying. Most unions have their own documents on dealing with bullying, which are available to members and non-members. Read the literature from all of them (you may have to pay for booklets from the unions you do not belong to).

- Ask for a copy of your school's policy on workplace bullying.
- Read about workplace bullying. There are some excellent books available (see Appendix 9) and these will serve to reassure you that this problem is widespread – you are not alone.
- Gather support for your cause by speaking to carefully selected colleagues. Divulge a little of what is happening to you and you may find that other members of staff come forward as sufferers too.
- Document all communication you have with your bully – even relatively informal contacts. This is not being unnecessarily paranoid, but will serve you well at a later stage if you need to refer to previous conversations. Aim to ease any possible stress and anxiety.
- Refute all unfair claims that have been made against you – in writing if necessary – and keep records of anything you say or write.
- Monitor changes in your work performance due to bullying. This might include getting behind on marking and preparation, or feeling inhibited in your teaching. Keep copies of any induction assessments, appraisals and OFSTED reports you may have and read all the positive comments when your confidence is low.
- Visit your GP, even if your health doesn't appear to be suffering. It is sensible to have formally recorded what is happening to you and whom you consider to be responsible. Your GP will be able to offer constructive stress-busting advice and will be a source of support should you need to take time off school. If your GP recommends sick leave, follow his/her advice. Time taken now could prevent a health crisis. You should record any ill health resulting from bullying in your school's accident/incident book.
- Never be encouraged to 'slide out gracefully' or leave the profession if that is not what you want to do.

Seeking help

It is an unfortunate character trait of many competent professionals, such as teachers, not to ask for help when they could benefit from it. In the case of workplace bullying and other abuses of power, the more advice you can get from different agencies and individuals the better.

ABOUT REDRESS

Redress is an organization set up to offer advice to teachers who feel they may be suffering from workplace bullying and/or abuses of power. It offers many forms of support and aims for fast, effective intervention in order to bring an end to the bullying and abuse.

The success of Redress can be attributed to many factors. With the consent of the sufferer, Redress may make public the person's situation before it escalates, or inform the governors or senior management of a school about what is happening. The organization realizes that the umbrella of confidentiality can sometimes hide a multitude of sins, including professional misconduct, and seeks to stop this from happening. Redress also uses the services of lawyers who are expert in both employment and education law. If you think you might benefit from the services of Redress, do make contact sooner rather than later.

Possible sources of help from within your school

Anyone who is not your bully could be the source of valuable support, from the caretaker to the headteacher, so be open to the advice you are given. More specifically, try these sources:

- your induction tutor/mentor;
- other NQTs;
- your union rep;
- the person with responsibilities for staff welfare (usually a deputy head-teacher);
- a governor who is attached to your class or department.

Possible sources of help from outside your school

These sources include:

- your union;
- Redress;
- your LEA education personnel department;
- books on dealing with bullying;
- your GP or other healthcare practitioner;
- family and friends;
- the Internet (take a look at www.bullydissolver.com).

ABOUT ACTING PROMPTLY

As soon as you think you may be victim to bully tactics, seek help. Acting promptly can help to circumvent more serious situations such as a disciplinary or incompetence claim being made against you. Gloomy as it may sound, the longer you leave it to act, the harder the situation will be to resolve. There is a wealth of support for victims of bullying – you don't have to suffer alone. Just don't sit on any experiences of bullying you may have had without talking to someone.

UNIONS

Without wanting to sound alarmist, the importance of membership of a professional association or union cannot be overstressed for new teachers. You may have joined a union while you were still training, but if you haven't join one now. Don't leave it to chance that you will not be involved in any number of the many disputes that arise between teachers, employers, parents and pupils.

The benefits of membership

Unions perform many functions for their members, but for NQTs these are the most useful:

- They give advice over work-related matters.
- They represent members at many levels of discussions with employers.
- They provide welfare benefits, personal legal help, professional insurance and financial services.
- They offer confidential crisis support.

On a more general level, your membership will enable unions to continue their work towards improving pay and working conditions for teachers everywhere in the country and give you national representation.

ABOUT UNION MEMBERSHIP

Although the 'beer and sandwiches' days of the government/unions relationship are certainly over, there are many issues today that unions can use to gain ground lost previously. A good way to contribute to change in teachers' pay and conditions is to be part of a union from your first day of teaching. However, choose wisely and question thoroughly.

Questions to ask before joining a union

Think carefully before you decide what union to join. Unions are usually under the impression that, once a new member has joined, they can count on that membership for life, so they always covet NQTs. The assumption is that NQTs have their whole career ahead of them – a career during which they will perhaps encourage others to join the same union they did.

The services offered by teaching unions vary little from union to union. The difference lies in the way these services are delivered, the extent of the support offered and the amount of time it takes to receive *appropriate* help.

Resist the wooing, and obtain answers to these questions before making your decision:

- 'If I am involved in a disciplinary matter, will you supply a *legally qualified* representative to defend me?' (Some unions don't consult a solicitor – who may or may not be an education or employment law specialist – until after dismissal, preferring regional representatives to deal with hearings.)
- 'Will you ensure that any case in which I am involved will be passed on to a suitably qualified person at an appropriate stage?' (You don't want representatives to struggle at a local level if someone higher up the union ladder will be able to settle the dispute sooner.)
- 'What responsibility do you take for the advice you give me?' (If union advice causes you to lose a case, or significantly disadvantages you, will you have recourse to redress?)
- 'If I choose not to follow your advice or want a second opinion, will you still represent me?' (You don't want your case to be dropped with this excuse.)

Being aware of these issues will ensure that you can glean maximum advantage from the fees you will pay throughout the course of your career.

Regardless of which union you join, do take out your own professional insurance as extra protection. It is inexpensive, and can usually be added to your car or house contents insurance. Make sure the policy allows you to choose your own legal representative and covers you for at least £50,000 legal expenses.

EXAMPLE David needed union representation after suffering a breach of contract. The case went to court but when, nine days before the hearing, David still had no legal representation from the union, he arranged his own. His union dropped the case on the grounds that he had gone against union advice. The personal cost to David was £35,000. This is an exceptional case – many teachers are happy with the level of support they receive from their union – but it does illustrate how important it is to arrange your own professional insurance.

ABOUT SEEKING PROFESSIONAL ADVICE

If you find yourself needing professional advice, do remember that you should remain at the centre of the way in which your case is handled. Your permission should be sought at each stage of the proceedings and, if you feel a particular route should be taken, throw in your suggestion. Seek second and third opinions about what you can do to move towards a resolution and never absolve yourself of the responsibility to stay in control.

PARENT–TEACHER ASSOCIATIONS

Most schools run a parent–teacher association (PTA), which usually has responsibilities for raising funds for the school to be spent on items not allowed for in the school's budget. It may be a registered charity and/or affiliated to the National Confederation of Parent Teacher Associations.

Their value to the school

Given that PTAs raise money (that all too rare resource) they are generally of great value to the school that they serve. If it were not for the PTA in some schools, it would be impossible to provide equipment such as mini-buses, videos and sports and computer equipment or to pay for end-of-term celebrations such as a Christmas meal for staff and pupils.

In addition to the funds that PTAs can raise, they also offer the opportunity for parents to become more directly involved in the work of the school, without taking on the responsibilities of governorship. A well-functioning PTA draws from the parent, teacher and pupil community of a school and therefore can consider itself, in many ways, at the hub of school life.

The pros and cons of membership

As an NQT you will have the opportunity to become involved in your school's PTA at some level. Before deciding how much commitment you would like to make to the PTA, you should consider the pros and cons.

Pros are:

- Membership gives you the opportunity to influence the decisions of the PTA, for example the way funds are spent.
- Membership gives you the chance to contribute to constructive ways of improving the teaching and learning environment in your school.
- You can become known to a significantly involved group of parents in a relatively relaxed atmosphere.
- Membership gives you contacts for use in your lessons. Many parents are able to make valid contributions to the curriculum.

Cons are:

- Some schools see PTA membership as a burden and 'nominate' the newest member of staff to join.
- Being a member will commit you to evening meetings at times when you may prefer to be preparing, marking or relaxing.
- You may end up being committed to turning up early on Saturday mornings to prepare for car boot and jumble sales.
- If membership becomes a 'duty', your enjoyment will be seriously affected.

PART III

Working through your induction

I THINK COMING IN THROUGH THE WINDOW WITH STUN GRENADES IS A LITTLE O.T.T FOR YOUR FIRST LESSON WITH A ROWDY CLASS.

CHAPTER 5

Induction – all you need to know

THE CAREER ENTRY PROFILE

The Career Entry Profile (along with the notes of guidance and standards) should accompany all NQTs with QTS to their first job. Designed by the TTA, it is a framework for target setting and action planning to enable your school to deliver to you the necessary support in a structured manner based on your strengths and development needs.

It consists of three sections, the first two of which (sections A and B) are to be completed by you and your ITT provider between May and June of your final year of training. The last part (section C) is to be completed in agreement with your new school once you are in post (ideally in September).

The three sections are as follows:

- Section A forms a summary of your ITT. When completing it, do include any distinguishing features such as additional qualifications (perhaps a first aid certificate) or opportunities for learning beyond those usually encountered while training (for example, a visit to a school overseas).
- Section B summarizes your strengths and priorities (up to four main areas for each) for development during the induction period, based on your training experiences and in relation to the Standards for the Award of Qualified Teacher Status (see Appendix 1). It is essential that these are 'genuinely individualized' so that they can become an effective part of your induction.
- Section C is the planning part of the profile and the core of the statutory induction arrangements, to be completed by you and your induction tutor/mentor once in post. You will need to take into account the priorities for development identified in section B as well as the induction standards and

any specific needs that have immediately arisen out of your new circumstances. It is intended that this section will be reviewed regularly and revised and updated if necessary in order to keep the focus sharp.

Section C will record:

- your *agreed* objectives (agreement is the essential part of this process);
- the actions that need to be taken and by whom;
- the success criteria;
- the resources needed to achieve success (which can only be achieved if resource allocation is *realistic*, so be honest about what you think you will need to reach a target);
- the dates by which these targets should ideally be met;
- the dates by which your progress should be reviewed.

The purposes of the Career Entry Profile

There are two main purposes of the Career Entry Profile: to provide information about your strengths and development needs in relation to the Standards for QTS; and to assist in setting objectives and prioritizing your needs for further professional development, thus playing a central role in your induction into the profession.

It is a way of linking your skills directly to the Standards for the Award of Qualified Teacher Status and the Induction Standards and recognizing the transition from training to working in post. What it is not, however, is a reference or a definitive record of all your achievements and progress. You will still need to keep your own records of work completed with classes and of particularly successful lessons for the purposes of future appraisals, inspections and personal gratification!

Used to its best advantage, the Career Entry Profile will enable schools to deploy NQTs in the most appropriate way, according to their skills and strengths. It is a part of a process, but is not an end in itself.

Who is responsible for the Career Entry Profile?

There are three main people with responsibilities for your Career Entry Profile under the statutory induction arrangements:

- your headteacher, who will have to ensure that all the monitoring, support and assessment that you receive takes your Career Entry Profile into account;
- your induction tutor/mentor, who will help to set up a suitable programme of monitoring, support and review that should be firmly based in your action plan as set out in your Career Entry Profile;
- you yourself will be responsible, as you will be expected to work with your headteacher and induction tutor/mentor in target setting and generally be 'fully engaged' in your induction period.

What the Career Entry Profile does for you

The Career Entry Profile does actually allow you to take control of your career, providing it is treated as intended by your training institution and your school. You can identify aspects of your skills base that need improvement. Don't think of these aspects as weaknesses, but as areas you would like to develop further. When you start your first teaching job you are not expected to be an expert at everything – far from it. Most experienced teachers agree that it took them at least three years before they felt they had a strong understanding of what it meant to be a teacher, and even then they continued to learn. In order, moreover, to be in the position of taking up a teaching post, you have satisfied high standards of competence.

Think of the Career Entry Profile as a way of helping to bridge the inevitable gap between training and working in post. The fact that there probably is a gap between training and working should not necessarily be considered as a shortcoming of your ITT provider – whatever the standard of your training, there will always be a period of transition at this time.

Maximizing the use of the Career Entry Profile

- Use it as evidence of progress. It can then serve as an excellent foundation for future professional development.
- Adapt it as necessary to take account of progress made in the early days and the context of your school. Don't consider it to be set in stone. Voice your needs if they change as a result of your first few weeks of teaching and talk about the possibility of accommodating them in your profile. What knowledge would make it easier for you to perform your job? Think of short-, medium- and long-term goals.

- Use it to support your induction programme at your new school – it should help you to receive the support you need rather than the help your school wants to give.
- Allow it to strengthen your bargaining position when it comes to further training – in the past in some schools, new teachers have been at the bottom of the INSET pile and missed out on valuable professional development. There should be a file of forthcoming INSET courses in your school. If not, ask the adviser with responsibilities for NQTs about what is coming up.
- Think of the *processes* by which you will achieve desired *outcomes*. Both process and outcome are relevant to your development. What do you want? How will you get it?
- Use it to establish sound reflective practices – vital for lifelong learning.

QTS SKILLS TESTS

The 1998 Green Paper, *Teachers: Meeting the challenge of change*, published by the DfEE, proposed national skills tests for trainee teachers to ensure that they all have a thorough grounding in numeracy, literacy and ICT. Returning teachers don't have to take the tests.

Table 5.1 is from the TTA's *Career Entry Profile 2002: Notes of guidance and standards*, available on www.canteach.gov.uk, or on 0845 606 0323. It explains the requirements regarding the skills tests.

You cannot be awarded QTS until you have passed all of the skills tests, as they are part of the Standards. There is no limit to the amount of times you can sit the tests.

The literacy test covers:

- spelling;
- grammar;
- punctuation;
- comprehension.

The ICT test covers (through the use of word processor, presentation package, database, spreadsheet, e-mail and Web browser):

- researching and categorizing;
- developing and modelling;
- presenting and communicating.

Table 5.1 *Requirements regarding the skills tests*

For teachers qualifying between:	To be awarded QTS:	To successfully complete induction:
7 May 1999 and 30 April 2000	they did not have to pass any of the skills tests	they did not have to pass any of the skills tests
1 May 2000 and 30 April 2001	they did not have to pass any of the skills tests	they have to pass the numeracy skills tests
1 May 2001 and 30 April 2002	they have to pass the numeracy and literacy skills tests	they must already have completed the skills tests and therefore have been awarded QTS before they can begin induction
1 May 2002 and 30 April 2003	they have to pass the numeracy, literacy and ICT skills tests	they must already have completed the skills tests and therefore have been awarded QTS before they can begin induction

The numeracy test covers:

- mental arithmetic;
- using and applying general arithmetic;
- interpreting and using statistical information.

Keep an eye on the TTA Web site www.canteach.gov.uk/support/skillstests/index.htm for the latest information on these skills tests as well as useful support materials.

INDUCTION

Be aware of your own achievements.

(Dan Millman)

Not only is it vital that you receive induction into working at your new school, but you will also need inducting into the profession as a whole. In order to ensure that NQTs across the country receive equitable induction (as far as possible), a statutory induction period exists, which combines support, monitoring and assessment of your performance as an NQT.

The induction you receive in your first year in the profession can really influence your attitude to, and opinion of, the teaching profession. For some, it is the main factor in whether they remain in teaching and it certainly forms the foundation of your further professional development.

For this reason, it is essential that you become familiar with the induction arrangements for NQTs. Get a copy of DfES Guidance 582/2001, *The Induction Period for Newly Qualified Teachers* (telephone the order line on 0845 602 2260 or visit the DfES Web site to download a copy: www.dfes.gov.uk), for the finer details and copies of the forms that will be used for your assessment. The main points of Guidance 582/2001 are summarized below, but the most important aspect of the statutory induction period is that, if you are ultimately unsuccessful, you cannot work as a teacher in maintained schools and non-maintained special schools – there are no second chances.

The TTA has a set of booklets called 'Supporting induction for newly qualified teachers', which are available free of charge from the TTA publications centre: 0845 6060 3223, or to download from the TTA Web site: www.canteach.gov.uk. It would be useful to have these close to hand, as well as any literature on induction that your union may have produced.

The statutory induction arrangements

- All teachers who gain QTS after 7 May 1999 in England must complete a statutory induction period satisfactorily. Failure to do so will result in ineligibility for employment as a teacher in a maintained school (or non-maintained special school).
- The induction period to be served is the equivalent of one school year (three, four or five terms, depending on the system in place in your school), pro rata for part-time teachers.
- You must complete at least a term for that period to count towards your induction. This is particularly important to NQTs working as supply teachers in their first year. The headteacher will be able to tell you if your time at his/her school can count towards your induction period. Induction cannot be done retrospectively.
- You will be given a reduced timetable, which will be 90 per cent of the normal timetable for teachers at your school (this applies pro rata to part-time and supply NQTs).

- You will have at least three formal assessment meetings. These meetings normally take place towards the end of each term in a three-term year.
- Your headteacher must write to the appropriate body (usually your LEA) within 10 working days of the completion of your induction period with his/her recommendation on whether you should pass or fail.
- Within three working days of the decision being made, the appropriate body must write to inform you as to whether you have passed or failed your induction period.
- Your induction period will be extended if you miss more than an aggregate total of 30 school days. It will be extended by the number of working days you have missed.
- If you have to take maternity leave during your induction year, you may extend your induction period if you choose to do so.
- If you have started but not completed your induction period within five years, you may apply to your appropriate body for an extension 'not exceeding a full induction period'. This may or may not be granted. There is no time limit for starting induction.
- If you are deemed to have failed your induction period, you may appeal against the decision within 20 working days of receiving notification. The General Teaching Council for England deals with appeals.
- Failure to complete successfully the induction period will mean that you will not ever be eligible to teach in a maintained school or non-maintained special school.
- Failing induction does not mean that an NQT will lose QTS.

Overview of the induction process

The timeline in Figure 5.1 indicates the key stages in the induction period as set out in the DfES Guidance 582/2001, *The Induction Period for Newly Qualified Teachers*. It has been taken from the TTA booklet, 'Overview'.

Who is responsible for your induction period?

Responsibility for your induction period is shared between you, your head-teacher, your induction tutor/mentor, the 'appropriate body' and the governing body.

ABOUT WHERE YOU CAN AND CANNOT COMPLETE AN INDUCTION PERIOD

The following types of school can provide you with an induction period:

- maintained schools;
- non-maintained special schools;
- sixth form colleges where, before the start of the induction period, the governing body of the college and an LEA have agreed that the LEA shall act as the appropriate body in relation to the college;
- independent schools:
  - if primary pupils at the school follow a curriculum that meets National Curriculum requirements;
  - if pupils at key stages 3 and 4 are taught a curriculum including all the core and foundation subjects you are employed to teach;
  - if there is an agreement between the school and the Independent Schools Council Teacher Induction Panel or an LEA that they will act as the school's appropriate body.

You will not be able to complete an induction period at the following schools:

- pupil referral units;
- schools requiring special measures (unless one of Her Majesty's Inspectors certifies otherwise);
- FE and tertiary colleges;
- independent schools that do not meet the requirements for providing induction periods.

If you are working through your induction year in a school that requires special measures (in other words, your school is inspected during your induction year and is deemed not to be offering a high enough standard of education to its pupils), you can complete your induction in that school.

Contact the TTA's Induction Team on 020 7925 3728 and/or your union if you are in any doubt as to whether or not you can complete an induction period in a particular school.

The NQT's responsibilities

- You must make your Career Entry Profile available to your headteacher and induction tutor/mentor as early as possible and use it as a basis for your induction period.

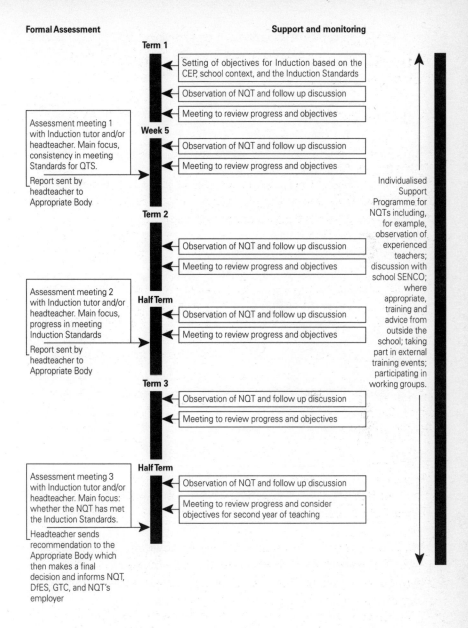

Figure 5.1 *Overview of the induction process*

- You should be actively involved in the planning of your induction period, taking increasing responsibility for your professional development as the induction period progresses.
- You must raise any concerns you have through the appropriate channels as soon as they arise. Failure to do so could mean that your chances of successfully completing your induction period are severely limited.

- You should keep copies of all induction reports and records of monitoring etc.

ABOUT RAISING CONCERNS

If you have any concerns about the way that your induction period is progressing, it is essential that you discuss these sooner rather than later. Your school must have an internal procedure set up for NQTs to raise concerns and it is best to use this first. If this route does not bring a satisfactory result, contact the named person at the appropriate body with responsibility for dealing with NQTs' concerns. This person should be someone who does not also have responsibilities for supporting and monitoring NQTs and making decisions about passing or failing the induction period. It would also be sensible to get advice from your union at this stage. Document all concerns you have for your own reference. Include details of why you are concerned, who else is involved, what you have done to help the situation and what you consider may alleviate your concerns. Also keep a record of what your induction tutor/mentor and headteacher do to solve any problems you raise. Do not leave anything to drift in the hope that things will resolve themselves. It is not overdramatic to say that your future in the teaching profession could be at stake.

The headteacher's responsibilities

- Your headteacher (along with the appropriate body) has overall responsibility for ensuring that the induction you receive is suitable and individualized.
- He/she will have to keep in close contact with the appropriate body regarding all aspects of your support, monitoring and assessment.
- He/she must liaise with other headteachers if you are completing your induction period in more than one school. When a teacher is doing induction in more than one school, only one headteacher can take the lead.
- He/she must ensure that NQTs teach a timetable that is 90 per cent of the normal teaching timetable in your school. This is a legislative duty and there are no exceptions. Your school will receive funding from the Standards Fund to cover the cost of this reduced timetable and other costs associated with induction. The remaining 10 per cent of your timetable is for focused induction and development activities.
- He/she must keep copies of all induction reports and records of monitoring etc.

- Your headteacher will recommend whether you should pass or fail your induction period.

The induction tutor/mentor's responsibilities

- Your induction tutor/mentor is, in effect, your line manager as far as your induction goes and he/she must be fully aware of his/her duties.
- He/she must devise a suitable programme of induction for you that is individualized and will allow for fair and thorough assessment of your abilities as a teacher as well as suitable support and monitoring on a day-to-day basis.
- He/she must formally assess you at regular intervals and make fair and rigorous judgements about you.
- He/she must make recommendations to your headteacher on the outcome of your induction period.

The appropriate body's responsibilities

- With your headteacher, the appropriate body is responsible for your training and supervision during your induction period.
- It is responsible for quality assurance of induction arrangements and may give guidance and assistance to schools and individuals.
- It must ensure that your headteacher and governing body are aware of what they should be doing and are doing it.
- It must make the final decision on whether you are deemed to have completed the induction period satisfactorily (in other words, whether you have met the Induction Standards) based on your headteacher's recommendations.
- It must inform you and your headteacher of its decision.
- It must give the NQT at risk of failing additional support, and assure itself that the induction being offered is of the highest quality.
- It must ensure that there are no conflicts of interest arising from its duty to support an inductee at risk of failure and its responsibilities for making the final decision on satisfactory completion of induction.
- It must ensure that if you qualified between 1 May 2000 and 30 April 2001 you have passed the national test for teacher training candidates in numeracy (this is one of the Induction Standards). If you have not passed the numeracy test before the end of the induction period (through illness or, for example, jury service) and you intend to resit it, the appropriate body may extend this period by one school term.

- It must inform the General Teaching Council for England of its decision regarding your induction period. It will do this by supplying an electronic list of successful inductees and also those who fail induction or who have induction extended.

The governing body's responsibilities

- The governing body must be fully aware of the implications of employing an NQT and ensure that the key personnel involved in the induction of NQTs are in a position to perform their duties to the highest standards.

What the induction period means for the NQT

There are many distinct advantages for NQTs undergoing statutory induction, providing all concerned are aware of their responsibilities and are keen to maximize the benefits of the situation. For this reason, it is worth knowing these points:

- All concerned in your induction period must be conscious of its developmental purpose.
- You should be fully involved and actively participate in self-monitoring and assessment against the Standards for QTS and the Induction Standards (see Appendices 1 and 2).
- You should be informed from the start of your responsibilities for your professional development.
- The induction you receive should be equitable to induction received by NQTs in different schools, as the statutory arrangements and the monitoring procedures (OFSTED will look at the quality of the induction NQTs receive when schools and LEAs are inspected) encourage national standards.
- Your induction should be individualized and well targeted rather than vaguely supportive.
- You won't be expected simply to meet the Induction Standards but to build on the Standards for QTS consistently and draw together your other skills and achievements as well.
- If your induction tutor/mentor is also your headteacher (be extremely wary of this set-up, although in some very small schools this may be unavoidable), a third party should also be involved at formal assessment meetings.

- Your teaching post should be one that does not require you to teach outside your age range and subject specialism, that means you teach the same classes regularly, that doesn't involve extra responsibilities (without preparation and support) and that does not present severe discipline challenges. However, there is nothing legally preventing you from teaching primary or secondary, irrespective of the age range you studied during your training.
- Your timetable should be reduced by 10 per cent and this must allow for targeted induction rather than extra preparation or non-contact time. The timetable reductions should be evenly distributed throughout your induction period.
- If your school is unable to provide induction of a high enough standard, your headteacher is responsible for arranging experience for you in another school. Be sure to talk to your induction tutor/mentor and named person at the appropriate body if you suspect this should be happening.
- You will be observed at least once in any six- to eight-week period and certainly within your first four weeks (and ideally in your first week). After these observations you should be given the opportunity to discuss the lesson and the conclusions your observer has reached.
- Assessment observations must be focused and a written record must be kept including details of any action needed as a result of the observations. Induction objectives can then be revised.
- You must have a professional review of progress at least once in every six- to eight-week period (every half-term in a typical three-term year), and these reviews should be informed by evidence drawn from all aspects of your work. These reviews must be informed by evidence of your work, and your objectives should be revised as necessary. Again, a written record should be kept, including any steps needed for further development.
- Your induction period must include the opportunity to observe experienced teachers. This could be colleagues in your own school or teachers in a local 'Beacon school'. Each observation must have a focus.

DfES Guidance 582/2001 states that induction tutors:

will wish to consider arrangements for NQTs to:

- receive information about the school, the specific post and the arrangements for induction, in advance of the first day of the post;
- receive information about their rights and responsibilities and those of others involved and the nature and purpose of assessment in the induction period;

- participate in the school's general induction arrangements for new staff;
- take part in any programme of staff training at the school, for example on the national literacy or numeracy strategies;
- know about any whole school policies, including those on child protection, management of behaviour and health and safety, and contribute, with other teachers, to specific school improvement activities;
- spend time with the school's SENCO to focus on specific and general SEN matters;
- receive, where appropriate, training development or advice from professionals from outside the school, eg from other schools, LEAs, Higher Education Institutions, Diocesan authorities, professional bodies and subject associations;
- attend external training events that are relevant to identified individual needs.

ABOUT THE INDUCTION STANDARDS

These are designed to build on the Standards for the Award of QTS in that they require you to show that you can perform all standards independently (as opposed to being under supervision when training). They also aid the focusing process so that professional development is valued and useful. The crux of your role here is to move towards performing all standards consistently.

Overview of NQT assessment

Figure 5.2 has been taken from the TTA's booklet, 'Assessment'.

ABOUT FOLLOW-UP DISCUSSIONS

It is really important that any discussions that you have with your induction tutor/mentor after an observation are focused and constructive. Although there may be time pressures for both of you, the benefits of talking through your collective impressions of what took place should far outweigh any inconveniences. These ideas may help:

- Make sure that all observations have an agreed focus so that the discussions afterwards have a relevant purpose.

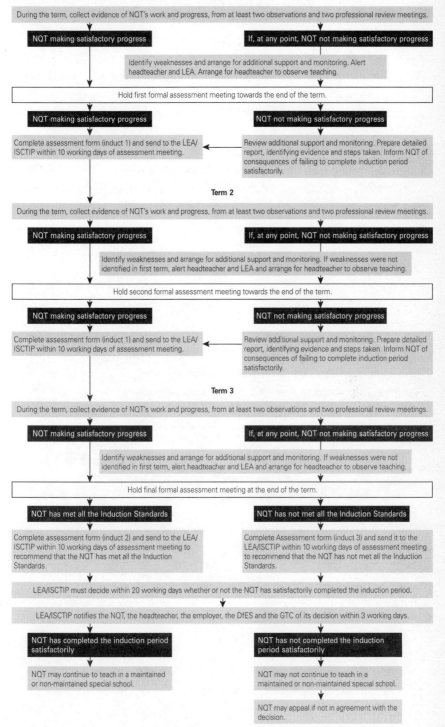

Figure 5.2 *Overview of NQT assessment*

- Aim to analyse the observed lesson and evaluate it for yourself before you discuss it with your induction tutor/mentor.
- Be honest about the positive points. Don't shy away from a bit of personal praise, but be sure to identify the evidence for your views.
- Likewise, ask for evidence to back up any statements that appear to be founded in opinion.
- Prioritize the points you want to discuss in case time pressures prevail.
- Aim to identify, through professional dialogue, any future action that needs to be taken.
- Keep a written record of any post-observation discussions.

ABOUT SUMMATIVE ASSESSMENT MEETINGS

The best way to view assessment meetings is as markers of your progress throughout your induction period. It is important that you feel free to discuss all your concerns, achievements and needs for further professional development. You should have at least three formal assessment meetings (ie one at the end of each term in a three-term year) with informal assessment meetings in between. At no point should you be surprised by any conclusion that has been reached on your work as, if everyone involved is performing their duties as they should, opinion on your progress should be made known to you throughout your induction period and not saved for formal assessment times.

These meetings should be informed by written reports from at least two observations and two progress review meetings that have taken place within the last term and any judgements must relate directly to the Standards for QTS and the Induction Standards. Further sources of evidence, says DfES Guidance 582/2001, could include:

- formal and informal assessment records for pupils for whom the NQT has had particular responsibility, including test and/or examination results;
- information about liaison with others, such as colleagues and parents;
- the NQT's lesson plans, records and evaluations;
- the NQT's self-assessment and record of professional development.

The first formal meeting will look at how consistently you are meeting the standards for QTS and beginning to meet the Induction Standards based on evidence from meetings and observations as well as your self-assessments, evaluations and lesson plans etc.

The second formal meeting will look at how well you are meeting the Induction Standards.

The third formal meeting is the final assessment of whether you are to be successful or not. If it is thought that you will be deemed to have passed your induction period, the meeting can also be used to discuss your development needs and to set objectives for the next academic year. For this reason it is worth thinking about what these may be in advance.

You should be asked to sign the assessment forms, which will then be sent to the appropriate body within 10 working days of each assessment. You should also be given the opportunity to make your own comments on these forms and you should receive copies of every written report on you, which should be kept.

ABOUT MAKING UNSATISFACTORY PROGRESS

It is expected that the vast majority of NQTs will be successful in completing their induction period, especially as concerns on both sides can be raised very early on. You should be informed of any chance that you may not be successful as soon as concerns arise, and the summative assessment forms from your formal assessment meetings must record that you risk failing the induction period. Individual weaknesses must be identified and a structured plan of action to guide you towards success must be put in place. You must be told exactly why you are thought to be at risk of failing, and a third party (ie your head-teacher) must observe your teaching. The appropriate body will be informed that you are considered to be at risk of failing the induction period and your headteacher should write to you about the improvements that you need to make in order to be successful. You must be told formally of the consequences of not making the necessary improvements.

If, at any stage of this process, you are unhappy with your treatment, talk to the named person at the appropriate body (usually this will be your LEA) as soon as possible. Also seek advice from your union.

In the event of being informed that you have failed your induction period, you are no longer eligible to be employed as a teacher in a maintained or non-maintained special school. You must be told the exact details of your right to appeal. If you decide to appeal, you may not be dismissed, but your teaching duties will be restricted before the appeal is heard. If you decide not to appeal, you will be dismissed within 10 working days of announcing your decision, or from the date when the time limit of 20 working days for appeal expired without an appeal being brought. Do not attempt to take yourself through the appeal process. Always seek union advice.

ABOUT THE COMPLETION OF YOUR INDUCTION PERIOD

There are three stages to go through once you have completed your induction period:

- Your headteacher must write to the appropriate authority within 10 working days of you completing the induction period. This is to recommend whether or not you should pass or fail, and you should be given a copy of this letter. You are entitled to send the appropriate body your own representation within 10 working days of your headteacher's letter, but, if this is necessary, it is essential to seek urgent union advice.
- Within 20 working days of receiving this letter, the appropriate body must satisfy itself that this recommendation is fair.
- Within three working days of the final decision being made and recorded, the appropriate authority must inform you, the headteacher in whose school you completed induction, your employer (if different) and the GTCE of the outcome. If you have passed the induction period, congratulations! If you have not passed, you should be told clearly about your right to appeal.

THE APPEAL PROCEDURE

This section has been taken from DfES Guidance 582/2001, *The Induction Period for Newly Qualified Teachers* (Annex D).

Introduction

1. This annex sets out the arrangements for appeals against decisions to extend or fail the induction period. The General Teaching Council for England (GTCE) is the Appeal Body and any decision of the Appeal Body will be final.

Making an appeal

2. If an NQT fails induction, or has the induction period extended by the Appropriate Body, that body must tell the NQT of the right to appeal, who to appeal to, and the time limit for appeal.

3. The NQT (the appellant) must send a notice of appeal to the GTCE (Appeal Body) within 20 days beginning with the date the appellant received notice of the Appropriate Body's decision. The Appeal Body will have discretion to extend this time limit where not to extend the time limit would result in substantial injustice to the NQT.

4. The NQT can appeal to the Appeal Body by sending a notice of appeal which can be a letter. NQTs can present their appeal in whatever way they see fit. The notice of appeal should include all of the following information:

   a. the name and address of the appellant;
   b. the appellant's DfES reference number and date of birth;
   c. the name and address of the school at which he was employed at the end of his induction period;
   d. the name and address of his employer, if employed in a teaching capacity, at the date of the appeal;
   e. the grounds of appeal;
   f. the name, address and profession of anyone representing the NQT in this matter, and an indication of whether the Appeal Body should send appeal documents to the representative rather than to the NQT;
   g. whether the teacher requests an oral hearing or not;
   h. if the appeal is going to miss the deadline, the NQT may give any justifications for the delay, and the Appeal Body must consider them.

   The NQT must sign the appeal for it to be valid.

5. The NQT should send the following additional material with the appeal:

   a. a copy of the document from the Appropriate Body notifying the NQT of its decision;
   b. a copy of any document from the Appropriate Body outlining its reasons for coming to this decision;
   c. a copy of every other document on which the NQT relies for the appeal.

6. The appeal should be addressed to:

Paul Fantom
General Teaching Council for England
3rd Floor, Cannon House
24 The Priory Queensway
Birmingham B4 6BS
Direct line: 0121 345 0087
Switchboard: 0870 001 0308

7. Appellants can amend or withdraw their grounds of appeal or any part of their appeal material and they can also submit new material in support of the appeal. They can do these things without permission up to the date they receive notice of the appeal hearing date (or notice of the outcome of the appeal if it is decided without a hearing). After the hearing date has been arranged the appellant needs the permission of the Appeal Body to amend or withdraw his or her appeal or submit further material.

8. Once an appeal is withdrawn it cannot normally be reinstated. An appeal which has been withdrawn in error may be reinstated in exceptional circumstances.

9. The correspondence for an appeal is handled by the 'proper officer'. Within three working days of receiving the notice of appeal, that officer will:
   a. send an acknowledgement to the appellant;
   b. send copies of the notice of appeal and accompanying documents to the Appropriate Body;
   c. send a copy to the head teacher who made the end of induction recommendation and any current teaching employer, if not the LEA.

   The proper officer will also copy any later amendments or additions or notices of withdrawal to the Appropriate Body.

10. The Appeal Body will be able to request additional material from the appellant if it thinks the appeal could be more fairly decided. If the appellant decides to provide such material in response to a request he should do so within 10 working days of the date of the request. The Appropriate Body will be informed that a notice has been sent, and sent copies of any material supplied by the appellant.

11. The Appropriate Body has 20 working days from receiving the notice of appeal to reply. If the Appropriate Body decides at any time that it does not want to uphold the disputed decision, it should inform the Appeal Body, who will allow the Appeal. The reply must contain:

a. the name and address of the Appropriate Body;
b. whether it seeks to uphold the disputed decision;
c. where it seeks to uphold the decision:
    i.   its answer to each of the NQT's grounds of appeal;
    ii. whether it requests an oral hearing;
    iii. the name, address, and profession of anyone representing the Appropriate Body, and whether documents should be sent to them instead.

12. The Appropriate Body should also send any document on which it wishes to rely to oppose the appeal, and, if the NQT has not supplied it, a copy of the written statement giving its reasons for the decision.

13. The Appropriate Body can submit further documents and amend or withdraw its reply. The rules are as described in paragraph 7 above.

14. The proper officer must send a copy of the reply from the Appropriate Body to the appellant within three working days.

15. The Appeal Body can make a decision without a hearing if the Appropriate Body has not replied in time: if it does so it may only allow the appeal. Where the Appeal Body considers an oral hearing is not necessary and neither party has requested one, the Appeal Body can also decide the appeal without a hearing. In other circumstances there must be a hearing. The Appeal Body must notify the parties of any such decision within 20 working days from the day after the expiry of the time limit for the Appropriate Body's reply.

Decision by oral hearing

16. The Appeal Body must fix a date for a hearing within 20 working days from the expiry of the time limit for the Appropriate Body's reply by sending the appellant and the Appropriate Body notice of the time and place of the hearing. The notice of the hearing must be accompanied by guidance about the procedure at the hearing, a warning about the consequence of not attending, and information about the right to submit written representations if they do not attend. The hearing will be at least 15 working days from the date of the notice.

17. Both the NQT and the Appropriate Body have to reply at least 10 working days before the hearing, to say if they will attend or be represented, what, if any, witnesses they wish to call, and if they are not proposing to attend or be represented at the hearing to provide

any further written representations they wish to make. Any written representations submitted will be copied to the other party.

18. The procedure at the hearing will be decided by the Appeal Body, but will be subject to the rules of natural justice, with full and open disclosure of documents. Both sides will be able to call witnesses, though it will be up to the parties to arrange for their witnesses to appear. Hearings will be in public although the Appeal Body has the power to decide that a hearing or some part of it should be in private.

Cost of appeals

19. The appellant and the respondent will have to bear their own costs. There will be no requirement to bear the costs of the other party in the event of a decision against one party.

The appeals committee

20. Induction Appeals Hearing Committees of the GTCE will be responsible for considering appeals. The GTCE will ensure that committee members receive appropriate training to undertake this role.
21. The GTCE took on the role of Appeal Body from the Secretary of State on 1 July 2001. The GTCE will keep its procedures under review to determine the most effective way to consider appeals.

Considering the importance of your induction period in determining your future in the profession and the detail and finality of the appeal process, it would be worth keeping a file in which you collect all documentation relating to your induction period and records of conversations about any concerns you may have. This may seem overcautious given that the vast majority of NQTs are expected to pass their induction period, but in the event of having to make an appeal will greatly ease your task. Do not attempt to go through the appeal process without seeking extensive advice from your appropriate body and your union at least.

MENTORING

The quality of the mentoring you receive is central to your experience of induction and being aware of this can help to ensure that you don't miss out.

Mentoring is no longer a new concept in the teaching profession and has been the subject of much research in recent years, perhaps reflecting the fact that the role involves far more than simply coordinating the support you receive. There has to be a real partnership between you and your induction tutor/mentor and a culture of effective, challenging support for your induction period to be of value. It would not be unrealistic for you to have high expectations of the mentoring process. At the very least you can expect:

- a carefully selected induction tutor/mentor with excellent interpersonal skills who knows the exact details of his/her role;
- an induction tutor/mentor with sufficient time to devote to your induction period so that fair judgements can be made on your progress;
- a relationship with your induction tutor/mentor that can develop over the time of your induction in response to your progress and changing needs, with support always remaining a constant.

In addition to this, the TTA, in its document entitled *The Role of Induction Tutor: Principles and guidance* (available on the TTA Web site: www.canteach. gov.uk or from the publication line: 0845 606 0323), has identified three principles that should set the right climate for successful induction:

1. Everyone in the school who is involved in the induction of NQTs should have a clear understanding of the responsibilities and role of the induction tutor.
2. Induction tutors should have, or should be developing, the specific knowledge, skills and understanding they need to carry out their responsibilities effectively.
3. The role of induction tutor should be well supported and recognised as important within the wider school context.

ABOUT TEACHERS FROM OUTSIDE ENGLAND

This information has been taken from Annex E of the DfES Guidance 582/2001, *The Induction Period for Newly Qualified Teachers*, and relates to teachers in Scotland, Wales, Northern Ireland, Guernsey, Jersey, Isle of Man and Gibraltar:

1. Scotland has a two-year probation period, and any teacher who has completed that will count as having satisfactorily completed induction in England. Northern Ireland has an induction stage in their teacher education, so teachers who have completed that stage are exempt from induction in English schools.

2. Wales does not yet have induction arrangements, but plans to introduce them. A person who qualifies as a teacher (in England or Wales) after 7 May 1999 and who takes up his or her first teaching post in Wales will be exempt from the requirements to serve induction in England provided he or she completes at least two terms in post before the introduction of induction in Wales.

3. Guernsey, Jersey, Isle of Man and Gibraltar have induction arrangements which are identical to the English arrangements. Any UK-trained teacher who successfully completes a one-year induction, which commenced on or after 1 September 1999, at a school in one of those territories, and under the supervision of the territory's government, is exempt from the requirements to serve induction in English schools.

The European Economic Area (EEA)

4. Teachers who are nationals of the EEA who fall within article 3 of the Council Directive 89/48 EEC on a general system for the recognition of higher-education diplomas awarded on completion of professional education and training of at least three years' duration are exempt from induction.

5. For the award of QTS teachers who are EEA nationals should apply to:

General Teaching Council for England
Teachers' Qualifications Section
3rd Floor, Cannon House
24 The Priory Queensway
Birmingham B4 6BS
Tel: 0870 001 0308
Fax: 0121 345 0100
e-mail: tqhelpdesk@gtce.org.uk
and ask for application form EC1.

Outside the EEA

6. Teaching qualifications gained outside the EEA do not lead automatically to the award of QTS. Non-EEA trained teachers may need to undertake some form of training before they can be granted QTS. However if they have at least two years' full time teaching experience they can present themselves for assessment against the QTS Standards without necessarily completing further training. Those with at least two years' full-time teaching experience may also present themselves for assessment against the Induction Standards and, if successful, will be exempt from the requirement to complete induction.

Research from the United States suggests that the better the start you have in a profession, the greater are your chances of success. While mentoring and induction form only part of the picture, with conditions of service also playing a role in your levels of job satisfaction, it is important to be alert to the quality of mentoring you are being offered and the impact it can have on this consequential year.

ABOUT POSSIBLE TOPICS FOR FOCUS

Throughout your induction period there should be plenty of opportunity to focus on myriad topics. Your targets for development as set out in your Career Entry Profile will form the basis of many of your meetings, but you may also like to consider the following ideas (if they are not already targets). This book covers many of them and can be used as a basis of any such sessions:

- accidents;
- additional adults in your classroom;
- anger management;
- assemblies;
- assessment;
- behaviour management;
- body language;
- bullying (of adults and children);
- child safety/protection;
- circle time;
- citizenship;
- classroom atmosphere/organization;
- community involvement;
- cover lessons;
- Curriculum 2000;
- differentiation;
- displays;
- effectiveness in the classroom;
- English as a second or other language;
- equal opportunities;
- extra-curricular activities;
- first aid;
- governors and their roles;
- health and safety;
- homework;
- ICT across the curriculum;
- inspection;

- moderation of children's work;
- motivating children;
- multiple intelligences;
- parents' evenings;
- pensions;
- performance management;
- planning;
- prioritization;
- questioning skills;
- record keeping;
- refugee children;
- reports;
- rewards;
- rights and responsibilities;
- sanctions;
- school visits;
- self-evaluation;
- social, moral, spiritual and cultural education;
- special educational needs;
- stress;
- target setting;
- teaching styles;
- tutoring;
- voice protection and projection.

Your relationship with your induction tutor/ mentor

While you should expect great things of your induction tutor/mentor, there is an obligation on NQTs to work at this relationship to help ensure that your induction period is an extremely positive springboard into the profession, allowing for your skills to be built on year after year.

If, for any reason, your relationship is not working effectively, make every effort to resolve this diplomatically within your school. If you are unsuccessful, the named person with responsibilities for NQTs at your LEA will almost certainly be able to help. Do keep records of your attempts to improve your situation. Usually, however, good communication skills will be sufficient in making your needs known.

Figure 5.3 was used as part of University College Chichester's Mentor Training Programme (2000–01). It clearly depicts the fine balance the induction tutor/mentor must strike between challenging and supporting NQTs.

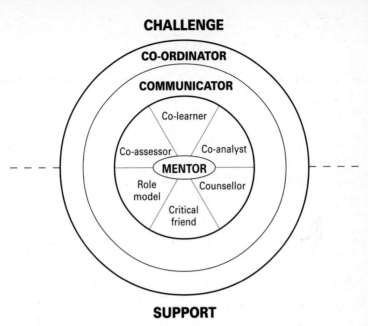

Figure 5.3 *University College Chichester: Mentor Training Programme (2000–01)*

What is known to be helpful

- The opportunity to visit your school and even take part in team teaching as much as possible before taking up your post.
- Early observations, particularly in your first two weeks at the school. These are helpful in identifying early idealism.
- A relationship with your induction tutor/mentor that facilitates frank discussions. This should include having the opportunity to discuss your respective roles and share professional reflections.
- Frequent informal support from your induction tutor/mentor as well as other colleagues, perhaps through a 'buddy' system (where you are allocated a particular person who does not have responsibilities for assessing you in whom you may confide). This way, each meeting need only cover a few issues.
- An induction tutor/mentor trained in listening skills, and willing to question his/her own practice, while being competent and confident in his/her own understanding of teacher effectiveness.
- The opportunity to observe and then analyse with colleagues *why* a particular technique works.
- Support that covers curriculum issues as well as day-to-day job management.

- Encouragement off plateaux through a wide range of helping strategies so that consolidation does not turn into stagnation; pushing limits within safe boundaries.
- Coordinated approaches to mentoring rather than *ad hoc* arrangements.
- A school ethos of learning from mistakes.
- Asking for support before problems develop.
- Clearly focused observations with the opportunity for NQTs to discuss their rationale for the lesson content and their reflections following the event.
- Specific, timely guidance on problem areas identified by NQTs.
- Encouragement to risk failure.
- Recognition and celebration of success.

However, there are some potential pitfalls to be aware of:

- If your induction tutor/mentor is not supported in his/her work, time constraints may mean that your induction depends heavily on the good will of colleagues.
- Your school may have little or no experience of mentoring NQTs.
- Your mentor may be untrained.
- Your reduced timetable may not be constructive if the time is frittered away through lack of planning.
- Your reduced timetable may be withdrawn part-way through the year (this is against schools' statutory duties).

If you suspect any of the above to be the case in your school, discuss your situation with your induction tutor, your union and the named person at your LEA with responsibilities for NQTs.

ABOUT OBSERVING COLLEAGUES

When you observe colleagues as they teach, it can be easy to be swept along by the pace and content of the lesson without making clear sense of the 'how' and 'why'. Keep these questions in mind for discussion afterwards (to enable you both to deconstruct the lesson), and aim to spend most of your time *experiencing* the lesson and not taking notes!

'Why did you choose… activity?'
'Would the lesson have worked if…?'

'How could I employ. . . technique with my class(es)?'
'Will you explain why you introduced. . . when you did?'
'If I did. . . are there any pitfalls I should avoid?'
'How have these techniques developed over time?'
'What other methods of explanation do you use?'

You will undoubtedly have your own questions to add to this list.

ABOUT RECEIVING FEEDBACK

When your induction tutor/mentor has observed a lesson, he/she will have reached certain conclusions about your performance with reference to the Standards for QTS, the Induction Standards and your agreed focus for the observation. These conclusions then have to be passed on to you in the form of *constructive* feedback.

The feedback you are offered must take place in total privacy and certainly not within earshot of pupils. You should be given the opportunity to ask questions and seek clarification on what has been said if necessary. A written record should always be kept of any discussions that take place as a result of an observation for several reasons, the most important being that it can be extremely difficult to *absorb* all that is being fed back. A natural tendency is to latch on to the potentially negative and forget the positive.

When receiving feedback, it is helpful to consider whether you have any blocks to receiving feedback. Do you respect the person doing the observations? Are observations always undertaken to an agreed focus? Are you seeking praise or a critical assessment? An excellent working relationship with your induction tutor/mentor will be invaluable here to enable your personal needs (such as encouragement) and professional needs to be met.

If you feel that the feedback you have received is not as constructive as it should have been, you may have to employ the following strategy:

- Attempt to determine what the person debriefing you *intends*. For example, is there any *positive* intent, or does it appear to be purely negative (which would be extremely unusual)?
- Feedback should be objective. If you sense that it has become subjective, aim to discuss whether this has in fact happened. It would also be wise to ask for specific examples to illustrate the debriefing you are being given.
- Reflect back to the person debriefing you what you understand to be the key points from the feedback. Use constructive, positive language.

- Do be aware of the power of language. Could it be that you have been oversensitive in your interpretation of what has been said to you? Or do you genuinely feel that you have been treated unfairly?
- Always discuss any concerns you have about your relationship with your induction tutor/mentor with the named person within your LEA. Don't let anything slip by; this is the only shot you get at induction.

ABOUT ENCOURAGING EFFECTIVE MENTORING

There are certainly things that NQTs can do to encourage effective mentoring during the induction period. Use these points as starters:

- Get to know the Induction Standards and Standards for the Award of Qualified Teacher Status thoroughly.
- Attend all the induction sessions you are offered.
- Work hard at building a solid relationship with your induction tutor/mentor.
- Be aware of the time constraints your induction tutor/mentor may be facing, but don't let that put you off asking any questions or raising any concerns.
- Be receptive to new ideas that may be different from those you have encountered in the past.
- Express your needs related to your workload as early as possible – be honest about this, as seemingly confident and capable NQTs can miss out on support.
- Put forward your ideas for your induction and think carefully about how challenging you want your targets to be.
- Get to know last year's NQTs and draw on them for additional support.
- Get to know the areas of expertise of your colleagues.
- Do regular evaluations of your work and acknowledge your progress. Keep records of incidents that have happened in your classroom to use as the basis of discussion.
- When possible, give feedback on the quality of the mentoring you are receiving.
- Facilitate constructive discussions by displaying good listening skills and asking for clarification on anything you don't understand or don't agree with.
- Aim to integrate what you learn from colleagues into your work on a daily basis.

Learning styles

A significant aspect of your induction year will be continuing professional development: in other words, continuing to learn. Having a clear understanding of the way in which you take in information has a profound impact upon the way you approach the lessons you learn as well as the way you approach teaching others. For this reason, it is well worth taking some time to identify, or at least consider, your preferred learning style(s).

A vast amount has been written about learning styles, and a quick search on the Internet will reveal thousands of relevant sites all with a take on this important aspect of teaching. The often-quoted Kolb's Learning Cycle is an interesting place to start. This cycle identifies four phases of learning: experience, reflection, conceptualization and action. The likelihood is that, rather than moving through all four phases over time, learners in fact come to prefer one or two phases over the others.

Since Kolb's Learning Cycle, other thinkers have looked at learning styles in a different light. The work of Howard Gardner and his theory of multiple intelligences is an example.

IN-SERVICE TRAINING (INSET)

This is met with mixed feelings in schools across the country. Some relish the opportunity to spend time with teachers from other schools, or work on projects and concepts for a longer period of uninterrupted time than is usually the case. Others would rather spend the time catching up with marking and preparation.

Although INSET is only a small part of your overall induction, aim to cultivate a healthy attitude to it (regardless of the prevailing view of your staffroom) because there are undoubtedly benefits you can gather from attending.

The INSET offered to new teachers covers a wide variety of topics, from the generic, such as classroom management and assessment, to the specific, such as special educational needs at your school. It may be delivered by specialists from outside your school at a central location (such as a teachers' professional centre) or by colleagues in your school.

Maximizing the benefit of INSET

The best way to glean the most from any INSET you are offered is to make a conscious decision to gain from each session. Whether this is from the information that has been presented, teachers from other schools or inspiration for the formulation of an idea to incorporate in your teaching, there will always be something that you can leave the session with. Think about these points too:

- Before attending any INSET, be it in your school or provided externally, think about what the course is about and what you hope to gain from it.

- Plan some questions to ask those giving the INSET.
- Use the tutors/advisers as a resource – find out their specialisms and get names and numbers if you think they may be useful in the future.
- Take the opportunity to meet NQTs from other schools and perhaps build up your own support network for the exchange of resources.
- Tell INSET providers if there are any areas you think NQTs would benefit from covering – you could inspire a new course.

Using the information given

You may well leave a session of in-service training with a bundle of handouts and an array of ideas floating around your mind. As most teachers then return home with the usual demands on their time (marking, preparation, family etc) it is no surprise that the information collected may never make it into everyday use.

- Keep a record of any INSET you attend that includes what was covered and how you can incorporate what you learnt into your work.
- Review these records regularly throughout each term. Even if this only takes a few minutes, you may be inspired by something you read at just the right moment.
- Photocopy any handouts that may be useful for colleagues at your school.
- Talk about the impact of INSET you have attended at meetings with your induction tutor/mentor.

ABOUT GETTING YOUR FAIR SHARE OF INSET

There is no set quota of in-service training for NQTs, but you can expect to be sent on a variety of courses throughout your induction period, simply because no school can provide all aspects of the training and support that NQTs need. Ask your induction tutor/mentor how many courses you will be sent on over your induction period and, when you get the opportunity, ask the adviser with responsibilities for NQTs the same question. If there is a discrepancy, raise this at your next meeting with your induction tutor/mentor.

Most LEAs provide each school with a folder of forthcoming INSET. Look through this to see if there are any suitable courses for you. If there are and you have not been informed of them, ask your induction tutor/mentor if it would be possible for you to attend. Unfortunately, money for INSET is limited so those in charge of the budget will have to make difficult decisions about who gets training.

CHAPTER 6

Developing effective teaching skills

YOUR DOMAIN – THE CLASSROOM

Whether you work in a classroom or an open-plan environment, the area in which you teach is your domain. The changes you make to this space can greatly affect the organization and ambience of your lessons, and the effectiveness of your teaching.

Before you go ahead and redecorate, do check with your line manager and induction tutor/mentor what house rules there are regarding classrooms and displays and always follow the guidelines given. For example, some schools insist on double-mounting or triple-mounting pupils' work before it is displayed, or will only allow work and posters to be put up within notice/display boards. Even within such restrictions, there will still be plenty of scope to make your mark.

Creating the environment you want

If you are fortunate enough to have a room assigned to you, without having to share, you can start your interior design from scratch. While the amount of work you do in any holiday should be kept to an absolute minimum, preparation before the start of a term can help to give you an empty space in which to create the environment you want, a learning environment:

- Throw out any clutter from previous years as well as anything that does not serve a purpose.
- Aim to zone your room – you could have an area for you and your administration and areas for different aspects of the work that takes place within the room. For example, many teachers have set places for books to mark

and books that have been marked, and separate display areas for written work and design work or the efforts of different year groups. This all helps to establish order and routines in your space.

- Brighten dingy corners with plants. You could involve pupils in their care.
- Think about creating a 'peaceful' corner. Look out for pictures of natural scenes and place them where you can see them when addressing the class. If possible, swathe the background of this corner with paper or fabric in a shade of blue or green.
- If space permits, allow your class or tutor group to decorate a small area of your room.
- Be aware of the light in your classroom. Try not to let the room get too dark, as this will make for gloomy lessons and gloomy pupils.
- Keep the air in your room circulating; have a window open all the time. Anyone who has walked into a room after 35 sweaty adolescents have just vacated it will know exactly how important fresh air is – and infants can be just as fragrant!
- Watch the heating levels – too cold and your pupils will grumble, too hot and you'll all become sleepy. Either extreme can lead to negative stress.
- Keep your room tidy and safe on a day-to-day basis. Don't wait until the end of term for a tidying blitz because the chances are you won't want to be bothered then. Utilize storage drawers and cupboards and avoid using your own unique filing systems. Label *everything* so that anyone can use your room and understand your systems. This will also encourage others to keep your space tidy.
- You could try spraying your room with a well-diluted essential oil to help keep the air fresh. Get an empty spray bottle (available from most chemists and toiletries shops), half-fill it with water and add 8–10 drops of a pure essential oil of your choice. Shake the bottle well before spraying the room. Neroli is said to be stress-reducing, juniper stimulating, lavender relaxing and lemon uplifting.
- Think about the use of colour in your room. You may not be able to do anything about the colour of the walls, but most teachers are free to choose what colour they use as a background to wall-mounted work. Reds and oranges are said to be stimulating while greens and blues are relaxing. Black can be a stunning base for mounted work. Be aware of the way colour affects your classes both in the classroom surroundings and in the clothes you wear – do you want unnecessarily to stimulate your pupils?
- Explore the possibilities of using music in your room. The use of appropriate sound can have a positive effect on learning situations (Plato considered it

to be 'a potent instrument for learning') and some teachers consider it as an additional resource, particularly for art and history (as well as music) lessons. Some teachers use music to signal cues for learning such as marking the start of a lesson, or when pupils are to be on task. There is also research to suggest that knowledge gained when listening to music is easier to retrieve. For further information, look at the work of Don Campbell of 'Mozart Effect' fame (www.mozarteffect.com). Do, however, be aware of the effect that time signatures and numbers of beats per minute in a piece of music can have on pupils. Music can entrain the body, regulating brain, breathing and heart rhythms. For this reason, it is best to go for music that has 60–70 beats per minute as that is the rate at which the heart beats when relaxed.

- Wipe your board clean as soon as you have finished with the work. This will help to keep lessons flowing smoothly, as you won't have to waste time with chores like this when you really want to be writing on it.
- Keep a stock of tissues and paper towels in your room. This will help in the event of spillages and will also prevent requests to go to the toilet for a tissue. If you teach the very young, you may want to consider keeping a stock of spare children's pants for little disasters.

ABOUT BEING AN ITINERANT TEACHER

You may be unfortunate in your first year in that you do not have your own classroom. However pushed your school is for space, you should at least be given a base from which to work. Although it may not be appropriate to start redecorating a colleague's classroom, you could ask for a display area of your own. Use the time without your own classroom to formulate ideas for classroom design. Observe the displays around the school and note the ones that seem to work and the ones that don't. Think about why this might be so.

How far can you go?

The changes that can be made to your workspace depend entirely on the school in which you are employed. Some have very strict rules on the way classrooms are set out and decorated while others allow for individual teachers to impress their style on the environment around them. Teaching is an inherently creative occupation and this is a great area in which to set your ideas to work.

Rather than bedeck your room as soon as you arrive, have a look at other classrooms and talk to colleagues. It would be fairly unusual for an NQT's ideas on classroom decor to be totally squashed. Teachers spend a great deal of their working day in the classroom and it is important to think of that space as a metaphor for you. How far does it reflect your nature? It is usually possible to implement any sound ideas subtly – even surreptitiously!

Getting the most from your space

Work on the assumption that change and movement are more advantageous than stagnation. Make sure, though, that you can always see all the pupils, that they can see you and any materials you use, and that you can see the door if you have one:

- Try different seating arrangements. Horizontal rows, vertical rows, conference style, grouped tables – all are useful for different purposes and it may be appropriate to change the furniture around at regular intervals. You could ask pupils to create seating plans.
- Alter the position in the room from which you function.
- Change displays regularly, making sure they are clearly labelled.
- You don't have to do everything in one go – altering displays on a rotation basis is fine. Aim to change at least one aspect of your room once every half-term.
- Make sure that everything in your room is functioning as it should. This includes such things as power points, windows and blinds.

ACTION Contact one museum, one publisher and one bookshop to ask for display materials for your classroom. You may be pleasantly surprised by the selection you receive.

ABOUT ADVERTISING

Be aware that you may be advertising certain products and places inadvertently through the resources you use to decorate your classroom. Advertising in schools is at the discretion of the headteacher and the governing body, so it might be best to check first if anything you want to use bears a brand name.

Every now and then it is worth reassessing the environment in your classroom. Think about how you would describe:

- the atmosphere you have created;
- the noise that your pupils make whilst on and off task;
- the effectiveness of the communication in your classroom;
- the way your pupils relate to you and vice versa;
- the degree to which your classroom rules and routines are adhered to.

Are there any changes you would like to make? It can be helpful to discuss these with your induction tutor/mentor.

BEHAVIOUR MANAGEMENT

Not surprisingly, one of the areas of greatest concern for new teachers is behaviour management. The need for this is certainly not a recent development; pupils have been misbehaving since schools began and people have been devising methods of managing misbehaviour for just as long. Yet teachers appear to be experiencing a worsening in pupil behaviour, and this has been recognized at the highest levels. Whether this is real or a symptom of reduced tolerance because of the other demands of teaching remains to be seen. Nevertheless, these views of teachers need to be addressed.

The following section draws on commonly accepted good practice and cannot be attributed to any one behaviour management method. The first thing to remember when thinking about behaviour management is that you are human. For all the rules you may devise with your classes and all your good intentions, there will be some days when they are harder to implement than others. This is natural, so don't give yourself a hard time. Also, it is not violence and serious confrontation that cause the most problems in schools, but the persistent interruptions of chatterers and comedians. This relatively low-level misbehaviour is what is most likely to stress (negatively) new and established teachers. Being aware of this can help you protect yourself from the harm that such antagonisms cause.

When thinking about your own model for behaviour management (for that is, in effect, what will emerge – teachers may use a model as a base but the reality is that only you can develop systems that work with the dynamics between you and your classes), find out how much freedom you have in this area. If your school has set discipline procedures you will have to follow them but, to a certain extent, within your own room, you are free. It hardly needs to be said that any behaviour that contravenes the school's code on equal opportunities and discrimination needs to be dealt with promptly and severely.

It does seem to be the case that classes behave best when teachers are working in a style most natural to them. If you like order and calm you are never going to be happy with the apparent 'chaos' of the teacher who likes to work less formally. Do also be aware of the fine line between order and anarchy. Good behaviour can be dependent to some extent on the good will and acceptance of pupils, which is why every minute spent on nurturing good relationships is time well invested.

Here are some more points to consider:

- Anger is often at the heart of a child's misbehaviour. Be aware of the many battles that the child may have already fought that day before he/she started messing around in your class. Don't greet a child's anger with your own. Remember what it was like being the age of the children you teach.
- Think about how you have behaved in lectures, seminars and meetings. Can you honestly say you have never talked when someone else is speaking, or looked bored, or yawned?
- Don't think of discipline as a means of control, but accept that everyone needs discipline for a variety of reasons, not least security and protection.
- Plan your ideas around the rewarding of success.
- Think about how children gain your attention in your lessons – is it through good or bad behaviour?
- Are there any changes you could make to the way you teach in order to minimize the need to correct behaviour?
- When implementing a behaviour management plan, never give up on your expectations. It may be a long (continuous) haul, but you cannot plant seeds today and pick flowers tomorrow.

Eight points to remember about managing behaviour:

- Don't speak too fast or too loudly and try not to blush; all these reactions can be interpreted as weakness.
- Give known troublemakers a responsibility that involves an element of trust. This is a good way to make your 'worst nightmare' your 'best friend'.
- Explain the stages of your displeasure. Never go from cold to hot, as you will only confuse the folk you are trying to nurture.
- Don't look as though you are expecting trouble, even when faced with the toughest of classes.

- Address your displeasure specifically, not to the whole class, and avoid public reprimands, as these are always counter-productive.
- Time your interventions carefully. Does every misdemeanour need correction? Can you express the point (for example, about dropping litter) without falling into a confrontation?
- Frequently convey to your pupils how much you enjoy your job and what specific aspects you like.
- Don't take on the world single-handed. Get support from your induction tutor/mentor or head of department. These people should be involved in rewards and sanctions anyway.

Above all, never resort to saying, 'This couldn't work with my classes.' Something certainly will, so what aspects can you modify for your own use?

Learning styles and behaviour management

Loosely linked in to the literature on the theories of multiple intelligence are theories on the learning styles of children. It can be particularly useful to attempt to ascertain the learning style of any pupils giving you particular difficulties. Don't, however, attempt to do this yourself. The special needs coordinator at your school should be able to provide you with the means of achieving this and there may well be some simple diagnostic tests available for teachers in your school to use. Failing that, a search on the Internet will reveal the extent of information out there on this approach to teaching.

In brief, it is thought that children are either visual learners, auditory learners or kinaesthetic learners.

Visual learners
These learners learn through seeing. They observe body language, facial expressions, visual displays, illustrations, diagrams and so on. They often like to be seated at the front of the room where they can enjoy a clear view of what is going on, and tend to think in terms of pictures rather than text. Spoken instructions can be difficult for visual learners to understand as they may have a tendency to misinterpret words. These learners often have a strong sense of colour and its uses.

Visual learners are helped by:

- colour diagrams and graphics etc;
- written instructions;

- the opportunity to create visual prompts and learning aids such as flow diagrams, flash cards and written brainstorms.

Auditory learners

These learners learn through listening. They like to talk to others and listen to what they have to say while paying particular attention to the tone and speed of voice etc. Such learners will become frustrated if the atmosphere in your classroom is such that it becomes difficult for them to have the quiet they need in order to hear.

Auditory learners are helped by:

- having written instructions read out to them;
- having the opportunity to talk through what they have learnt and verbally answer questions;
- listening to key concepts from each lesson, preferably several times, rather than reading from a book, board or worksheet.

Kinaesthetic learners

These learners learn through doing and touching. They are the children eager to get out on the field to get on with the lesson, or to get their hands on the equipment so that they can conduct their own experiments. Sitting still and listening are not what these folk like to do!

Kinaesthetic learners are helped by:

- the opportunity for experiential learning;
- brain breaks (see section on 'smart moves', page 168);
- being prompted to think, review and revise while *doing*.

For more information on learning styles and how they can link to behaviour management, take a look at www.geocities.com/-educationplace/ls.html and www.howtolearn.com/personal.html, both of which are useful US sites on the topic. Also, www.ldpride.net has an interactive learning styles test and interesting teaching strategies that are sure to be of use. Alternatively, a search on an engine such as Google.com will come up with over 270,000 sites!

Classroom rules and routines

The only reason to have classroom rules and routines is to make life easier and safer, so improving the quality of learning that takes place in your room. By articulating the behaviour you expect through rules and routines, you are specifically organizing your expectations of pupils. The act of making explicit what may be implicit in the way that you teach helps to create further security for your pupils by removing uncertainty about what is expected of them. Appropriate rules and routines also help to steer pupils towards effective learning, and you towards effective teaching.

This book cannot provide a list of rules and routines for you to adopt because they must be specific to you, your pupils and the subject(s) you teach. However, you may like to think about devising rules around these areas, but be aware that they can at best provide a framework on which to develop your learning relationships with pupils further:

- the way pupils speak to each other and to you;
- the way pupils listen to each other and to you;
- pupils' attitudes to homework and classwork;
- pupils' attitudes to time management and the completion of work;
- the way pupils sit and move around the room;
- eating and drinking in the classroom;
- the beginnings and endings of lessons;
- the handing in (and out) of work.

Many teachers like to devise rules with the help of pupils. This serves to emphasize the fact that behaviour management is a continuous dialogue between pupils and teachers with commitments on both sides. When you actually write the rules with your pupils, keep them positive. 'In this room we sit in silence when Mr Brown is talking to us' is infinitely better than 'Don't chatter when Mr Brown is talking.' Certainly don't create rules that put ideas into pupils' minds. Just think about the consequences of 'Don't throw chewing gum at teachers.' Does such a rule actually need to be written?

Here are some hints for using rules:

- Make sure your rules reflect the ethos of the school.
- Don't relax your rules or expectations, however familiar you become with pupils; they will appreciate the stability and security your lessons give them.
- Think about ways of using peer mediation/pressure to ensure your rules are met.
- Build on respect for the right to learn and to teach and pupil accountability. Forget any desires for popularity; respect will serve you far better.
- Once you have devised your rules and routines, stick to them, use them, refer to them and discuss any changes with pupils.

- Use the rules that you devise with your class(es) to build on a sense of community in your classroom.
- Don't just aim to be 'captain of the ship'. You also want a happy crew. Ask your pupils what it is about your lessons that helps them to learn, and what hinders their learning.

ABOUT UNDERSTANDING THE CLASSROOM

In his Association of Teachers and Lecturers document, *Managing Classroom Behaviour* (available to members and non-members – see www.askatl.org.uk for further details), Chris Watkins identifies five key features of the classroom situation:

1. Classrooms are busy places – apparently, teachers engage in 1,000 interactions a day!
2. Classrooms are public places – the behaviour of teachers and pupils is visible to everyone in the room.
3. Classroom events are multidimensional – personal–social aspects of pupils' and teachers' lives are always affecting classroom life.
4. Classroom events are simultaneous – they do not occur on a step-by-step basis.
5. Classroom events are unpredictable – despite the development of routines, no one can predict events with complete accuracy.

Keeping these factors in mind when thinking about what happens in your classroom can help you to develop and retain perspective about your expectations of yourself and your pupils.

Being slick

Behaviour management is not about fighting every battle. If you do, your lessons will become far too stilted and pupils will become desensitized to your rules. The key is to be slick and deft, brisk and businesslike in your behaviour management from the very first second of a lesson:

- Start work promptly. If pupils are taking a while to settle, give them a task to do in limited time. Make this first task simple, straightforward and achievable.
- Identify the cause of a disruption. Is it due to boredom, peer pressure, inappropriately pitched work or concentration difficulties?

- Use these three steps with any child who seems to be unfocused:
  - *Anticipate* bad behaviour. This is much easier when you know your pupils well.
  - *Distract* with simple instructions for work. Try written and verbal instructions to cover most learning styles.
  - *Praise* as soon as you can.
- Don't get into a dialogue about behaviour while the lesson is going on; this is unfair on the rest of the class and wastes valuable time.
- Go to where pupils are sitting rather than the other way round. This prevents the need for crowd control around your desk or chair.
- Don't be afraid to scan the room and say 'That's good, Ben', 'I don't like that behaviour, Angie', 'Nice work, Mustapha', 'That's better, Annie.' Quick-fire feedback can whip a class into shape with speed.

EXAMPLE I was getting increasingly incensed by a year 9 boy who was clearly passing something around the room. Instead of responding calmly, I shouted, 'What are you doing?' I was really embarrassed when the boy said that he was passing a Christmas card for me round for the class to sign. I'd lost my temper when I could have dealt with it earlier and minimized the disruption to the lesson.

(Second-year teacher, West Sussex)

ABOUT DEALING WITH INTERRUPTIONS

The best way of dealing with interruptions is to pre-empt them. Explain, in your first lesson and every lesson that follows, that you will allow plenty of time for questions so interruptions aren't necessary. Respond to all interruptions firmly – they are a huge source of stress for teachers and there is no harm in telling pupils how infuriating it is to have someone talk when you are trying to explain something, not to mention the violation of the most fundamental classroom rule.

Always give jobs to interrupters, such as tidying the room at the end of the lesson or picking up litter, and connect the sanction to the interrupting. If you are able to anticipate an interruption, block the offender by raising your voice slightly, or move towards where he/she is sitting, which sends the signal that you will not be stopped from finishing. Other non-verbal cues include making eye contact and subtly shaking your head, or dropping a card saying 'Listen, please' on his/her desk without interrupting your flow.

ABOUT LARGE CLASSES

With some classes numbering over 40, behaviour management becomes a real skill. If chatting out of turn is the main cause of disturbance, this is only compounded by large classes.

Minimize the hassles of misbehaviour by thinking about the space that pupils have to work in. Are they piled on top of each other with left-handed and right-handed pupils locked in eternal elbow battle? Is there an EU rucksack-mountain blocking your freedom to roam? You could also think about ways in which you may need to modify your teaching. Does group work increase the decibel level to such an extent that it causes actual damage to the eardrums? Can you make eye contact with each pupil? Can they all hear you? Can you hear them?

Appeal for cooperation by developing a strong group identity and a sense of belonging. The 'Dunkirk spirit' – we're in this together – can work well.

Motivation

> The ultimate goal of the educational system is to shift to the individual the burden of pursuing his own education.
>
> (J W Gardener)

The development of natural internal motivators must be at the heart of all behaviour management (and is in some of the management models). This is an ongoing task for teachers that cannot ever be forgotten. Motivated pupils have no time to misbehave.

In order to motivate your class, you need to know what their general mood is. Are pupils buoyant, mad, angry, petulant, playful, tired or slothful? You can use the time while they are settling to assess this and it may be necessary to adapt your lesson plan. A series of very short tasks may be more suitable than a longer project. This doesn't mean rewriting your plan, but it may mean changing the way you deliver it.

If pupils appear to be angry, it can be worth sacrificing some of your lesson to establish what the problem may be. Spend some time talking about it and focusing on solutions before attempting to start your lesson. This is more likely to result in receptive students and you have shown yourself to be aware of the greater picture of their school experience.

EXAMPLE I had one year 9 class all through my NQT year that seemed to really drain me. Individually, I liked the pupils, but together they were awful! The start of every lesson was a battle and I never felt I had them on side. I decided to follow this advice and at the start of one lesson I asked them what I could do to make the lesson more enticing for them. I didn't intend that the discussion should take all the lesson, but it did in the end. We got loads out in the open – I learnt so much about them all in that one lesson. It didn't solve all my problems with them, but it did more than any other technique. Best of all, they now see me as someone who will listen to them, and even those that I had thought really weren't interested in learning have shown me that they want to know that I'm interested in them. It's been a big lesson in understanding that delivery of a subject has to come second to creating an environment for learning.

(Secondary NQT, Cumbria)

Man is so made, that whenever anything fires his soul. . . impossibilities vanish.

(La Fontaine)

Try some of these ideas to help motivate your classes:

- Give pupils the chance to plan part of a lesson. Ask them how they want to do something and allow them to create their own conditions (within your parameters, of course). You could then ask them to assess the lesson.
- A step up from this is to allow children to teach part of a lesson. This shares the 'power' and allows you to take a back seat (literally).
- Time tasks throughout the lesson. This is a great motivator and also teaches time management. Do be flexible though. You want to motivate, not stress.
- Think of ways of teaching through the interests of your pupils. If a particular craze is sweeping your class, how can that be incorporated into your lessons?
- Shun labels. Some children (and whole classes) get inextricably attached to a label they may have been given in the past, for example 'I'm thick, sir – got anything else for me to do?' or 'We're the bottom set, miss.' You could reply by saying 'You can't be. I don't teach thick kids [or troublemakers, lazy tykes etc]', and move quickly on to a positive aspect of the group or child.

ABOUT SPENDING YOUR OWN MONEY ON
CLASSES

All teachers spend some of their own money on their classes at some stage,
especially as little extras can allow you to make your mark on your pupils.
However, it is worth asking your head of department or induction tutor/mentor
if you can claim back any expenses. Some PTAs raise money for just this
purpose.

Creating the habit of work

If, lesson after lesson, you allow time at the beginning and end that does not
have a constructive purpose, pupils will certainly learn one thing – that work
is not the habit in your room. Your starting work cues need to be totally
understood and respected, and your expectations for good behaviour high. If
you know that what you are teaching is useful, that you would want to learn
it and that it has an immediate application for pupils, you can easily create a
sense of urgency to start work.

You could also think about how to use the peace of silence in your lessons.
It can give children a boost, as it offers temporary respite from having to
respond to the many stimuli around them. Silence also creates a sense of
common purpose – everyone is working under the same conditions.

Why not ask pupils if there is anything you can do to improve their work
habits? You may be pleasantly surprised by the suggestions of even the most
demotivated of classes.

ACTION Think about an occasion when a lesson has gone really
well with little or no misbehaviour. What characterized that lesson? Can you
harness those factors for future use?

Rewards

There is no such whetstone, to sharpen a good wit and encourage a will
to learning, as is praise.

(Roger Ascham)

This is where your ingenuity can really shine. The more original and inspiring your rewards, the more likely pupils are to want them. Use these general ideas as a basis for any reward structure that you may devise:

- Follow school policy. There may be an existing house points or merits scheme or perhaps letters can be sent home detailing achievement. This still leaves you free to introduce some of your own incentives in your lessons.
- Think about power differentials when you praise a child. For example, are you communicating with your heads at the same height? This can make all the difference.
- Can you celebrate achievement in public? Do remember though, that this may seem more like a punishment for some pupils!
- Do your pupils have any preferred activities as a reward, such as being allowed extra time on a computer, being able to play a game in class or being given an edible treat? Discuss this with them, and remember that these activities may well change. What's popular this week may be out next.
- Your rewards should be worth the effort and certainly not too easily attained. You want them to be held in high esteem by pupils and for them to know that you will be consistent.

ABOUT APPROPRIATE AND EQUITABLE REWARDS

There is nothing more annoying to staff trying to build up respect amongst pupils for a system of reward than a maverick teacher dishing out praise lavishly and indiscriminately. The danger here is the slippery slope to piling on the praise because a child hasn't done something (eg hit his/her neighbour) rather than has done something (eg listened attentively and contributed to the lesson when usually this is not the case). Those members of the class who do not require this 'encouragement' will see this as grossly unfair.

Do also be aware of the many stages of praise before you reach for the high-prestige rewards. For example, a positive comment written in a book, a memo sent to the form tutor etc could be more appropriate than a merit.

Sanctions

> It is better that 10 guilty persons escape than one innocent suffer.
>
> (William Blackstone)

Schools vary tremendously in their attitudes to sanctions and it is essential that you absorb school policy. The hints on sanctions below will provide additional support.

ACTION Whenever you have to deal with indiscipline, ask yourself how many pupils it involves. This will help you see that the 'subversiveness' is not that extensive.

EXAMPLE My tutor told me a great analogy to remember. . . A retail manager does not discipline his shop. He manages it. He does not wait for problems to occur and then wonder what to do about them. He has a plan in place.

(Primary NQT, London)

Hints on sanctions
Do:

- Avoid sanctions that simply reiterate what the rules are, such as repeatedly copying out the school code. They *know them*; that's why they broke them! Aim to *teach* through sanctions, preferably about emotional intelligence, awareness of others and citizenship.
- Be courteous to pupils when punishing them. Always offer a good example and explain exactly what you believe to be right and wrong in the situation. Be sure to convey the fact that your preference would be to reward them for deserving achievement rather than punish for indiscipline.
- Be extremely wary of detaining a child other than in a formal school detention. Laws apply regarding a school's right to detain a child (see your school's policy on detention for further information) and a notice period must be given. In addition, detention is rarely considered by pupils to be anything more serious than a nuisance.

- Listen to a child if he/she offers an explanation or an apology.
- Address problems and administer sanctions after the lesson. You will not gain the respect of the child through humiliating him/her in public.

Don't:

- React impulsively to a 'crime'. Think about an appropriate sanction – perhaps have some ready-prepared. Instant reactions will not lead to consistency.
- Threaten punishment and not follow through precisely.
- Be alone with pupils when reprimanding them. Always ask for another member of staff to be present to witness what happens.
- Refer to siblings. The child may have had a lifetime of listening to cries of how well behaved his/her brothers and sisters are.
- Give collective punishments. Have you ever taught a class in which every child deserves exactly the same level of punishment?

Avoiding punishing yourself

A smooth sea never made a skilful mariner.

(Anon)

Think about these questions:

- Do you respond and punish automatically? Could you halve the amount of sanctions you deliver?
- Do you talk to pupils about their behaviour at a time that is convenient to you, when you have cooled off?
- Do you take misbehaviour as a personal insult? (It is extremely rare for this to be the case. There are always other factors affecting a person's behaviour and there is no harm in letting pupils know that you are not the cause of their anger on this occasion.)

If you have a really bad day, when you feel as though all you have done is respond to poor behaviour, use this recovery plan:

- Put the day in perspective. Was it the whole day that went wrong or just part of it?
- Identify *what* went wrong and *who* contributed.

- Resolve to talk to the pupils and/or staff who contributed to your bad day before you go home if possible.
- Write down two things that you can do to prevent the same circumstances occurring again.
- Ask yourself why you expect to have perfect lessons and great days every day. Does it really matter if you don't?
- Give yourself an evening off – no marking, no preparation. What is not done now can wait. Don't even take work home; you need the break.
- Treat yourself to whatever makes you feel good, eg nice food for dinner, some flowers, a novel or a bottle of wine, etc.
- Book something enjoyable for the near future – cinema tickets, a night out or even just some time with a loved one.

ABOUT CONFISCATING PROPERTY

This is a potentially problematic area best avoided. If a pupil has an illegal item in his/her possession a member of the senior management team should be dealing with the situation and your role is to pass on any information you have as soon as possible. If you want to remove any other item from a child's possession, make sure that you have given the opportunity for the child to put the item away, that the child knows exactly why it is being removed and when and from whom (perhaps the pastoral head) the child can retrieve the item. Never seize something or force yourself into a corner by saying 'Give me that now.' You could easily be met with refusal. If something (eg a note) is being passed around the room, don't destroy it yourself – ask a pupil to. Take the dustbin to the child to minimize disruption.

Social inclusion

Regular attendance and high standards of behaviour are specific educational goals. An underlying view is that misbehaviour should not be accepted as inevitable, regardless of the circumstances facing a school. To help support this goal of the social inclusion of all pupils, guidance (Circular 10/99) was issued by the Social Exclusion Unit, the Department of Health and the Home Office in 1999 and this is summarized below. Copies of the circular can be ordered from the DfES publications centre: 0845 602 2260, or viewed on the Internet.

The good practice principles that the guidance highlights are:

- setting good habits early (habits of punctuality and good behaviour);
- early intervention;
- rewarding achievements;
- supporting behaviour management (through models such as assertive discipline);
- working with parents;
- involving pupils;
- commitment to equal opportunities;
- identifying underlying causes;
- study support.

The guidance suggests that the following groups are particularly at risk of becoming excluded from education and it would be worth taking some time to consider what your contribution to their inclusion could be:

- those with special educational needs;
- children in the care of local authorities;
- minority ethnic children;
- travellers;
- young carers;
- those from families under stress;
- pregnant schoolgirls and teenage mothers.

As well as taking a look at Circular 10/99, visit http://inclusion.ngfl.gov.uk. This is a free catalogue of online resources that seeks to assist teachers, parents and carers in supporting individual learning needs. The resources have already been carefully catalogued so you won't have to spend hours sifting through free-text Web searches!

Classroom folklore

There is no particular order to this list; just look through it for inspiration to perhaps trigger you own ideas. Teachers of pupils of a variety of age groups and subjects have implemented these ideas, so they can work:

- Give A level and year 11 classes a short break mid-lesson. This gives them a chance to chat briefly and can result in everyone feeling refreshed.

- Do simple stretching exercises with young children (year 6 and below) mid-session. This can help to prevent fidgeting especially in those who cannot sit still for long. When the children are standing, ask them to stretch up as high as they can from toes to fingertips, and then flop over and slowly come up again. This can be invigorating for the teacher too.

ABOUT 'SMART MOVES'

Learning is experience. Everything else is just information.

(Albert Einstein)

There is a good deal being written now on what have become known as 'brain-gym activities'. Much of what is seeping into schools now (under various 'schemes' and 'approaches') has roots in the work of Carla Hannaford, a neurophysiologist and educator. Her book, *Smart Moves: Why learning is not all in your head* (1995), explores the body's role in thinking and learning, and how movement can lead to enhanced performance.

Simple activities can improve fine and large motor movement, laterality and generally wake up the mind/body system. While you can find endless lists of such activities to try with your class in several popular texts for teachers, it will be most useful to you to explore a book such as Hannaford's for a solid background and explanations of the relatively few key moves that will improve learning most effectively in your classroom.

EXAMPLE One NQT was having problems controlling a class with a particular child interrupting persistently. After numerous warnings she offered a final 'If you carry on I'll move you out of the class.' He continued protesting so she sent him to the head's office. Grudgingly he pulled his crutches out from under the desk and hobbled off. His original complaint was that he needed to stretch his legs.

- Be spontaneous. This worked well for the teacher of a year 10 boy who was being particularly disruptive. She was working with a child at the back of the room when there was a sudden outburst of laughter. The boy was trying on her jumper that she had left at the front of the room. She laughed spontaneously simply because he looked so ridiculous and after a while everyone got back to work without the need for the teacher to say anything. Her relationship with the boy was much improved afterwards, as she had shown that she was human and able to overlook some aspects of his behaviour.

- Ask a child who has misbehaved to help you through part of your lunch break. You could use the opportunity to get a job done, eg mounting work, as well as chat to the child about aspects of his/her behaviour. This helps to minimize the chances of either party seeking to dominate and can work with all age groups. Don't do this too often – working through a break is not a good habit.

- Introduce a 'stop' law. If anyone does anything that adversely affects another, anyone can say 'Stop.' This can create a very safe environment and, if managed well, with clear consequences for violation of the law, empowers everyone in the room.

- Offer the opportunity for pupils to visualize the way they would like others to behave towards them. Link this in with their understanding of the way they behave towards others.

- Keep a marble jar. When someone in the class does something good, put a marble in the jar. When the jar is full, give the class a treat. Don't take marbles out of the jar if someone misbehaves. You don't want to punish the whole class.

- Give out a token (eg a plastic disc or a raffle ticket etc) for good behaviour. At the end of the day/week/term pupils can purchase treats with the tokens. For example, 10 tokens might mean they can buy the choice of an end-of-term video, two tokens might pay for some sweets etc. Build up your own 'shop'.

- Offer the best worker the choice of what song you listen to when you pack away. You could play CDs through a PC, laptop with speakers or a portable CD player.

ABOUT BEHAVIOUR MANAGEMENT MODELS

There are many models for behaviour management, most with their own ideas on why children misbehave. Many of these draw from existing good practice and require whole-school approaches for their effectiveness. However, you may like to find out more about the following:

- the *Canter model*: this is based on assertive discipline with teachers firmly insisting on good behaviour through certain techniques;
- the *Jones model*: this aims to help students support their own self-control through effective body language, incentive systems and efficient individual help;
- the *Rogers approach*: this is based on the conscious awareness of the steps of teacher action – such steps include the tactical ignoring of behaviour, taking pupils aside and giving simple choices.

There are also the Kuonin, Neo-Skinnerian, Ginott, Glasser, Dreikurs, Gordon, Curwin and Mendler, Redl and Wattenberg models of behaviour management, to name but a few, but don't feel obliged to absorb them all!

ABOUT CIRCLE TIME

Circle time is talked about with zeal in some schools and the idea can certainly work with pupils of all ages, and adults too. There is nothing new about the concept of circle time. Some tribes and cultures have long used such a system for discussion and, as a tool for educational purposes, it is thought to date back to Sweden at the turn of the last century.

Much of the literature on circle time draws heavily on the original research of Ballard (1982), and his work is the best place to start for the underlying principles of circle time. You might also like to consider two points.

Firstly, circle time should not be associated with discipline or problem solving. 'Issues' should not be brought to a circle. Rather, it is a tool for developing self-awareness, self-image and group awareness. Acceptance of each other must be unconditional.

Secondly, it is possible to use circle time to teach pupils that we all have feelings that need to be expressed, that we need to be able to respond constructively to the feelings of others and that from this starting point we can express ourselves without fear of criticism or judgement.

PUPIL–TEACHER CONFRONTATIONS

Time cools, time clarifies; no mood can be maintained quite unaltered through the course of hours.

(Thomas Mann)

Regardless of how well you establish routines and explain your expectations, there will inevitably be occasions when pupils cross the boundaries of acceptable behaviour. This then gives you cause to confront the miscreant. The nature of pupil–teacher confrontations is even something that OFSTED looks at during an inspection.

However you decide to approach these confrontations, you should aim to do it rationally and honestly. These solutions should perhaps be avoided:

- sarcasm – some bright teenagers may understand sarcasm but generally it is lost and only serves to frustrate the teacher;
- humiliating pupils – this is unproductive and certainly not supportive of pupils' welfare;
- losing your temper – this is rarely beneficial especially if it happens in front of the whole class for the sake of one pupil.

Serious misdemeanours need to be dealt with immediately in accordance with the established policies in your school. The most effective method is to remove the offending pupil from the room and deal with the problem after a 'cooling-off' period. Asking a trusted pupil to get a member of the senior management team to come to your class to collect the child is effective. This sends clear signals to the rest of the class that boundaries have been crossed and that teachers are united. It also ensures that you don't have to face the public humiliation of having your requests for a pupil to leave the room ignored.

ABOUT BEING ASSAULTED AT WORK

If a colleague, pupil or parent assaults you at school, you will need to record the incident with your headteacher (who may need to report it to the Health and Safety Commission). Also talk to your union and seek medical advice. Such a situation needs to be treated most seriously.

When you do face the child to resolve the situation, remember these points:

- Explain quietly, clearly and calmly (with 'soft words and hard arguments') what it is about his/her behaviour you cannot tolerate and why. Avoid ranting 'How dare you. . .', as this simply shows you have lost your cool and makes it very hard to bring the conversation to a constructive conclusion.

- Calmly insist on eye contact and general respect. Pupils should look at you when you talk to them and you may want to ensure that they don't slouch or overtly show that they simply aren't bothered. Pupils should always listen without interrupting.
- Don't exaggerate the behaviour. You can expect pupils to see that you are not unreasonable without the need to embellish.
- Aim to establish what the pupil got out of the misdemeanour; was it a win/win situation for him/her? Does the pupil think what s/he did was a good idea? The response will almost certainly be negative.
- Avoid raising your voice during a one-to-one as this is always counter-productive:
  - there is no physical need;
  - you will alienate the pupil you are trying to encourage to see reason;
  - you will raise your blood pressure unnecessarily;
  - you risk losing reason and saying something offensive – 'How can I get this into your (thick) head?';
  - you will earn a reputation for losing your temper;
  - you will disturb classes trying to work in the vicinity.
- Aim to understand how you feel about the situation. A teacher trainer in the US 50 years ago suggested that teachers should consider whether they are irritated, challenged or hurt by a child's behaviour. His theory was that, if you are irritated, the child is likely to be an attention seeker, so good behaviour should be reinforced. If you feel challenged, the child may be a power seeker. This is more difficult to handle, but not impossible. Restate rules and expectations as frequently as necessary. If you feel hurt, the child may be a revenge seeker. In each situation, it can be helpful to explain to the child what you think is happening. However, dealing with these character types is complex and your response is bound to change from day to day. Seek the advice of your induction tutor/mentor, as it may be time to set up a meeting with the child and his/her carers.
- Initially, don't spend a long time trying to sort out the problem. Once you have explained why you have had to reprimand the pupil, dispense your punishment and leave it at that. However, you should arrange a mutually agreeable time when you can discuss both the child's behaviour and ways of enabling him/her to improve. Be sure to explore how the pupil views his/her behaviour as well as the view the pupil has of him or herself. This stage is vital in this process and allows you both to talk rationally while sufficiently distanced from the original misdemeanour. Your aim is to reach an understanding of each other's needs and a commitment to improving your relationship.

This whole process may take a long time. Some pupils may be resistant to your methods and it is important to persevere. You're not going to succeed with all pupils all the time, but calm determination can go a long way. Be consistent in your expectations and praise any subsequent improvement in behaviour. Never give up on a pupil.

'Difficult' children

Unless children's crimes are so heinous as to warrant exclusion, you are going to have to exist in the same institution with children who have behaved unacceptably towards you. Whatever methods you adopt to deal with the situation, keep this in mind. It is not enough to agree to disagree or to write a relationship off. Go for peaceful, constructive resolutions even if they take a term or year to achieve, or if they result in you having to face your own role in the situation's demise (if you had one).

ABOUT CONFRONTING CHILDREN

When you are confronting children with your disappointment and anger at their poor behaviour, always keep in the forefront of your mind what the best possible outcome would be. How do you want the situation resolved? Visualize your perfect scenario. There is no harm in telling children the hopes you have for an improvement and involving them in creating some appropriate criteria by which you can both assess whether progress has been made. This approach can be taken with whole classes as well, and some teachers periodically set aside a part or whole lesson to discuss behaviour and attitude. It is extremely difficult for even the most deviant of pupils to completely ignore such reason from a teacher.

- When it looks as though a relationship with a child is beyond repair, you need, initially, to go for damage limitation.
- Think of examples when the child has worked well for you. Is there a common theme here? Tell the child what you have liked about him/her in the past.
- Seek advice from colleagues who teach the child, including the form tutor, or colleagues who have had success in dealing with 'difficult' children.

- Don't get into power games – you are the teacher and therefore always 'in charge'. However, that should be taken as read, so don't humiliate yourself by reiterating it in front of pupils.
- Avoid saying things like 'When you're away the class works really well.' The child may already be battling with feelings of rejection to be misbehaving, so adding to these will do nothing for your relationship.
- Aim to reach an understanding of each other's needs and be prepared to concede something to the child.

ABOUT YOUR PERSPECTIVE ON 'DIFFICULT' CHILDREN

When you feel you are spending disproportionate amounts of time on certain pupils it is easy to start viewing the whole class as being difficult. This is very rarely the case and it is important to retain a sense of perspective. You may find teaching a particular class difficult because of the actions of one or two pupils – don't let that taint your enjoyment of the group.

Changing your perspective

It is very easy to make judgements of pupils that are extremely hard to remove or change. Sometimes it is appropriate to review your perspective of a child and situation:

- Do you really need to fight every battle? Perhaps some situations can be overlooked in order to preserve the overall ambience of a lesson. The fact that Johnny is doodling this week may be a huge improvement on his previous behaviour. You should have high expectations of all your pupils, but the reality of teaching means that you are sometimes going to have to ask yourself 'Does it matter? Is it worth it?'
- Be prepared to question your own attitudes. Do you find that pupils' behaviour is much worse on days when you are tired or angry at some aspect of your life? Be aware of fluctuations in your levels of tolerance.
- Try to find out as much as possible about children who you consider are being 'difficult'. There will be something you have in common and you may be able to build on that as a basis for a better working relationship.

An often-used quote from Lord Elton is worth keeping in mind when thinking about behaviour and discipline:

> Members of staff who treat their pupils with discourtesy, impatience or contempt, or are late for those from whom they demand punctuality, who scribble illegibly on words which they insist must be impeccably clear and tidy, who will not listen to those from whom they demand absolute attention, who bawl their heads off at those from whom they demand soft and respectful speech, who hold up to ridicule those whom they instruct to treat all men with respect, or who treat any of their own colleagues with anything but courtesy and respect in the presence of any of the pupils, are suffering a painful and obvious discontinuity of logic.

Attention Deficit Hyperactivity Disorder

This condition, known as ADHD, is being diagnosed with increasing frequency in school-age children. It is believed that the condition is caused by a minor brain dysfunction affecting the part that deals with behaviour inhibition, perhaps due to an imbalance of neurotransmitters. The condition affects more boys than girls; the ratio is about 6:1.

Stimulant medications can be used to try to correct imbalances, but recent research has shown that fatty acid supplements can lead to significant improvements for children with ADHD.

Symptoms of ADHD include impulsiveness, overactivity, clumsiness, disorganization and an inability to sustain attention. In the classroom this may manifest itself as fidgeting, being easily distracted, being forgetful, being disrespectful of authority, interrupting others, having difficulty listening, talking incessantly and being incapable of following instructions.

This can all be incredibly frustrating for a teacher (as well as for the pupil). You should have been told about any sufferers in your classes, and given management strategies for their particular learning difficulties, but there may be some others who are undiagnosed for various reasons. If you suspect that a child you teach may be suffering from ADHD, talk to your SEN coordinator.

Bear these general points in mind when teaching ADHD sufferers:

- Many children who have been diagnosed with ADHD suffer from poor self-esteem. They may be aware of their shortcomings, probably from years of criticism before their condition was diagnosed, but are somehow unable to remedy them. Use techniques to boost esteem as frequently as possible. Any behaviour that could warrant positive reinforcement should be praised.

- ADHD children may be very impatient and might use waiting time destructively. Try to avoid this situation by making sure they are occupied, even if this means dealing with them first within the class.
- Many ADHD children respond well to routines. Try to make your classroom routines consistent from the start, including the sufferer's seating arrangements, and explain any changes clearly and in good time wherever possible.

ABOUT OTHER EDUCATIONAL AND MEDICAL NEEDS

There will be a wide variety of conditions and circumstances affecting children's learning in your classes. While it would be ideal if you could find out all about the conditions suffered by the children you teach, that is quite impractical. If you get a chance, read about Asperger's syndrome, dyspraxia and autism, and lean on your SEN coordinator for ideas and guidance on educating children with extra needs.

Management strategies

When teaching ADHD pupils, these tips will be useful:

- Make sure the ADHD child sits as close to you as possible and away from distraction (eg windows and doors). Seat some positive role models nearby.
- When talking to the pupil maintain eye contact for as long as possible.
- Encourage the child to use tools to structure his/her day, for example timetables, daybooks, diaries etc. These all help to create routines.
- Break any tasks down into timed sections. Aim to do this surreptitiously so that the ADHD child does not feel different. Avoid giving multiple commands and make sure the child has understood the instructions before beginning the task. You should already have a culture of tolerance in your group for children who feel the need to clarify and question.
- Make sure that when you explain tasks the child is listening and not holding, touching or fiddling with anything.

- Calmly insist on consistent rules for politeness in the classroom. For example, no child should call out or interrupt another person. You may need to spend time teaching and reteaching the ADHD child these rules.
- Work with your SEN department to modify work as necessary. You may agree that an ADHD child should have more time to complete certain tasks.
- Think about the way ICT can be used in your lessons, as this can help to focus an ADHD child.
- Be aware of the amount of stimuli surrounding a sufferer. Is there anything you can do to reduce this?
- Be prepared to adjust your expectations of the ADHD child in terms of self-responsibility. There may be days when you have to explain tasks calmly several times and monitor each stage religiously. Perhaps these are the days when frequent rewards would provide the incentive for the child to carry on.
- Stress and fatigue can affect the ADHD child more profoundly than other children. Be sensitive to their personal circumstances and try to avoid overload.
- As soon as behaviour starts to deteriorate, use distraction strategies. Point out good work and behaviour and as far as possible ignore the child's challenges to your expectations. However, if other children are distracted then you will have to correct his or her behaviour. Aim to reward more frequently than you punish and, instead of focusing on the negative, express the positive, eg 'Sit still please' rather than 'Stop fidgeting.'
- Discuss the consequences of misbehaviour.
- Utilize the concept of breaks during lessons by giving the ADHD child a 'job' to do. This gives the child temporary respite from classwork and also serves to boost self-esteem, as the child feels trusted.
- Encourage the child to reward him or herself. Teach him/her methods of positive self-talk. For example, when you praise good work ask the child what his/her opinion is. Try to draw out of the child the aspects that he/she is particularly pleased with. The aim is to get the child to say 'I'm pleased with my work' or 'I did that well' or 'This is good.'
- The therapeutic value of play has been shown to be great for ADHD children. Apparently the more play you have as a child the more rational and less impulsive you are as an adult. Avoid restricting an ADHD child's opportunities for play. This is most clearly illustrated by the stresses of teaching a class that has been prevented from playing because of a wet break – they all seem to have ADHD then!

EXAMPLE For me personally, what helped was to be told exactly what to do stage by stage. If I was given something to do and told to go away and do it then I struggled, but if I was given a task at a time I could go away and complete that, and then go back to the teacher for the next task. I found it very difficult working for myself. It helped when the teacher outlined specifically what I had to do but not when he or she made a big deal of it in front of the class because it just made me feel stupid and inferior.

(Alex, 18, diagnosed ADHD)

ABOUT MEDICATION FOR ADHD

Medication for ADHD is still highly controversial. Some teachers fear that it is being used to calm disruptive children and there has been a steep rise in prescriptions for drugs used to control the condition and other similar ones.

Medication cannot cure ADHD but used in carefully controlled conditions it is thought by some to moderate its effects. However, this can only be successful as part of a package of help – medication cannot teach and encourage, nurture and support, but may provide a backdrop against which help can be absorbed by the child.

CLASSROOM BODY LANGUAGE

There is no doubt that the non-verbal communications that we give convey messages more efficiently than the spoken word. For no profession is this more the case than teaching. When your greatest weapon in the battle for control is sheer force of character, your body language can serve as an excellent reinforcement.

There is an element of acting in all teaching, and attention to body language and posture is a quick way into character. Exponents of the Alexander Technique know clearly the extent to which the way we use posture affects physical and mental health.

> **ACTION** Before focusing on your own body language, observe colleagues in action. How does their body language and posture change to deal with different situations? Now turn your attention to yourself. What posture do you adopt when talking to the whole class, talking to individuals, reprimanding, praising and joking? Do you stand defensively (abdomen and chin pointing outwards) or protectively (shoulders rounded and pelvis tipped back)?

In order to achieve 'free' posture, whereby your body is able to function efficiently, you need to pay attention to your body's extremities – your head and your feet.

Imagine your head is filled with helium, eager to float upwards. Notice the immediate lengthening effect on your spine, while your shoulders fall naturally into place.

Now focus on your feet, making sure that when you stand they take your weight evenly and that when you sit both feet are placed comfortably on the ground (crossing your legs does nothing for circulation).

By remembering these simple ideas, your basic posture will not only be physically correct, but will also have a positive effect on your mental state.

Subtleties for the classroom

Consciously using body language in the classroom can be an excellent way of correcting or recognizing behaviour without speaking or interrupting the flow of your lesson. Do try to be aware of habits that may be annoying to pupils as these can totally dominate their concentration. Think back to your own schooldays – did you ever do something like count the number of times a teacher said a certain phrase or touched his beard?

Do:

- Smile. Forget the old-fashioned notion that no teacher should smile before Christmas! You're a human not a robot and showing that to pupils can only strengthen their respect for you.
- Use eye contact. Make a direct link with a pupil when you talk to him/her to encourage the pupil to feel that he/she has your undivided attention.
- Look at the class when you talk. Some teachers don't bother to look up from what they are doing to issue further instructions to a class, or continue to speak when facing the board and writing.

- Use hand and arm gestures to illustrate points. This will help to guard against stagnation in the delivery of your lessons.
- Use professional touch. For example, a hand on a pupil's shoulder can give reassurance or positive reinforcement.
- Observe the body language of pupils for signs of boredom. This will help you pace your lessons.
- Actively give the impression of listening. This conveys a sense of the importance you are attaching to what is being said.
- Lean or walk towards a child who is talking. Again, this is a way to engage directly in what is being said.
- Use encouraging gestures to help a child to continue talking if he/she is stumbling when answering a question.

Don't:

- Point at pupils. Always use names, even when trying to correct behaviour. Pointing can be perceived as far too aggressive for the classroom.
- Frown. It can be easy to hide behind a permanent frown, which forces you to tense your facial muscles. Reserve frowns to indicate displeasure at a specific individual or incident.
- Cry. As an expression of emotion, crying is fine, but you will save yourself unnecessary embarrassment if you can hold back the tears until there are no pupils around. However honest it may be to cry in front of children, there will be some who will only remember the loss of control.
- Clench your jaw or fists. Pupils will spot the rising tension before you do and may play on your stress.
- Habitually touch parts of your head or face. This can be associated with insecurity.
- Invade a pupil's personal space. Allow the pupil some territory. This is perhaps more important for older pupils.
- Adopt a 'hands on hips' posture. This is negative (and tedious).
- Move around the room in a manic fashion. Gently paced movements will help to set the tone of lessons.
- Make unnecessary sound to get attention, such as banging on desks etc. The noise is unsettling in itself, not to mention what it does to your own stress levels.

What to wear

Gone are the days when teachers paraded in gowns, although some schools do still use them for assemblies and similar occasions. This, in one way, is a pity; at least the problem of what to wear would not be so profound for some teachers!

You will need to find out what the dress code is for your school by asking colleagues if you are not formally told. It is pretty unusual for suits to be compulsory now – most schools allow teachers to be smartly comfortable:

- Respect the dress standards your school is trying to achieve.
- Don't use clothing as a way of expressing discontent.
- Think about the image you portray through your clothing.
- Aim to blend in with staff rather than stand out dramatically. Perhaps confine flamboyance to the weekends.
- Wear stimulating reds and oranges with caution and go easy with accessories.
- Aim to throw out any shoes or clothes that are beyond repair. This may be difficult considering the immense financial pressures NQTs are under, but there's no doubt that your self-image is reflected in your outer appearance.
- Build up a wardrobe of clothes that 'work'. A few good-quality, coordinating items will be most useful.
- Think about whether you need to dress for occasions such as meeting parents or visitors. Perhaps dressing up a little may boost your confidence.
- Whatever guidelines you have to follow when working out what to wear to school, do remember that it is still possible to convey individuality within the tightest of restrictions and extremism is rarely constructive.

Using humour in the classroom

The most wasted of all days is that on which one has not laughed.

(Nicholas Chamfort)

The physical benefits of laughter are well documented and such that most teachers would do well actively to seek amusement on a daily basis. It is infectious, relaxing and an excellent reliever of tension, exercising hundreds of muscles in the face and neck.

We don't know for certain why laughter evolved, but, from a behaviourist viewpoint, it is clear that it is a social signal. Research has shown that we are

30 times more likely to laugh in social settings that when we are alone. We use laughter to strengthen bonds and show that we are willing to be free and open. Therefore, say researchers, the more laughter there is within a group of people, the closer the bonds are likely to be.

Laughter is a disarming mechanism: a universally understood signal of trust. When we laugh, physiological responses take place within our bodies, such that it is impossible to suffer the effects of negative stress at the point of laughing. In addition:

- Immune function is enhanced.
- The fight or flight response is inhibited (leading to a reduction of stress hormones).
- The diaphragm receives a workout.
- The effects of pain can be less pronounced.
- Muscles relax.
- Intellectual performance is boosted through increased flow of oxygen round the body.

Psychologists also believe that humour helps individuals to confront personal problems in a more relaxed and creative state, generating heightened flexibility of thought.

You don't have to earn yourself the reputation of the one who tells terrible jokes all the time in order to employ a little humour in your lessons. There is no government circular stating that classrooms must be devoid of laughter and, in fact, some teachers work laughter breaks into their lesson plans.

Don't worry about overexciting children and not being able to bring them down again. They will soon get used to your routines and quirks, and you will work out the best time to employ a little humour. If you fear an inappropriate response from your pupils at any time, leave the humour for another day. The key here is balance. Use too much humour and you risk appearing to need adulation and affection from your pupils. Aim to throw in occasional high points of humour. But:

- Be sure not to waste time.
- Be aware that any jokes or funny tales you tell will be repeated outside the classroom.
- Never employ humour at the expense of a pupil, however well you know the pupil. This could easily be misunderstood.

ABOUT HUMOUR AT SCHOOL

You only have to glance through a newspaper and see all the cartoons and humour-based columns, or look through TV listings, to see the amount of humour that surrounds us. There is nothing wrong with injecting some light-heartedness into school life. Some schools have humour boards in staffrooms so that staff can read them for light relief. Perhaps establish one in your school, or dedicate a small area of your room (perhaps a cupboard door) to appropriate humour.

WHAT MAKES LESSONS EFFECTIVE?

A teacher is one who makes himself progressively unnecessary.

(Thomas Carruthers)

Thousands of lessons are taught across the country every day, the effectiveness of which varies tremendously. Effective teaching is not something that can be taught, understood and regurgitated consistently; the effectiveness of your lessons is bound to fluctuate, but one thing is certain – if you have the skills to respond to the dynamics of the moment, the overall value of your lessons will be great.

During an effective lesson, experienced teachers perform with a degree of intuitiveness. They make decisions about the pace and content of a lesson with ease and there is almost subconscious use of established routines to ensure that the lesson flows smoothly and effortlessly.

As an NQT, don't place such expectations on yourself. Allow time to develop your own skills of effectiveness and don't expect everything to work all the time. Use your experiences to propel you towards the goal of effectiveness through regular evaluation and analysis of your lessons.

When OFSTED visits your school, inspectors will be looking at questions of effectiveness, particularly regarding your planning, use of time and resources within a lesson as well as the overall pace, flow and rhythm of a lesson.

ABOUT EFFECTIVENESS

What does 'effective' mean? If you consider effectiveness to mean having 100 per cent of pupils on task 100 per cent of the time, then no lesson that has ever been (or will ever be) taught can be thought to be effective! However, if learning has taken place you can consider the lesson to have been effective on some level. Even the teacher who abandons a planned lesson to respond to the behavioural needs of a class sets standards for future lessons and so facilitates effectiveness. The perfectly effective lesson is something that good teachers continue to strive for throughout their careers.

Useful habits

Get into the habit of sticking to certain routines that keep your lessons moving and minimize the opportunity for misbehaviour. The emphasis is on pace and rhythm.

ACTION Think about what it would be like to experience one of your lessons. Would you feel safe enough to take part and offer your ideas, and feel stretched but not rushed, at peace in your environment? 'Be' one of your pupils for a moment. What image of you as the teacher do you see? Are you stimulated, inspired and motivated by what is being said? Is the presentation filled with vitality? Do you understand the purpose of the work you are given?

Before a lesson

Once in the flow of the first term, effective lessons presuppose good relationships with the pupils, adept group management and slick organization of resources. These are all aspects to work on from day one until retirement!

- Make sure your planning is sound. Know what you want to teach and how. Do you know how the group is organized? Is it streamed, set or banded? Is the group 'mixed-ability'?

ABOUT THE HAY MCBER MODEL OF TEACHER EFFECTIVENESS

In June 2000, Hay McBer published a model of teacher effectiveness. The descriptions were based on research into what it is that effective teachers do in practice. There is not the space here to cover the minutiae of the report (which can be downloaded from www.dfes.gov.uk/teachingreforms/leadership/mcber/index.shtml) but, in brief, it supports the often-held view that it is a combination of interconnected factors (teaching skills, professional characteristics and classroom climate) that contributes to overall effectiveness.

The report does identify a 'Dictionary of Characteristics' for main-scale teachers, teachers at the threshold and outstanding teachers. These characteristics have been summarized below:

- professionalism:
  - challenge and support;
  - confidence;
  - creating trust;
  - respect for others;
- thinking:
  - analytical thinking;
  - conceptual thinking;
- planning and setting expectations:
  - drive for improvement;
  - information seeking;
  - initiative;
- leading:
  - flexibility;
  - holding people accountable;
  - managing pupils;
  - passion for learning;
- relating to others:
  - impact and influence;
  - teamworking;
  - understanding others.

Do get a copy of this report, as it will not only be helpful in focusing on your own effectiveness in the classroom but could serve as a basis for many a discussion with your induction tutor/mentor.

- Don't aim to plan too far ahead especially if you are teaching a topic that is unfamiliar. You can't be an expert in everything.
- Check any equipment you plan to use to make sure it works properly. Do all you can to avoid pupils having to share resources. If you prepare any of your own resources (and most teachers do), guard master copies closely.
- Prepare your room as much as possible, including the board. Be creative with your board space, be it black, white or a murky shade of green! If you have a rolling board, you can design board work in advance and roll the prepared section away until you need it. This means you don't have to turn your back on pupils, and pupils don't have to look at a board displaying irrelevant information, which may be confusing for some. Think of board routines you can teach your class. Perhaps put directions in boxes and questions in bubbles. Once you have created your own formula, stick with it. Use the board as a way of presenting the lesson – a valuable resource. Some teachers write statements about what the lesson is about on the board, for example 'Today we will explore the causes of World War I.'
- Whenever possible, be waiting for your class to arrive, even if that means missing a few minutes of your break. You can, perhaps, ask pupils to line up quietly (or in silence) outside if space permits, before they enter your room. Reiterate your need for pupils to enter quietly and calmly.
- Welcome pupils with confidence. The first two or three minutes of a lesson are crucial.
- Allow some time for pupils to unpack and settle and again insist on silence before beginning the lesson. Give a clear signal when the lesson is to begin. Be consistent so that pupils learn your cues.

During a lesson

- Introduce each lesson. Think of lessons as works of art worthy of an introduction. You are, after all, composer and conductor.
- Link each lesson to the previous lesson through the use of questions and answers. It is essential that pupils see how the work they do is related. Aim to build on existing knowledge and offer the opportunity for your pupils to demonstrate what they know.
- Think about when you want to hand out books, paper and materials – before your introduction or after? Try to hand books out yourself and comment on the quality of the work of either individuals or of the class as a whole. Avoid broad generalizations. Put the name of absent pupils on the top of any materials they have missed out on. Then you will easily be able to ensure they get them when you next see them.

ABOUT LESSON PLANNING

The OFSTED document, *Lessons Learned from Special Measures* (available free of charge from the publications order line: 07002 637833), includes a summary of what effective lesson plans include. This is a useful summary, regardless of whether or not you are teaching in such a school.

Effective lesson plans include:

- clear learning objectives;
- approximate timings for each part of the lesson;
- activities that relate to the learning objective;
- the subject-specific language to be used;
- the deployment of, and tasks for, additional adults;
- briefing notes for support staff and others;
- special resources that are needed for that lesson;
- indication of where work is differentiated;
- assessment details for individuals, groups or the whole class;
- evaluation notes;
- information for use in the next lesson.

You may be involved in the development of individual education plans (IEPs) for your pupils. These plans must be achievable and measurable with a long-term vision if they are to be of value to both pupil and teacher. With specific targets, precisely worded, children can recognize when they are achieving and begin to move themselves forward. If would be useful to discuss IEPs with the SENCO and with your induction tutor/mentor.

ABOUT OVERHEAD PROJECTORS

If you have an overhead projector and screen in your classroom, you can create acetates with overlays that can be used again and again, as long as you use permanent pens or computer-print them. Remember to use a large font size though. This is particularly useful for cover lessons and last-minute planning.

- Don't let latecomers disrupt the lesson. Deal with them at an appropriate time during the lesson or at the end.
- State the lesson's subject, context and purpose. Pupils should always know what will be expected of them, how and why. What is the key competency they will be learning? How can they apply it to real life?
- Announce activities in advance if appropriate, for example 'In five minutes we will move on to role-playing.'
- Use examples that your pupils can directly relate to. Clarify points throughout. Find the simple starting point and develop it. This helps to bring the distant within easy reach.
- Keep the lesson bubbling. Be enthusiastic about what you are teaching and, if you can introduce a 'wow' factor, all the better.
- Encourage enthusiasm for related learning, for example through visits to the library, museums, further reading, visits from experts and the use of ICT (including video, radio, TV etc). Make lessons interesting and dynamic through the use of themes. Guide each child's discovery. This encourages children to take responsibility for their learning.
- Be flexible and adaptable. Abandon your lesson plan if necessary. Be a 'leader' in your classroom.
- Vary the timed activities you give children. Keep individual abilities constantly in your mind and draw on the practical, intellectual, oral and written. Can pupils keep track of their progress and take part in target setting? Are they surprised by the activities or can they predict them?
- Allow only minor digressions before pulling the group back to the topic. Minimize blocks to learning. Catch pupils doing things right rather than wrong.
- Think of ways you can draw key concepts from pupils. Are you appealing to their curiosity and encouraging them to respond creatively? Anecdotal input from teachers can have a profound effect on the learning environment that is created.
- Allow time to recognize and celebrate attainment in your lessons.
- Give pupils the opportunity to develop skills in your lessons by allowing them to apply intellectual, physical and creative effort to the work you set. Nurture imaginative thinking and encourage problem solving.
- Be sure to include memory aids in your lessons, for example mnemonics, prompt cards, bulleted summary sheets and so on.
- Allow plenty of time to set homework and check that all pupils know exactly what they have to do. You could ask specific questions such as 'Annie, when is the homework due in?', 'William, where will you find the information you need?', 'Emma, what page are the questions on?' etc.

- Allow time to clear away before recapping and reflecting on the lesson. Connect the threads of new learning with past and future learning.
- Dismiss the class clearly, perhaps a few at a time. Don't allow them simply to wander out.

EXAMPLE As a student, Amanda, a secondary teacher in Greenwich, had to teach a class after the sudden death of a pupil had been announced. She had to abandon the lesson she had planned and simply respond to the children's reactions.

ABOUT MIXED-ABILITY CLASSES

The notion of streamed classes as an alternative to mixed-ability classes is a little nonsensical. All groups are of mixed abilities and for this reason you will need to take into consideration the ability of each child in every class you teach.

Most schools have some mixed-ability classes but not necessarily mixed-ability teaching. A skill all teachers need is in finding the optimum level of differentiation needed – too much and you launch yourself into a planning nightmare while too little means that it's unlikely that you will stretch any child.

True mixed-ability teaching involves enabling children to work independently. Make sure you always have supplementary materials for the faster and slower learners and be aware that pupils' abilities will appear to change depending on how inspired they are by the topic. Underachievement is to be avoided at all costs and at all levels of ability. Watch out for pupils who:

- occasionally offer flashes of brilliance in their work;
- may seem permanently distracted;
- lack confidence in the classroom;
- overcriticize their own efforts;
- apply creativity and originality to problem solving;
- ask probing questions;
- show you extra work they have done in their own time.

Gently raise your expectations of such pupils, praising and nurturing at every stage.

ABOUT USING TAPES AND VIDEOS

Contrary to popular belief, showing a class a video or playing a tape actually involves a great deal of work. You will have to ensure that all the necessary equipment is available (in some schools this means booking it in advance) and is working properly. You also need to be able to justify its connection with the work in progress. Above all, never play a tape or video without either giving pupils a list of points to listen out for or stopping it in pertinent places to discuss what has happened. Be aware of any biases you may be presenting to children. Think about what alterations you need to make to seating and lighting and do as much of this yourself as possible to cut down on opportunities for indiscipline.

ABOUT EXPLAINING

> The mediocre teacher tells. The good teacher explains. The superior teacher demonstrates. The great teacher inspires.
>
> (William Arthur Ward)

Whatever you teach, the basis of all lessons will be explanations. The universal law here is pace, although it is surprisingly difficult to assess this objectively. Think about the speed at which you talk. Are you too fast or too slow? Too loud or too quiet? Do you vary the tone, volume and speed of your speech?

Start with the real basics – you can't begin too simply. From this point, you can always build on the complexity:

- Make good use of key terms and phrases in appropriate language. Use a natural, logical progression of concepts and repeat, repeat, repeat.
- Ask pupils to demonstrate their understanding of your explanation. Look out for misinterpretations.
- Remember to vary the way you deliver explanations to accommodate the ways different children learn (eg verbal definitions, hands-on experience and so on).

After the lesson

Only the mediocre are always at their best.

(Jean Giraudoux)

- Insist on an orderly exit from your room or to another area of your teaching space.
- Clean your board for the next lesson.
- Be available to talk to pupils between lessons. Even a chat in the corridor can keep a pupil's enthusiasm bubbling.
- Evaluate the lesson and resources you used – even if only mentally.
- Be realistic about what you first think to be a disastrous lesson. Was it really? What can you change for the future? Don't expect to sparkle all the time and don't dwell on mistakes. There isn't an advanced skills teacher in the country that doesn't make mistakes – and learn from them.
- Praise yourself!

ABOUT GROUP WORK

Many teachers like to set group tasks for pupils to offer the opportunity for collaborative learning. If you choose to use group work in your lessons, these ideas may help:

- Think about how you will group your pupils. Common choices are by friendship, by ability (either deliberately mixed or streamed) or by location in the room. You will also need to consider the size of each group. If it is too large there may not be enough work to go round.
- Plan each stage of the group work carefully, with the emphasis on cooperation and interdependence. There would be little point in pupils working independently within their group.
- Make sure your pupils know exactly why they will be working in the groups you have chosen, and how you intend to assess them. Emphasize the relevance of what you have asked them to do.
- If your pupils are not used to group work, they may need to be given skills to make the situation work. For example, can they fairly divide labour? Do they know how to keep a group together?
- Help each group to get started and plan the work they have ahead of them.
- Encourage the groups to deal with their own problems. Only step in if

absolutely necessary. That said, you will need to keep a close eye on what is happening in each group.

- Don't let the task pass by without giving pupils the opportunity to evaluate how well they worked in the group and to consider what would make things easier in the future. This needs careful management on your part so that such evaluations don't degenerate into finger-pointing sessions.

ABOUT QUESTIONING

I was gratified to be able to answer promptly. I said, 'I don't know.'

(Mark Twain)

- Announce questions in advance if appropriate, for example 'I'm going to be asking you about ocean trenches in a few minutes.' This provides pupils with a little advance processing time.
- Aim questions at particular pupils and don't lean on the reliable few. Adapt questions to individuals.
- Asking questions to the whole class can prove to be a discipline debacle as some patiently put hands up and others yell out the first thought that comes to mind.
- Word questions carefully – you may be asking for a witty or glib answer.
- Aim to draw knowledge rather than a one-syllable grunt. Get pupils to analyse and synthesize in their answering. Higher-order questions will do this. Avoid lower-order questions such as basic comprehension, as it is possible to answer these without any knowledge at all.
- Allow sufficient time for the pupil to think of an answer. Encourage through non-verbal cues.
- Select something positive about a wrong answer.
- Ask the same question to different pupils for variety in response.
- Repeat answers for the benefit of the class – they may not all have heard.
- Encourage pupils to ask you questions, and be honest if you don't know the answer. Do, however, make a note to find the answer to tell pupils the next time you see them.

Use questioning to intervene when a child's understanding is off target. Think of an appropriate tactic, such as posing a question that contains a clue to the answer, and be sure to take a step back when understanding has taken place: you don't want to fire developmental questions immediately, but should seek to consolidate what the child has achieved.

Personal evaluation

For a lesson to be effective, you need to plan, deliver and evaluate it. Your training probably saw you furiously writing out an evaluation for every lesson you delivered, as well as every resource you created. If it didn't, start evaluating now.

Keeping up good habits

It would be ridiculous to expect new teachers to fill in a pro forma after every lesson documenting how it went, what resources were used, what worked and what failed, whether pupils were challenged and how you could improve things in the future. However, if you don't spend time reflecting on the lessons you deliver and your teaching, you are unlikely to be able to give effective lessons in which your skills as a teacher continue to develop.

Even if only for a few minutes you consider the lessons you have taught during a day, you will get into the habit of being a reflective practitioner, ever open to learning and improving. If you can get into the habit of jotting your thoughts down, all the better. A small resource evaluation notebook will enable you to keep track of improvements you can make and successes you've had. It can make great reading on a bad day!

Ask yourself:

- Did pupils achieve my learning intentions?
- Has learning actually taken place?
- Did pupils participate?
- Can I assess what pupils have achieved? (Think qualitative and quantitative assessment.)
- Did I enjoy the lesson?

You could even ask your pupils at the end of a lesson what they learnt. Did they enjoy the lesson? Would they like to do it again?

EXAMPLE For Sam, the evaluation process was much more natural once he was in his first job. It became an automatic mental assessment of what was achieved and learnt: a running commentary.

A group of West Sussex teachers developed the checklist below for use in lesson evaluation. It is used effectively in Worthing High School among others, and it can easily be adapted for use with classes of all ages.

Checklist for lesson evaluation

Did I:

- introduce the lesson?   YES/NO
- put the lesson in context?   YES/NO
- make sure the pupils listened in silence?   YES/NO
- introduce the key words to be used?   YES/NO

Did I:

- maintain the pace of the lesson?   YES/NO
- maintain high expectations?   YES/NO
- differentiate the tasks appropriately?   YES/NO
- regularly interact with the pupils?   YES/NO

Were the pupils:

- on task?   YES/NO
- actively engaged in their learning?   YES/NO
- aware of when they could talk and when they should   YES/NO
  remain silent?

Did I:

- respond to the previous homework?   YES/NO
- set homework?   YES/NO
- make sure that the homework task was clearly understood?   YES/NO
- make sure that all pupils entered the task into their organizers? YES/NO
- set a deadline for completion?   YES/NO
- provide differentiated opportunities?   YES/NO

Finally, did I:

- restate the learning intentions?   YES/NO
- summarize what had been achieved?   YES/NO

- explain the intentions for the next lesson?   YES/NO
- ensure that pupils were focused and listening in silence?   YES/NO

Observations

An excellent way of helping you to improve the effectiveness of your lessons is to observe colleagues in action from all areas of the school's curriculum. This can give you good ideas to utilize yourself and bad ideas to avoid at all costs.

Before you observe a colleague, discuss why you want to watch him/her teach. Keep in mind that it can be intimidating to have a new teacher fresh from training in your class. Make sure your colleague is in full agreement that you should be there. This process can help to create some strong, trusting relationships. Ask in advance if your colleague minds you taking notes or moving around the room at appropriate times.

Learning from colleagues

- How did the teacher gain the attention of the pupils?
- How was the lesson introduced?
- What motivated the pupils?
- How were resources used?
- How did the teacher employ questions?
- How was the lesson paced?
- Did the teacher respond to the needs of the pupils with flexibility? What links were made to previous and future lessons?
- Was there an air of enthusiasm from both teacher and class?
- What would you have done differently? Why?

Aim to have a specific focus for your observations.

Spiritual, moral, social and cultural education

This extremely complex area of education is a major focus of OFSTED inspections and it is important (although not just for this reason) that teachers devote time to the development of spiritual, moral, social and cultural (SMSC) education in their lessons. Don't leave SMSC education to chance; pupils cannot be relied upon to catch the knowledge they need in this respect.

Think about how you can make SMSC education specific and identifiable in your lessons. These ideas may help but are by no means definitive:

- Is pride in achievement something that you encourage?
- Do your pupils display a 'have a go' mentality?
- Is creativity nurtured in each child?
- Do you encourage courtesy and trustworthiness in your pupils?
- Do you offer them the opportunity to work collaboratively and to develop skills of cooperation?
- Do your pupils form constructive relationships with one another and with teachers and other adults?
- Do your pupils work in an atmosphere free from oppressive behaviour, such as bullying, sexism and racism?
- Do you actively promote equal opportunities in your classroom?
- Do your pupils reflect on what they do and understand the impact they have on others?
- Do you appreciate the role of emotion in your classroom? Are you an *emotional coach*?
- Do you encourage your pupils to respect other people's differences, particularly their feelings, values and beliefs?
- Do you encourage initiative in your pupils?
- Do you encourage a sense of awe and wonder in pupils at their existence and what surrounds them?
- Are all aspects of human existence celebrated as welcome and valid experiences?
- Can the natural environment be brought into your teaching?

HOMEWORK STRATEGIES

Your school should have a clear homework policy outlining how much homework should be given to each class and how frequently it should be given. At best, this will be written into schemes of work, making the setting of homework relatively painless for new teachers. At worst, common practice in your school will be to yell out the homework at the backs of departing pupils as they rapidly disappear into the corridor!

The notion of homework suffers from the hugely differing interpretations of what constitutes good practice. The line from the DfES is that homework is not an 'optional extra', but is an 'essential' part of a child's work. There is more on this to be found at www.standards.dfes.gov.uk/homework/.

If you do have an element of freedom in the way you set homework it is worth regularly affirming to pupils and parents your commitment to setting meaningful tasks. This tends to create a positive homework ethos that you can build on.

ABOUT SETTING APPROPRIATE HOMEWORK

Ask yourself these questions when you are planning and setting homework:

- Does it have a place in my scheme of work?
- Can pupils make use of libraries and study centres?
- Is it fair in length and context?
- Have I differentiated?
- Does the task discriminate in any way?
- Does the homework vary in length and nature?
- Does the class have access to the relevant information?
- Can the homework lead to pupil achievement?
- Am I encouraging motivation in pupils?
- Can pupils derive from the work set what I want them to?
- Do pupils know what my learning intentions and assessment criteria are?
- Can my pupils value the work set?
- Am I forging links between school and home?
- Can I ascertain whether the homework has been completed?
- Do pupils know I will follow homework up?
- Is my focus on quality (as it should be) or quantity?

When OFSTED inspectors visit your school they will look at how homework is used as an effective part of your lessons. While the actual work you set is important, you also need to consider such issues as how you will collect in the work. Do you have a space on a table for pupils to deposit books, do you ask a pupil to collect them or will you walk round the class, marking off in your register when you collect a book? Establish firm routines with your classes so that everyone knows your arrangements (which, incidentally, should be mutually helpful).

The OFSTED study, *Homework: Learning from practice* (Weston, 1999), identifies the various dimensions of homework, and these are reproduced in Figure 6.1.

Throughout any topic you should aim to set a variety of homework tasks, without relying on any one dimension.

DIMENSIONS OF HOMEWORK		
Completion	*versus*	**Preparation**
Finishing off class work, 'catching up', following up what has been done in class		Reading around new unit/text, research for project, learning new terms
Reinforcement	*versus*	**Research**
Practice exercises, learning, revising		Information retrieval, from school or home sources
Written work	*versus*	**Other modes**
Essays, notes, compositions, exercises, diagrams		Reading, oral inquiry, practical work, drawing, painting
Time-limited	*versus*	**Open-ended**
eg exercise timed to last 20 mins, set of 10 'spellings'		eg 'Research' task, TV review, practical design
Direct parent involvement	*versus*	**Pupil independence encouraged**
eg parent reading with/to child		eg Year 6 pupils, preparing for secondary, parental encouragement only
School resources only	*versus*	**Non-school resources important**
Homework can be completed with textbook or other school-supplied materials only		Pupils encouraged/expected to use library, home, family members' experience
'Overnight' task	*versus*	**Longer-term task**
Short-term task to be completed in one homework session		Homework used to contribute to progress of ongoing topic

Figure 6.1 *Dimensions of homework*

Getting what you want from a task

Homework that is hastily set is unlikely to produce the results you want. If you have placed the task within a scheme of work and your pupils know the context of what they have been asked to do, the chances of getting what you want from a particular task are much greater. Basically, the only way to *get* what you want is to *know* what you want:

● Have homework tasks pre-prepared on sheets of paper or written on the board.

- Allow plenty of time at the end of a lesson to explain the homework. You need to make sure that pupils have written down the details of the task, when it is due in and how it should be completed.
- Never explain the task while pupils are copying into their books. Wait until they have all finished reading and writing and then explain.
- Ask pupils to explain to you what their task is.
- Make sure every child has the resources to complete the task. Ask your SEN department to help differentiate the work you want to set.

Utilizing the homework notion

The best way to ensure that your classes actually complete the homework tasks you set is regularly to reiterate the value of independent study at home. You could also explain to your classes a few general tasks that they could do as homework in the event of your absence. Make sure you keep a stock of such tasks and that pupils know the circumstances in which they should complete them. They could even have them written down in the back of their exercise books or homework diaries and you could nominate someone from the class to inform the cover teacher which task should be done. Although it is harder to place such tasks in the context of current work, this does give pupils an element of choice and responsibility over their work. Tell other members of staff about your system. They will know what to expect if they have to cover your classes and may even want to adopt your idea.

Homework is another opportunity to do some positive PR for your school. View the tasks you set through the eyes of parents. Are they varied and relevant? Are the books that go home in good condition? Can parents easily discern the purpose of a task?

ABOUT SETTING 'WEAK' HOMEWORK

There are bound to be occasions when you have to think on the hoof as far as homework is concerned. Obviously this is not going to be a problem if it only occurs once or twice, but if classes get the impression that homework is not a priority for you, it certainly won't be for them. Try and ensure that the tasks you set will be useful in furthering or consolidating knowledge.

Avoid giving homework tasks connected to your subject or classwork as a punishment. You run the risk of putting the child off your subject for ever. Punitive tasks should be complete in their own right.

Be reasonable in your homework expectations. Just like you, your pupils have lives outside school.

Marking strategies

The whole point of homework is that pupils work independently at home, or at least outside school hours. An unfortunate by-product of this arrangement is the amount of marking that this can generate for teachers.

ABOUT GATHERING GOOD IDEAS

Keep a record of all the homework tasks you have set for each scheme of work. These will probably be suitable for future use and you can adapt them on the basis of previous evaluations on their effectiveness. You could even ask pupils what homework tasks they have enjoyed and have found inspiring.

Once you have decided whether your marking of a piece of work will be summative, formative or diagnostic, there are a number of strategies you can employ to cope with the burden:

- Create tasks that can be self-marked or peer-marked in class.
- Set some non-written homework.
- Pace your homework setting so that you don't have hundreds of projects to mark at the same time. It can take a while to get into the rhythm of a term but homework is one area of teaching you can control.
- Plan homework setting to complement your energy levels. There's little point in arranging piles of marking when you know you are coming down with a cold.
- Think about how you can create tasks requiring short answers. Some subjects lend themselves to this more easily than others. However, you should not rely on short-answer questions too heavily, in any subject.
- Have your marking criteria and the task set in front of you as you work through the books, for quick reference.
- Set a time limit for marking a set of work and stick to it. Minimize distractions and *focus*. Perhaps introduce an element of surprise by using different coloured inks – do you always want to use red?
- Find out if there are any possibilities of help with marking from your department or year colleagues.

ABOUT EXCUSES

Throughout the course of your career you will hear some of the most amazing excuses for non-completion of homework. Make your homework tasks excuse-proof by following these ideas:

- Be consistent with your sanctions for homework not completed. Giving the benefit of the doubt once is just about permissible but certainly no more. It would be a good idea to discuss with the pupil what the problems may be.
- Explain tasks carefully and slowly and offer your class the opportunity to talk to you about the task at a later stage if necessary.
- Create routines for the setting and collection of homework for each class. Have homework days.
- Make the reason for the homework clear. If pupils know the relevance of what they have to do they are more likely to do it.
- Where appropriate, explain to pupils the assessment criteria you will use.
- Think of how tutors can help you create good attitudes towards homework in pupils.
- You will need to discuss with persistent offenders exactly what the problems may be. Explain what your expectations are and what the shortfall is. It may be appropriate to adapt homework tasks or to work with the child after school for a while.

Penelope Weston's book, *Homework: Learning from practice* (1999), summarizes indicators of good practice in homework in both primary schools and secondary schools. These are reproduced below.

Indicators of good practice

Primary schools

Giving a lead

- Homework policy is led and co-ordinated by a senior manager.
- Staff and parents are actively involved in all aspects of the programme.

Developing and disseminating policy

- There is a written policy, developed consensually with staff and parents; the consultation process has taken time and reflected the local and school context.

- A range of approaches is used to continue to convey the ideas in the policy, including guidelines for pupils and parents, workshops and newsletters.

Managing time

- Homework allocations are clearly set out, probably in the form of a weekly and termly schedule setting out what work is due and when, and indicating an estimated time for tasks.
- Homework is structured to help pupils (with parental support) to develop regular study patterns they can manage.

Motivating pupils

- Pupils are encouraged to complete their work by regular feedback, praise and rewards for effort.
- Requirements are made clear to parents, and their support is enlisted so that homework is completed.
- Sanctions for non-completion are clear, but seldom need to be enforced.
- Failure to do homework is investigated before sanctions are applied.

Providing resources

- The school supports teachers by providing commercial resources or time and materials to prepare resources.
- Opportunities are taken to offer pupils additional resources where possible, eg access to computers or library books.

Reviewing performance

- Learning goals are defined for homework and teachers evaluate whether the tasks set are meeting these goals.
- There are systematic procedures for monitoring how programme requirements are being fulfilled (by staff and pupils), and how the programme meets their needs.
- The policy itself is regularly and fully reviewed against school development goals.

Secondary schools

Giving a lead

- Homework policy is led and co-ordinated by a senior manager.
- Other managers share the responsibility of planning and review.

Developing and disseminating policy

- There is a written whole-school policy, with common criteria for department policies.
- A range of approaches is used to continue to convey the ideas in the policy, including guidelines for staff, pupils and parents.

Managing time

- Homework allocations are clearly set out, probably in a homework timetable which is clear to parents and pupils and adhered to by staff.
- Deadlines for completing tasks are explicit and manageable.
- Homework is structured to help pupils to develop regular study patterns they can manage.

Motivating pupils

- Pupils are encouraged to complete their work by regular feedback, praise and rewards for effort.
- Requirements are made clear to parents, and their support is enlisted so that homework is completed.
- Sanctions for non-completion are clear and consistent, but seldom need to be enforced.
- Failure to do homework is investigated before sanctions are applied.

Providing resources

- The school enables staff to buy or prepare appropriate resources.
- Opportunities are taken to offer pupils additional resources where possible, eg access to computers or the resource centre.

Reviewing performance

- Learning goals are defined for homework and teachers evaluate whether the tasks set are meeting these goals.
- There are systematic procedures for monitoring how programme requirements are being fulfilled by staff and pupils, and how the programme meets their needs.
- The policy itself is regularly and fully reviewed against school development goals.

CHAPTER 7

Pastoral pointers – tutoring and you

GETTING PERSONAL

There are bound to be occasions when discussions with pupils move away from the curriculum. Being prepared for such situations will save unnecessary embarrassment and protect you from possible future criticism.

Your personal issues

Regardless of the age of your pupils, you will almost certainly face from them some degree of interest in your personal life. While keeping yourself a complete mystery is neither necessary nor desirable – it is good for pupils to have some insight into the lives of their teachers – the skill is in achieving professional balance.

How much should you tell?
This is entirely for you to decide. The main thing is to be aware of your motives for revealing aspects of your life to pupils. Is it:

- because they frequently ask you?
- because you really do see some of them as friends?
- because you feel it may excuse your mood/behaviour?
- because it is relevant to a particular lesson?

You will know when you have established a good relationship with your pupils and when you have crossed the invisible boundaries of professional discretion. Some points to remember:

- It can sometimes be appropriate to talk to a pupil about an aspect of your personal life to reassure him/her. For example, if a pupil is suffering from a broken heart, there can be no harm in empathizing and telling an anecdote about your experiences. This illustrates your understanding of issues facing your pupils.
- Never reveal something to a pupil that should then be considered a secret. This places unfair expectations on the child and crosses professional boundaries.
- Be prepared for distorted repetitions of your revelations.
- Keep certain aspects of yourself back from the full knowledge of your class. It's not desirable for them to know all about your partner, children, hobbies, home, family, aspirations or dreams and, in any case, they probably won't be interested.
- Divert attention away from yourself by focusing on pupils. If you feel uncomfortable under questioning from pupils, establish early on that you would prefer it if they did not ask personal questions.
- In many ways it is a compliment to your abilities to relate if pupils want to know more about you. However, flattering as this intrigue may be, inappropriate 'chumminess' can be damaging to your career, and your more astute pupils will interpret it as insecurity and sense weakness.

Pupils' personal issues

This is something you will face time and again throughout your teaching career, from dealing with a child who has wet him/herself (depending on the age range you teach) to helping a child through the grieving process.

How much should you ask?

It can be easy to work out which pupils are carrying burdens above those of childhood and adolescence. There may be changes in behaviour and character that need addressing or dramatic changes in work performance. Even improvements can be cause for concern as they can be indicative of a child who is escaping from a situation by throwing him/herself into work:

- It is important to tread extremely carefully when talking to a child you feel may be suffering a personal difficulty. Your school may have guidelines to follow but, if not, talk to the child's pastoral head before doing anything. He/she may know the family, or know how to approach the problem.

- Discuss the child with colleagues to establish whether others have noticed a change.
- Always get guidance from pastoral heads and tutors before asking to speak to the child's parents or carers.
- If you decide to approach the child directly, having spoken to colleagues, do so in a relatively light-hearted (but not flippant) way. Ask, in passing, if there is anything wrong. Avoid saying 'I've noticed you haven't been yourself recently', as this may place the child under undue pressure to discuss private matters. Pave the way for the child to come and talk to you if he/she wants to. You could say 'You know where I am if you want anything, don't you?' Then keep a close, surreptitious eye on the child for a week or so before trying again if things have clearly not improved.

Helping versus interfering

Your memory will tell you that many childhood and teenage issues often resolve themselves with time. Once you have established with pupils that they can talk to you, or a colleague of the opposite sex, whenever they need to, further questioning could well be construed as interfering. Unless you suspect some form of abuse or neglect, in which case you must speak to the named person dealing with all child protection issues, take a back seat and observe for a while, so as to preserve the relationship you have already created with the child.

ABOUT PUPILS GETTING PERSONAL

Intimate relationships (or even discussions) between teachers and their pupils should *always* be avoided. They represent a gross misuse of a teacher's professional status.

However, there may be situations when a pupil involves you in an issue of a personal nature – perhaps the pupil declares undying love for you. It goes without saying that you must respect and accept what the pupil says, but don't attempt to deal with the situation alone. Protect yourself by referring the issue to the child's pastoral head or tutor and make sure that, whenever you speak to the pupil, you do so either when there are others present in the room (preferably a colleague) or in a public place where others may be passing through.

TUTORING

The system of tutoring delivered through tutor groups or houses is one way in which a school cares for its pupils.

Pastoral care should never be confused with discipline – in fact, the two are quite separate. When you discipline a child you are reacting to his/her behaviour, not to the person. Effective pastoral care is proactive and responsive and cannot really be confined to the tutor group. Especially in the primary sector, the roles of individuals as teachers and tutors are inseparable.

Chris Watkins, of the Institute of Education, defines tutoring as being 'that aspect of teaching which helps the learner develop personal, social and learning strategies and choices to make the most of themselves and get the most from the school and from later life'.

Most people can think of times when they have not felt nurtured. Maybe this was at school or college, perhaps being ignored in a shop or failing to have needs met in a relationship. Those times usually result in demotivation, despondency, demoralization, frustration and even anger. Using those memories to empathize with the tutees in your care makes it easier to understand the importance of meeting all the needs of pupils to ensure that they believe in their personal value to the school community.

Ideally, you will not be given a new form in your first year of teaching, as problems can arise when both teacher and class are new. You may be a co-tutor in your NQT year but will almost certainly be a tutor in your own right in your second year. However, you are not expected to sink or swim. There will be a pastoral team for you to call on and even pastoral heads may bring in experts to deal with certain situations, eg bereavement counsellors or drugs-awareness experts.

This section is based on the assumption that personal, social and health education (PSHE) is provided for elsewhere in your school's curriculum.

Your role as a tutor

As a tutor, you are in an extremely powerful position. You can make (or break) a child's experience of school life through your care for, and interpretation of, the issues important to your tutees. Make sure you have been given all the relevant documentation regarding your job as a tutor. You could also get ideas from colleagues and select what you feel would suit your group. Seek help if there is any issue that you do not feel happy dealing with alone. There will be other members of staff to refer to for advice, for example the pastoral head, your mentor or the SENCO.

It is wise to take all opportunities to get to know the families of your tutees. In particular, be aware of those who do not live in nuclear families, and who the home caregivers are.

EXAMPLE One NQT taught a boy who only had one leg, but it took the NQT a year to realize this! Since then he has read all the information on his tutees carefully.

Aspects of your role as a tutor

A tutor is at the very least all of these:

- inspirer/morale booster;
- listener;
- counsellor;
- communicator;
- problem solver;
- administrator;
- nurturer;
- enabler;
- monitor of academic progress;
- monitor of social development;
- manager of behaviour;
- praise giver;
- motivator;
- team builder;
- confidant.

Inspirer and morale booster

There will be times when you will have to try to inject some enthusiasm into a demoralized group. Perhaps they are suffering under the pressure of exams, or have been reprimanded all morning for the poor behaviour of certain members of the group. Your role is to draw the group together and boost morale sufficiently for them to continue the day. Try to create in them a sense of enthusiasm for each other, and for learning.

ABOUT THE ROLES OF THE TUTOR

Be an actor, not a reactor.

(Dr Maxwell Maltz)

Whatever you read about the roles of a tutor, it is important to develop your own ideas. Use personal experiences to devise thoughts on what you want your role to be. As long as you fulfil your school's requirements of its tutors, you can expand your role as you see fit. For example, you may want to organize a trip for your group – perhaps to the cinema – as a way of creating the sense of being part of a team. However, keep the growth of pupils central to your thoughts, abide by local practice (which will be set down by your headteacher and governors) and strive to make school life a more humane experience for your tutees. Good pastoral care can enable pupils to become better learners, so keep in mind the power that your role as a tutor holds.

Listener

Listening is an important aspect of tutoring, and knowing how to listen is an essential skill. Pupils may simply want to express what they are feeling without the intervention of a problem solver, or may want you to act in their defence. Your job is to know the difference, and that will only become evident through listening. Allow pupils to describe their emotions.

Counsellor

There will be many occasions when pupils need the skill and understanding of a counsellor. As an NQT you may not be qualified in counselling, but will certainly use some counselling skills. You can always refer to a professional for anything that you are not happy dealing with, such as a child's bereavement.

Communicator

Not only will you have to relay messages from other members of staff, but you will also have to communicate your own requirements to your group. The way in which this is achieved will have an impact upon the tone of your group.

Problem solver

Tutors often have to inject a sense of reality into fraught and emotional circumstances. Your job here is to find solutions to the problems that your tutees present that are acceptable to all involved. However, there may be times when you will have to be honest and say 'I'm sorry, but I don't know the answer to that.' There is never any shame in this, as long as you find out the necessary answers – this could even be done as a group.

Administrator

Not only do you have a legal requirement to keep attendance records of your group, but you will also have to deal with all the administration related to your group, eg letters from parents explaining absence from school and other school business.

Nurturer

Being a nurturer involves boosting the self-esteem of all the pupils in your care – even the ones you simply cannot get on with. A tutor can help minimize what can be the cruelty of school life for children by boosting their self-esteem. Those with high self-esteem can retain perspective under pressure, and self-esteem is most likely to be nurtured when children are dealt with consistently. You will need to give tutees proof that they are gaining in competence and that you are genuinely interested in them.

Enabler

The role of enabler is closely linked to your nurturing roles and involves creating the circumstances in which your tutees can gain maximum benefit from their school life. You will enable them to succeed. You can also ensure that your tutees have the maximum opportunity to make informed decisions. However, be sure to educate rather than advise. Don't inflict your opinions – allow them to create their own against a backdrop of sound information. This links in with the current trend for schools to be proactive as opposed to reactive when it comes to pastoral care.

Monitor of academic progress

As a tutor you are in the optimum position to track the academic progress of your pupils including monitoring the time they spend on homework etc. When it comes to reports and assessments your input is essential. In some schools parents are invited to speak to form tutors as well as subject teachers at parents' evenings.

Above all, you want to encourage your tutees to become reflective practitioners and observe for themselves what is at the heart of all their schoolwork. What common threads are there? Why are they doing what they are doing? You could ask them to talk about what they have learnt and the processes they used to achieve a learning outcome. Create the environment in which it is safe for pupils to praise each other.

Monitor of social development

The time spent in tutor periods is likely to be when social development (or lack of it) is most apparent. The tutor's job is to monitor this to ensure that all pupils are given the opportunity to grow socially. Most children at some stage face difficult questions of identity such as 'Who am I?' or 'What am I?' They will have to develop self-knowledge, self-growth and the capacity to adapt to situations and go with the flow, not to mention rational autonomy and the understanding of the impact of the self upon others.

Pupils also have to develop the ability to be flexible and responsive to their environment, especially as they move through the school system and have to interact with increasing numbers of teachers and styles.

Manager of behaviour

There may be occasions when colleagues complain to you about the behaviour of a member of your group. While the colleague may have dealt with the misbehaviour, he/she may also look to you as a tutor to reinforce the standards that are expected. You will also have to keep an eye on the general level of behaviour in your group and praise or reprimand as appropriate.

Praise giver

An unfortunate fact of school life is that you are more likely to hear about the misdemeanours of your group than their successes. You should aim to praise the group as a whole and individuals as frequently as possible. Remember how good it feels to be on the receiving end of positive feedback. Help colleagues in this role by reporting to them the good behaviour of their groups.

Motivator

Whether it is coping with the mid-term blues or dealing with a defeat in the inter-form football contest, there are bound to be occasions when you will have to lighten the tone of your group and motivate your tutees.

Team builder

The only way to create a class that is happy to work together cooperatively is to spend time team building. As a tutor, you are at the centre of your team. Talk together, encourage unity and emphasize group successes, for example 'Mrs Evans said you worked very cooperatively in Art today – that's great to hear. Tell me about what you did.'

ABOUT REPRIMANDING INDIVIDUALS

If you do have to reprimand a member of your group, it is imperative that the pupil understands why. What was his/her role? How did he/she personally contribute to the situation? Ask the child to explain exactly what happened and be open to the possibility of a misinterpretation of events, without expressing doubt at a colleague's understanding of what happened. Throughout your dealings with the child, think of ways of enabling the child rather than pushing him/her into a corner. How can the child be guided to a solution? Encourage tutees to be honest about their feelings, even if it does mean listening to 'I hate Mr Boyd', so that you can seek to find ways of turning these negative emotions into positive ones. Whatever the outcome, it must allow for good working relationships to be re-established.

The best way around this sort of situation is to prepare for it in advance. Many teachers run 'What would you do if. . .?' sessions, which give pupils many ideas to draw on as and when the situation arises. This will help to enable tutees to express grievances constructively and deal with the outcome sensibly.

Confidant

There are likely to be situations when tutees confide in you. However, you do have legal obligations to look after the welfare of the children in your care. This may entail passing information on to other agencies if necessary; therefore you must never promise to keep secrets. A teacher cannot be bound by a pupil's request for total confidentiality.

ABOUT DETECTING SIGNS OF ABUSE

Tutors are obliged, as part of their role as teachers in safeguarding children's welfare, to observe tutees for signs of neglect and abuse. Be aware of changes in behaviour such as increased aggression, withdrawal or overdependence, as well as physical signs such as bruising etc.

Always follow your school's guidelines on dealing with suspected abuse. Never try to tackle this complex area alone.

Setting the tone of your group

Your personality will be the main factor controlling the tone of your tutor group. You can set your own rules and limits for your tutees, although involving older pupils in this can work extremely well.

Consider some of these points:

- If you are punctual, your pupils are more likely to be.
- Make the administration side of your tutoring duties slick and efficient. A stock of class lists will be extremely useful for keeping track of money collected etc.
- Place importance on preparation for the school day. Urge pupils to be fully equipped.
- Create routines and stick with them, for example silence when the register is being taken, any notices to be read out immediately after the register has been taken etc.
- Encourage tidiness and pride in your room.
- Constantly reiterate the purpose of your role – you are there for your tutees.
- Encourage togetherness and celebrate differences.
- Strive for balance and fairness.

Maximizing the opportunities of tutoring

Whatever the extent of your role as a tutor and the lessons you have to deliver, there are always methods of maximizing the opportunities that tutoring presents:

- Use any spare time in tutor periods to chat to your class, whatever their age group. Perhaps treat it as 'circle time' (see Chapter 6) – you can glean so much about your tutees, the way they work and what motivates them in this way. Just make sure that those who want to speak have the opportunity and that such chats are not dominated by the few.
- Create the opportunities for tutees to talk to you when they want to. Approachability is an important characteristic for a good tutor to have.
- Remember the finer details of your tutees' lives. Draw attention to birthdays (you could even give a card or small present) and celebrate the achievements of pupils in your group, as a group.
- Pay attention to your obligations to provide equality of opportunity for your pupils.
- Discuss the strengths and weaknesses of the group and devise strategies for improvement.
- Encourage a climate of openness.

- Never forget the role of the tutor in boosting self-esteem. You will probably find that this becomes a two-way process!
- Keep track of pupils who may need follow-up care after a personal trauma.
- Be prepared for tutorial periods, as you would be for a lesson. Leave your subject behind and get to know your tutees as individuals. You should aim to have learning intentions for tutor periods as well as lessons.
- Liaise well with the coordinator of tutor groups in your year and also with the person in charge of personal and social education. If someone else is planning activities for you to do with your group, let him/her know if there was anything that worked particularly well or anything that was a complete disaster.
- Know the line of pastoral authority in your school. You may need to seek help urgently to deal with a situation and should know exactly whom to turn to.
- Ask your tutees what they would like to do or discuss. You could set some time aside each week or month to focus on their choices.

ABOUT SYMPATHY

It is important not to mix sympathy and empathy. Too much sympathy can lead to draining emotional involvement and away from problem solving. It is usually best to keep the focus on finding solutions so that pupils don't fall into the habit of seeking sympathy from you for its own sake. Hearing the expression of sorrow or sympathy can become a prop for certain character types and there will come a day when you are no longer able to fulfil the sympathetic role. That leaves the pupil in a vulnerable position, no longer trusting of the relationship you have. Your role here is as a non-judgemental enabler.

Empathy, on the other hand, is an essential quality of a teacher.

ABOUT GIVING PUPILS BAD NEWS

There may be occasions in your career when you have to break bad news to pupils. This can stretch the skills of the most experienced teachers. If you do need to break some bad news to a pupil, bear these points in mind:

- Arrange it that a colleague is with you when you break the bad news. This is particularly important, as the pupil will need some form of comfort.
- Try to detach yourself from what has happened and focus on the immediate needs of the pupil. You may need to arrange for the pupil to be taken somewhere.

- Make sure you know all the facts and try to answer the pupil's questions as honestly and tenderly as possible. Have tissues and a drink ready (but not in view).
- Allow the child to express his/her emotional reaction as freely as possible.
- Think about how much you need to tell other pupils. Seek advice from your headteacher on what should be said and when.

ABOUT THE MENTAL HEALTH OF YOUR PUPILS

Mental illness is a feature not only of adult life. Increasing numbers of young children are being diagnosed with mental health problems and there is no doubt that teachers can play an important role in the healing process for such children.

Recognizing mental illness in the young can be very difficult; after all, when does the angst of growing up actually become a health issue? However, there are some tell-tale signs that should be looked for:

- excessive introspection;
- loss of appetite;
- tearfulness;
- dramatic changes in behaviour/character;
- obsessiveness;
- mood swings;
- declines in standards and quality of work;
- obvious anxiety/panic attacks.

If you are concerned about the mental health of a pupil, you should seek the advice of your induction tutor/mentor and/or the child's pastoral head. It may be necessary to contact the child's parents, but do not do this without the full backing of your managers. Once mental illness has been diagnosed, the child will begin what is likely to be a difficult haul back to health. During this time, he/she will need all the support you can give. Mental health services for young people vary tremendously around the country and, unfortunately, mental illness still carries a stigma that many cannot handle.

Your SENCO may be able to point you in the direction of literature on helping a pupil through mental illness, as may the Mental Health Foundation (www.mentalhealth.org.uk) or Mind (www.mind.org.uk).

TUTORING FOLKLORE

> Remember that a man's name is to him the sweetest and most important sound in the English language.
>
> (Dale Carnegie)

There is no doubt that sound tutoring is a skill that may come naturally to some teachers and not others. A great deal of your success in tutoring will come as a result of trial and error and it isn't possible to present a winning formula for this complicated task. However, you will pick up hints and tips from colleagues and books, which can inspire you into loving this aspect of teaching.

Ideas that have worked for others

Use these as inspiration, but don't feel under pressure to try them all!

- Take photographs of your tutees to put up on the wall. Pupils could add to the gallery photographs of sporting achievements or school trips etc.
- At the start of the school year, ask your group to write down their hopes and fears for the year/term. Store their ideas away and review them at the end of this period. This is a particularly good exercise to use to illustrate the personal development of your pupils over time.
- Keep a folder for each member of the group in which they can record the work done in tutorial periods.
- Some tutors keep their own records of their tutees in addition to the school records. These can be useful in monitoring progress over the year and for report writing. They also help for reference writing. These records should be considered confidential. You could also include references made to your group by other teachers.
- Encourage your pupils to help you to settle in to your new school (providing they aren't new as well). Ask them about the school and its history etc. Try not to get drawn into discussions about other members of staff – this is inevitable, but remain professional.
- Create a list of discussion topics that pupils can choose from for specific purposes. These could include just about anything from smoking, citizenship or rites of passage to animals, music or body language. Involve pupils in this process.
- Organize cards and/or presents from the group for your cleaner, certainly at Christmas time but at the end of each term too. This encourages pupils

to be more responsible for their actions as they become aware of the thanking process and why this needs to be done.

- Some tutors like to split their tutor groups into smaller 'care' groups. These groups can be responsible for making the room tidy at the end of each day, or doing any 'housework' tasks that need to be done. This encourages pride in the group's immediate surroundings, while ensuring the work is done on a rotation basis. End-of-term parties are relatively easy to organize yet will mark important transitions for you and your group. You would have to check this out with the powers that be in your school, but it may be possible to organize some food and drinks as well, perhaps with small contributions from your pupils. Be sensitive towards anyone who does not celebrate Christmas and Easter – it can be better simply to celebrate the end of the term or year, or the season.
- Ask pupils to write a 'this is me' letter to include details like where they live, who lives with them, likes and dislikes, hopes, fears and aspirations etc.
- Gain as much experience as possible. Observe other tutors in action and talk about ways of adding to your tutoring skills.
- Give pupils an inspirational quote as thought for the day/week.
- Encourage ongoing tournaments, perhaps with cards, a computer game or Scrabble etc.
- Work as a group to solve problems. For example, if the group is not responding to a particular teacher, work together to devise ways of remedying the situation.
- You could give pupils something to think about while you call the register, for example something they learnt that day, something that would improve their achievement, someone they would like to thank, the best thing they did that morning, someone they need to apologize to, etc. Do, however, make sure you allow time for a quick feedback.
- Always explain to your tutees why you are doing something. If you can't do that, the process or procedure doesn't need doing.
- Reassure colleagues that you will deal with their complaints of any member of your group. Both teachers and pupils have to believe that teachers are united.
- Some tutors write to their tutees' parents at the start of the year to introduce themselves. This is also a good opportunity to express your hopes for the group and explain the best way for parents and carers to contact you. Not only does this put you in control of the demands made of you, but also it establishes, from the start, lines of communication. Do get clearance from

the pastoral heads first, before going ahead and sending letters home – there are still some schools out there that believe a teacher must reach at least the age of 45 before having direct contact with the outside world!

- Observe your group while they are being taught by another teacher.
- Consider how you might use peer tutoring. This is becoming increasingly popular both overseas and in the UK.

ABOUT CHILD BULLYING

This is a hugely important aspect of school life – too great to deal with here in detail. Research indicates that over 50 per cent of pupils experience bullying at school at some stage, and the Professional Standards for Qualified Teacher Status state that teachers should 'recognise and respond effectively to equal opportunities issues as they arise in the classroom, including by challenging stereotyped views, and by challenging bullying or harassment, following relevant policies and procedures'.

Make sure that you read your school's policy on dealing with child bullying and any advice that is issued by your LEA. Talk to teachers who have tackled bullying in the past about techniques that have proved successful. It is also worth reading some of the excellent books on bullying (see Appendix 9) and discussing the issue regularly with your tutor group. You could devise a role-play or encourage your class to talk openly about bullying they have witnessed.

Taking time to look at language, how it is used and how it can be misinterpreted also leads to a greater understanding of bullying situations. Try to encourage pupils to view the bullying from both sides, thereby developing skills of empathy with all involved.

The Web site www.bullying.co.uk is a useful resource for teachers dealing with child-on-child bullying.

FIRST AID IN THE CLASSROOM

Accidents will occur in the best-regulated families.

(Charles Dickens)

Without being too dramatic, your ability to administer first aid can mean the difference between life and death. Quick action to help a child suffering a health crisis will greatly ease his/her distress and the physical trauma suffered.

Individual schools and LEAs will have developed their own procedures regarding first aid and the administering of medicines so make sure you have been appropriately informed (you should never be *directed* to give a child medicine). While responsibility for first aid will rest with the qualified first-aiders and 'appointed persons' in your school (know who they are and where they can be found at any time), knowing what to do in certain circumstances will add to your confidence in the classroom.

Your induction programme should cover first aid information, which should also be included in the staff handbook. As a teacher you are not obliged to give first aid, but you are expected to do your best for the welfare of a child according to the DfES document, *Guidance on First Aid for Schools*.

- Do find out as soon as possible if you are indemnified in the event of any claim of negligence made against you. Your employer will be able to confirm this in writing for you. Also find out if assisting with any form of medical procedure comes under the scope of your employment.
- You may consider obtaining a first aid qualification yourself – courses are run by the British Red Cross, St John Ambulance and sometimes LEAs. Becoming a first-aider should be undertaken on a strictly voluntary basis. Under no circumstances should you ever be persuaded or 'encouraged' to take this on.
- If you do decide to volunteer to undertake first aid training, your employer should provide it or, at least, pay for an outside agency to provide it.
- According to the *Dorling Kindersley First Aid Manual* (which is regularly updated and available through all good high street and online bookshops), an important rule of first aid is 'First do no harm.' Bear this is mind when looking after a child, and be aware of your limitations. If for example the sight of blood really does cause you to pass out, you need to get someone else to deal with the situation immediately so that there aren't two casualties in the classroom. A copy of the *Dorling Kindersley First Aid Manual* will probably be available in every school – if not, buy yourself a copy to keep in your classroom.
- It goes without saying that you must protect yourself at all times. If you have to deal with a child's body fluids in any way, always wear protective gloves. It's a good idea to keep a pair handy, but remember to throw them away and replace them after use.
- If there is a medical emergency while you are teaching, consider the rest of the class. There may be pupils who are shocked or affected in some way and it could be necessary to clear the room of everyone except the casualty. A

teacher in a neighbouring classroom should be able to help you out here. This will also help to protect the dignity of the casualty.

- Remember to follow your school's regulations on reporting accidents and incidents. In brief, you will need to know the date, time and place of the incident, the name and class of the injured/ill person, details of the injury/illness, details of the first aid given, what happened as a result, and the name of the first-aider dealing with the incident.
- You may feel perfectly calm and able to cope while you are dealing with a situation, but be prepared for a possible reaction afterwards. You may need to nurture yourself a little after the event.

Typical childhood ailments

There are a number of medical situations you could encounter in your classroom. The following advice is designed to give basic information and is not a replacement for qualified medical advice, which you should seek at the earliest opportunity. Send a child to the school office with a request for immediate first aid assistance, so that you don't have to leave the casualty.

Accident injuries

Depending on what subject and age range you teach you could encounter varying degrees of injuries from accidents that have happened in your classroom. The first thing to remember is that accidents do happen. There is usually little reason to blame yourself for an accident that has happened to a child in your care, as long as you are aware of basic accident prevention.

Bleeding

With gloved hands, apply pressure to the wound. Take great care if an object is embedded in it – you may only be able to raise the wound so that it is above the child's heart. Wait for help to arrive – a first-aider should do any bandaging or call for an ambulance if necessary.

Broken bones

While you are waiting for help, simply protect the injury site from further damage. Don't forget to reassure the child, who may be in great pain. You could talk the child through a visualization of a peaceful scene to prevent panic setting in. Only move the child with the help of a qualified first-aider.

ABOUT ACCIDENT PREVENTION

Some areas of a school are potentially more hazardous than others, such as science rooms, technology rooms and workshops. However, all classrooms present potential risks, so taking these steps could reduce the possibility of an accident taking place in your room:

- Take a look round your classroom regularly throughout the day to make sure there are no obvious hazards such as chairs out of place or broken furniture.
- Make sure the windows in your room are all safe, that the catches work and there is no cracked or broken glass. If necessary, make the window area a pupil-free zone.
- Check your room for leaks. One teacher had to spend a lesson that was being observed by an OFSTED inspector finding suitable receptacles for rainwater that was dripping through the ceiling on to her guest.
- Check the furniture in your room regularly for damage, cracks and splinters. Ask your classes to inform you of broken items.
- Make sure any necessary repairs are carried out promptly. You may have to remind the powers that be about what needs doing.
- Be strict about the way pupils enter and leave your room. Bundles can quickly become dangerous. Also be firm about the way pupils move around the classroom.
- Make sure pupils' bags are safely stowed away during lessons. Many a teacher has tripped on stray bag straps as he/she moved around the room to work with children.
- Be strict about food consumption in your room. Children who are trying to surreptitiously chew gum or suck sweets are more likely to choke.
- Check that any leads and wiring in your room are safe. If you are not sure, ask a colleague to check for you.

Eye injuries

Personal experience will probably tell you how excruciatingly painful an eye injury can be. Immediate medical assistance is required for anything more serious than simply dust or grit in the eye – use your discretion. You may need to comfort the child who should be sitting still. The child will probably be protecting the site of the injury with his/her hand – this is fine as long as he/she does not apply pressure.

Head injuries

If the child is bleeding, apply the same advice as given above. It is possible that the child may be suffering concussion, the symptoms of which may not become evident immediately. For this reason, a doctor must see a child who has suffered a head injury as soon as possible. Confusion, vomiting, sleepiness and uncharacteristic aggression are all signs of concussion.

Anaphylactic shock

Anaphylactic shock is a severe allergic reaction to a particular substance. This could typically be a bee sting, nuts or drugs, or anything that the particular individual happens to be allergic to. The onset of symptoms, such as increasing difficulty breathing, tends to be rapid and requires immediate medical attention. Sit the child somewhere quiet and try to stop him/her from panicking while you wait for help. The child may carry adrenalin (if known to have an allergy), which can be administered by either the child or a suitably qualified adult. Don't be fazed by the speed with which the child's condition may deteriorate. This is usual under the circumstances and can be corrected if the right medical assistance is given in good time.

Asthma

Children known to be asthmatics should know what to do in the event of an attack. Many will have their own inhalers, which they can administer themselves. It is essential to call for immediate assistance and while you wait encourage the child to sit upright as this eases breathing. Do not put your arm around his/her shoulders but offer verbal reassurance instead. The child may naturally place his or her arms up on a table; this is a natural reflex that also aids breathing. Try to encourage the child to breathe in through the nose and out slowly through the mouth. This helps to prevent hyperventilation.

Choking

This is a difficult situation to deal with unless you are a fully qualified first-aider. The only safe thing for you to do is to look for any obvious obstruction in the child's mouth that could easily be hooked out with a finger. Medical assistance is urgently required.

Diabetes

Many people suffer sudden drops in blood sugar and will recognize the urgency for food that this causes. In normal circumstances, blood sugar can be regulated by eating something sweet, but in diabetics treatment can be more complicated and the fluctuations in blood sugar more dramatic. The child may also suffer from sweating, shaking and loss of concentration. Your role, having called for assistance, should be to support the child's needs. Allow him/her to eat immediately, regardless of any rules about food in the classroom.

Epilepsy

You should have been informed of any children in your classes known to suffer from epilepsy, but remember a child's first fit may occur in your classroom. There are different classifications of fits, some more severe than others. Minor fits may simply involve temporary losses of concentration, in which case you may need to repeat instructions to a sufferer or offer some reassurance. However, in the case of a serious fit, after calling for assistance you need to ensure that the area around the child is cleared of any potentially dangerous objects. Lay the child on his/her side and watch for any changes in his/her colour or choking. Try to protect the child's head but do not restrict his/her movement in any way. Talk reassuringly to the child throughout the whole fit, as this is thought to ease anxiety. It may be essential to clear the other children from the room, as a fit can be frightening to witness and embarrassing for the sufferer on recovery, as it is common to be incontinent during a fit.

Fainting

Children can faint for a variety of reasons. For some, simply standing for an extended period of time will be enough to bring on a faint. There is usually little warning of an impending faint and the first you may know is when a child hits the deck! If this is the case, place something soft under the head, raise the feet above the level of the heart and talk reassuringly as he/she comes round. The child may be confused or disorientated. After a faint a child should be encouraged to drink water, eat something and rest until he/she feels fully recovered. Medical assistance should be sought, as fainting can be a symptom requiring further investigation. If a child reports feeling faint, place his/her head between his/her knees and talk reassuringly until the feeling has passed.

Headaches

Children can get headaches for a variety of reasons such as stress and tension, food intolerance, dehydration or the onset of a deeper ailment such as a virus or infection. Very occasionally, a headache can indicate a far more serious condition such as a tumour. If a child complains of a headache during class time, watch for accompanying symptoms he/she may have such as feeling nauseous or dizzy, or having a raised temperature or disturbed vision. Be guided by the child; he/she may prefer to remain in your classroom doing a quiet activity, or may want to be excused from the room. Headaches can often be cured by rehydrating the body so always offer the opportunity for the child to get a drink of water. Check the temperature in your room too. If it has become hot and stuffy, those sensitive to temperature will begin to suffer. If the same child appears to be experiencing a cluster of headaches over a period of time, discuss the matter with your induction tutor or with the child's pastoral head.

Nosebleeds

These are relatively common in children as receiving a hit on the nose or blowing and picking the nose can bring them on. Often nosebleeds are slight and do not require any intervention. However, if the bleeding shows no sign of abating, place the child's head in a forward position and pinch the fleshy part of the nose (not the bridge). Take every precaution to protect yourself.

Period pains

Period pain can be severe in some adolescent girls and it can be mistaken for other ailments such as appendicitis. A girl suffering from excessive period pain should be encouraged to seek medical assistance, as it could be indicative of an underlying condition such as endometriosis. This situation needs to be treated with sensitivity, particularly because the girl may not want to reveal why she feels unwell. For this reason it would be sensible to enable the girl to spend some time away from the class, perhaps doing some work in an office or sick room. A qualified first-aider may decide to send the child home where pain-killers can be administered.

Vomiting

Hopefully the child will have given you plenty of warning of feeling sick, but this is not always the case. If a child vomits in your classroom you need to arrange for it to be cleaned up as soon as possible. Usually the caretaker has this unenviable task! If possible, cordon off the area. In the meantime do your best to clean the child's face (or offer tissues for the child to do this him/herself) and reassure that all is well. A first-aider will probably suggest that the child goes home. In any case, arrange for the child to have a glass of water if the child feels he/she could manage this and to change his/her clothes if they are soiled.

PART IV

Managing the job

CHAPTER 8

Getting your work/life balance right

COPING WITH MEETINGS

Part of life in the teaching profession is attending numerous meetings. In fact, the end of your teaching day is only half the story for most teachers, not least NQTs.

You may be asked to attend any or all of the following:

- full staff meetings;
- induction tutor/mentor and adviser meetings;
- year or department meetings;
- union meetings/briefings;
- planning meetings;
- SEN meetings;
- ICT meetings;
- PTA meetings;
- special events meetings.

You will (should) also have informal meetings about your day-to-day planning and progress. For some this could amount to many meetings each week, requiring preparation and follow-up.

Over recent years there has been a strong focus on teacher workload and the bureaucratic burden facing teachers. This has culminated, to date, in a clear summary from the DfES entitled *Valuing Teachers' Time: Developing the role of support staff* (for further information, visit www.teachernet.gov.uk/remodelling) as part of the response to demands from the profession for this issue to be addressed.

This summary document lists the sources of advice and guidance on what schools can do to reduce workload. The list includes the DfEE Circular 2/98, *Reducing the Bureaucratic Burden on Teachers*, which sets out guidance for schools to follow in an attempt to reduce the non-teaching commitments of staff members. The circular states that:

> Well-run meetings are essential to the internal management and communications of a school. Schools need to have flexibility to determine the pattern and number of meetings. Those are matters for sensible professional judgement. But schools do need to establish a pattern of meetings which is fully justified.
>
> All schools should regularly review the number and quality of their meetings, and should assess their existing practice against the following considerations:
>
> - only hold meetings when they are justified and cancel unnecessary ones;
> - circulate agendas and papers in good time;
> - set time limits and stick to them;
> - ensure meetings are effectively chaired;
> - always set a clear purpose for a meeting;
> - encourage and take account of all points of view while guiding the meeting to definite conclusions;
> - communicate the conclusions to all with an interest;
> - ensure effective action is taken as a result.

As schools differ so greatly in their organization and administration, NQTs can have very different experiences of meetings. In order to maximize their use, consider these points:

- If you are unable to discern the relevance of a meeting, ask its organizer if you need to attend. If you can't contribute to or learn from a meeting, there is little point in attending.
- Make sure you know the purpose of the meeting.
- Send your apologies if you are unable to attend.
- Be particularly aware of any items on the agenda that directly relate to you or your classes.
- Ask for clarification on any aspect of the meeting that you don't understand, although the chair should have ensured that there was no possibility for

confusion. If you allow jargon to whizz over your head, the crux of the discussion could pass you by.

- Plan in advance any input you would like to have. Perhaps you could prepare some questions to ask or comments to refer to. Be clear and succinct in your speech and make sure you stick to the point. Try not to feel intimidated and don't be put off asking questions; it's only by questioning that progress through dogma can be made.
- If you feel the chair is being manipulative or dominating, keep your tone of voice consistent and maintain eye contact with calm assertion.

Organizing the information you need

Attending meetings invariably means gathering a small forest's worth of paper. Avoid information overload by:

- assessing what is relevant to you while you are in the meeting;
- using highlighter pens to colour-code what needs immediate action, what can wait and what can be thrown away;
- sticking to a rigid filing system. For each piece of paper that comes into your possession, you have only three options: file immediately for future reference, act on it immediately or destroy it (you could consider scanning important documents into a computer to cut down on storage space – this also allows you to 'manage' documents more efficiently);
- creating a 'recycle bin' for documents you cannot bring yourself to file or destroy – make sure you empty this bin regularly.

If a meeting results in you having a task to perform, make sure you have been given the means by which to achieve it. This invariably means time and resources. Any deadlines must be realistic.

Minutes

You should be given the minutes a few days after the meeting. Once you have read them, mention anything you disagree with to the person who produced them. Be especially vigilant if you are quoted. If you feel that an important matter has been omitted from the minutes, raise this as soon as possible. If necessary, you can have it recorded that you disagree with the minutes when they are discussed at the next meeting.

If you would like to have something included on the next agenda, ask the chair of the meeting. You may not be successful, but your request should at least be heard and discussed.

ABOUT RECYCLING

Schools use a tremendous amount of paper and consequently generate piles of paper waste. Unless your school makes the effort to recycle this waste paper, most of it will end up in a landfill site. Britain falls way behind other European nations in its attitude to recycling and this is now beginning to pose real threats to the environment and to health, with some areas of the country having only a few years of landfill space left. Recycling is now an urgent necessity, not a new-age fad. The order of preference for waste management is to reduce consumption (use less paper), reuse (as scrap) and recycle (anything that cannot be reused):

- Keep paper use to a minimum.
- Organize your waste so that paper can be easily recycled. Even if paper is not collected for recycling, most municipal tips offer paper-recycling facilities.
- Encourage classes to adhere to your systems of waste management and make sure they understand why this is important.
- Suggest a whole-school approach to recycling if there is not one in place already.

For information on recycling and the 'Are you doing your bit?' campaign, take a look at: www.doingyourbit.org.uk.

EnCams is an environmental charity, which runs the Keep Britain Tidy campaign and the Going for Green brand. For further information, visit www.encams.org and www.goingforgreen.org.uk, or e-mail info@encams.org.

Friends of the Earth also has details of waste reduction strategies: 020 7490 1555; www.foe.org.uk.

TIME MANAGEMENT

If it weren't for the last minute, nothing would get done.

(Anonymous)

Few professions rely on effective time management and awareness quite as much as teaching. As an NQT, it would be helpful to think of effective time management as a way of enabling you to live a full life outside your work – a life that allows for relaxation and rest as well as hobbies and relationships. It is not a way of creating time to do more work or of managing crises.

ACTION Think about your relationship with time. Do you have enough time to complete the tasks you want to complete, or are you always running against the clock? Are you in control, or does time control you?

In order to develop time management skills, you need to become *aware* of time. Teachers often suffer from time 'poverty' – too much to do in the time available. Added to this is the fact that, as an NQT, you are less likely to be in a position to delegate your tasks and, often, jobs will be delegated to you.

Pacing yourself

Working in such a structured environment, it is important for teachers to pace themselves, not only on a daily basis but on a termly and yearly basis as well. Just as each day has its own rhythm, so does each term and year. Therefore, your targets for a day, term and year need to be realistic and take into account rhythms and fluctuations. If you tend to collapse after pressured times with exhaustion or some other ailment, you are clearly not pacing yourself:

- First look at the calendar for the whole year and write down anything that applies to you, for example parents' evenings, reports, school plays and so on. This will give you an initial picture of the busiest times of the year.
- Then look at the term – where do your biggest commitments fall? Do you have extra departmental or curriculum work, for example writing exams or schemes of work to do? This will give you the basic shape of the term. Pinpoint the very busy times when other aspects of your job like marking and preparation will have to be minimized. Aim to ease your workload at these times. Lean on pre-prepared work and take opportunities for pupils to self-assess.
- Next, look at the rhythms of your week. Do you have any nightmarish days? Where are your opportunities to catch up on administration and marking?
- Throughout each day, get to know the times when you work most efficiently. If you suffer from a 4 pm low, don't attempt to work. The aim is to maximize productivity at your most productive times. It is simply a waste of time to attempt to work at the same pace all through the day. It is better to rest, or turn your attentions to other things, rather than work unproductively.

Once you have established the rhythm of your days, aim to give yourself treats at low points of the day, term or year. Perhaps plan a weekend away mid-term or spend some time indulging your interests. Planning is an essential part of this process, as anticipation and excitement are part of the enjoyment:

- When you are working slowly, don't punish yourself. Recognize it as a part of your natural rhythms and energy levels.
- Taking on piles of work will not add to your feelings of self-worth and esteem, but will add to your stress and anxiety levels.
- When you feel yourself working at a pace that is uncomfortable, slow down, regardless of any deadlines.
- Learn to know when to stop working on a project. There will be an optimum time to let it go.

Prioritizing

Rather than attempting to work through each task as it comes to you, manage the time you have by prioritizing. This means allowing yourself the time to *think* before launching into work. For every job ask yourself, does this *need* to be done? If the answer is yes, assess its importance as being:

- high;
- moderate; or
- low.

Another question to ask is 'Will this make life easier?' For example, spending time sorting through a pile of papers may be beneficial if it means you are now more organized. It is worth accepting at the start of your career that reaching the end of your list is highly unlikely!

EXAMPLE   One deputy head had learnt not to do anything his headteacher asked for only once. If something really needed doing, the headteacher would ask two or three times: an easy way to prioritize!

It is best to go through the prioritizing process as soon as you can so that jobs don't pile up. Once you have done this, you have created a 'to do' list that takes account of any deadlines and can be worked through systematically. If you find yourself getting behind, either knock something off your list or seek help. This is sensible and, at times, vital. Aim to empty your pigeon-hole daily and respond to memos or phone calls as soon as possible.

Prioritizing should not just be done in relation to work. Sometimes you will have to put your private life above work if you are to remain an effective teacher. In his book *Time Shifting* (1996), Stephan Rechtschaffen writes about the 'trickle-down' approach to time. He explains that, generally, we place our work first, followed by our primary relationship/family, then our everyday chores, then social life and finally ourselves – if there is any time left. We tend to neglect the bottom of the list upwards, so if you find you're neglecting your social life alarm bells should be sounding. If you find it hard to devote time to your primary relationships, your work really is dominating beyond reason.

Managing your preparation and planning

Preparation and planning, in combination with the resulting marking, make huge demands on your time:

- Take as much help as possible. If your department has a successful scheme of work for a topic, use it. If a textbook covers a topic well, use it rather than create your own worksheets. Only produce a scheme of work yourself when you have time. You may even be given some (extra) non-contact hours for the purpose. Be sure to familiarize yourself with the schemes of work available on the Standards site: www.standards.dfes.gov.uk/schemes/.
- Don't feel inadequate if you are only one step ahead of the class – it doesn't matter. However, if you can get a little ahead of yourself, you will relieve some of the pressure to plan every night.
- When you are planning for one lesson, see if there are ways of planning for two, three or four lessons at the same time. Block planning in this way helps to relieve pressure.
- Don't spend time filling in lesson plans unless this is your way of record keeping. For most teachers, keeping track of plans in a teacher's organizer (usually given out free at the start of the autumn term) is sufficient, as there is space to record the plan and the contents of the lesson as well as any homework set.
- Talk to colleagues and your induction tutor/mentor about your preparation and marking. Are you overdoing it? Do they know any short cuts you could be taking? Do you know when to stop?
- If, through your experience this year, you can see ways of saving time next time you have to plan and teach a topic, write them down.

- Keep good records of all your planning and preparation for the next time you cover the topic.

Working at optimum levels

Some people can stay longer in one hour than others can in one week.

(William Dean Howells)

Beware the law of diminishing returns. You will have an optimum level at which you can work effectively. Go beyond that level and you risk wasting your time and wearing yourself out. If your working hours are so long that you have to force yourself out of bed in the mornings, ask yourself what it is that you hope to teach your pupils. If you feel depressed about your work, it is likely that you are not working at an optimal level and it is essential that you reduce the hours you work before you burn out.

Working fewer hours does not mean that you get less done; it just means that the time you spend working is probably more productive. When you decide to work, focus on what you are doing. Minimize all distractions; better to do that for one hour and complete your task than spend three hours unfocused and still not finish what you have to do:

- Establish what it is you like to do and aim to spend time on that. For example, if you enjoy designing worksheets, create that job for yourself. Perhaps others in your department will tackle some of the tasks you don't relish.
- Take opportunities throughout the day to get work done. Your class may be needed for sport or music practice etc.
- Delegate as much as possible. If your school has reprographics staff, let them perform that aspect of your job. Fully utilize non-teaching assistants.
- Time your tasks, but be realistic with your deadlines. Giving yourself a specific time limit to complete a task is far more likely to result in success.
- Try to avoid feeling pressurized into working at the perceived pace of others around you.
- Do you have time-wasting habits or inefficiencies? Try to develop a conscious awareness when you work and assess how efficient you are.
- Take regular breaks from intense work like exam marking.
- Buddhists practise 'mindfulness'. This means being aware of the present moment, of what you are doing and how you are doing it. This is quite the opposite of doing A while thinking of B and C. Practising mindfulness tends to have the effect of apparently expanding time.

ABOUT ENCOURAGING YOURSELF TO WORK AT YOUR OPTIMUM LEVEL

If you suspect you are not working at a pace that is good for you, think about these questions:

- Do I avoid beginning tasks because it all seems like too much?
- Do I allow myself time to plan what needs to be done?
- Do I spend time on tasks that are not essential?
- Do I allow myself to be interrupted by colleagues and pupils?
- Do I help others to achieve tasks at the expense of my own work?
- Do I view deadlines as constructive encouragement or a source of unparalleled stress?
- Do I struggle with tasks that could or should be done by someone else?
- Do I underestimate how long something will take me?

If you answered yes to some or all of these questions, take the opportunity to discuss time management and awareness with your induction tutor/mentor at your next meeting. It may be a gradual process, but time management will get easier as your confidence and experience grow. Don't, however, give yourself a hard time!

BALANCING WORK WITH YOUR HOME LIFE

The intellect of man is forced to choose
Perfection of the life, or of the work.

(W B Yeats)

Personal relations are the important thing for ever and ever, and not this outer life of telegrams and anger.

(E M Forster)

Balancing work and home life is an extremely difficult skill, and one that many teachers never quite learn. This is mostly due to the extent to which school-work encroaches on the evening. The irony is that evidence seems to suggest that teachers who can maintain a work/life balance tend to be more effective in the classroom, not to mention more enthusiastic about their job. Teachers most profoundly affected tend to be those who live alone, as there is no one to say 'Stop working now; it's 11.30 – why don't you relax for a while?' or 'Can I help you with anything?'

The key word is 'flexibility'. It would be ideal if you were more than a day ahead of yourself, as this would enable you to take an evening off at short notice. However, the teacher who can avoid working at home at all is rarer than a heatwave at Christmas.

That said, there are going to be times when you will have to focus more intently on work after school – perhaps just before an inspection or at report time – and therefore need flexibility from those you live with:

- Always be aware that you need to maintain good relationships outside work. If you find yourself cancelling arrangements, ask yourself why. Are you over-committed to your work?
- Allocate some time for nothing and everything – whatever you most feel like doing. Keep spontaneity alive in your life.
- Make sure that at least 75 per cent of your holidays are work-free. If you do have to do some work, do it at the start of the break so you can then enjoy uninterrupted free time.
- Instead of thinking about how much time you spend working, calculate how much time you spend not working. How much of the time available to you do you have control over? Work/life balance can only be established when we seek out where our control lies.

Keeping your identity

It can be easy to work yourself into the belief that you are a teacher and *only* a teacher. Use time management and awareness to free up space when you can nurture hitherto neglected needs:

- Are there hobbies you would like to pursue but don't because of work?
- Have any aspects of your character changed since you started work?
- Are you forgetting birthdays and other events you would normally remember or paying more attention to the finer details of schoolwork rather than the finer details of your life?
- If you had to stop teaching, where would that leave you? Would you be at a total loss as to what to do?
- Have you had more or less fun in your life since you began teaching?

Help yourself maintain balance by the following:

- Spend time on indulging yourself. Whether you enjoy sport, going to the theatre or cinema, going out with friends or pursuing your favourite hobby, ring-fence time when you can do these things without feeling guilty.
- Have at least one evening a week totally devoted to relaxation.
- Allocate time to keep in touch with friends and family. Make phone calls, write letters or send e-mail – take an interest in the lives of those around you.
- Spend some time each day simply focusing on you. Some people meditate, others go for a walk, listen to music or take a long bubble bath. Whatever works for you, do it! Those you live with will soon learn that this time is sacrosanct to you, and that to allow you uninterrupted space makes you easier to live with.
- If necessary, take a sick day for the benefit of your mental health if nothing else. You would not be the first (or the last) teacher to take a day for catching up and resting.

STRESS BUSTING

> Instead of seeing the rug being pulled from under us, we can learn to dance on a shifting carpet.
>
> (Thomas Crum)

The degree of negative stress experienced by members of the same profession varies tremendously from individual to individual, but it is fair to say that workplace stress does appear to be on the increase. Negative stress is not to be ignored. Its effects are far-reaching and can lead to life-threatening conditions.

The *New Oxford Dictionary of English* defines stress as 'a state of mental or emotional strain or tension resulting from adverse or very demanding circumstances'. There is nothing intrinsically wrong with being stressed; it is virtually impossible to avoid being stressed at times and can lead to the necessary stimulation required to complete a task. It is when stress continues beyond the event for which you were preparing or the interview etc that you should start to take evasive action before mental, physical and emotional symptoms occur and the stress becomes negative.

Recognizing the symptoms of negative stress

Negative stress can be hard to identify despite the fact that it can cause your body to present a wide variety of behavioural, physical and emotional symptoms. If you think you may be suffering from negative stress, consider these questions:

- What do others say about you? How are you described?
- How do you interact with others? Are you patient and attentive or snappy and distracted?
- Are you less confident than you used to be? Shyer and more introspective?
- Is your mood stable and balanced or do you find yourself swinging from contentment to distress in one go?
- Is decision making more difficult than it used to be and concentration a thing of the past?
- Are your thoughts generally positive or negative? Do you have any thoughts of impending doom?
- Do you rely on stimulants more than usual? Has the occasional drink become a daily necessity?
- Has work taken over where leisure once reigned? Once you have completed your work do you have the energy for a full social life?
- What are your energy levels like? Do you experience the highs and lows of adrenalin 'dependence'?

Recognizing the symptoms of negative stress requires self-observance and honesty. Denial of stress-related problems compounds the situation and prolongs recovery time.

The causes of stress in teaching

It is impossible to identify the exact causes of stress in teaching especially when you consider that one person's stress is another's motivation. However, these factors do seem to have some responsibility for negative stress amongst teachers:

- *time*: feeling unable to perform the required tasks in the time available;
- *control*: not being in control of the number of tasks that have to be completed; external pressures;

- *information*: having to keep up with a rapid pace of change and feeling ill informed about the latest situation; ever-increasing expectations;
- *workload*: having to complete work at home in order to keep up to date; sometimes unrealistic expectations and possible inequality in work distribution; also the tremendously diverse nature of the job;
- *indiscipline*: having to control unruly pupils and deal with constant interruptions on a daily basis;
- *deadlines*: facing many deadlines each day as work must be prepared and books marked for each class or part of the day;
- *personality overload*: depending on what age group you teach, you could interact with over 100 different personalities each day;
- *fear*: about accountability, inspections, job insecurity and so on;
- *resource limitations*: having to prepare resources to supplement material in the school and for differentiation purposes; the poor condition of some classrooms;
- *aggression*: the potential threat from pupils and parents as well as possible bullying from staff members.

ACTION Think about areas of possible stress in your job. Are you able to identify clear factors that contribute to the pressures you face? Do any of these seem to be intractable? Talk about the stresses you have identified with your induction tutor/mentor and read on for further advice. What action can you take to reduce your stress?

Stress-busting skills

Begging your doctor for tranquillizers to calm your mind and ease your day is probably not a good idea without adopting some stress-busting techniques. However, stress is now thought to be a contributory factor in many diseases and it is well worth talking to your healthcare provider about any negative stress you feel.

Managing through a crisis

Whether you are experiencing the sudden symptoms of feeling overwhelmed or, worse, a panic attack, take these steps:

- Stop. There isn't *anything* that cannot be dropped, even if you are in the middle of a lesson. Someone will be free to take over from you.
- Focus on your breathing. Count slowly as you breathe in through your nose and out through your mouth until a sense of calm gradually pervades you body and mind. The more you practise this when you are already calm the easier it will be to do in a crisis.
- Look at ways of immediately reducing your workload. Go home if necessary.
- Talk to someone about your feelings before leaving school. Take support from senior colleagues and any stress counsellors your school or LEA may have. Don't worry about admitting your anxiety to a senior member of staff. Other members of staff would be lying if they said they hadn't suffered in the same way at some point in their careers!
- Release the stress of the day when you get home. Talk, cry, shout, exercise or go for a walk – whatever works for you.
- Commit yourself to undertaking some of the maintenance tips that follow. For example, book a massage. Now!
- Compose an affirmation that you can use the next day.
- Visit your doctor or other healthcare provider if you feel that stress is piling up. It may be best for you and the school to take some time out.

ABOUT THE PHYSICAL SYMPTOMS OF STRESS

A number of changes take place in the body when it is working under too much stress:

- The blood supply to muscles is increased.
- The adrenal glands produce more adrenalin.
- Pupils become dilated.
- The heart rate increases.
- Blood pressure can rise.
- The sweat glands produce more sweat.
- Breathing becomes more rapid.
- The menstrual cycle can become disturbed.
- The digestive system can become upset.
- The immune system becomes less effective.
- Skin problems can develop.

It is important to consult your GP or other healthcare provider if you find yourself suffering from any of the above sooner rather than later. It is easier to correct minor health disturbances than major ones.

ABOUT TEACHER SUPPORT LINE: 08000 562 561

Teacher Support Line is a free national information, support and counselling service for all teachers. It is open 24 hours a day, every day, as a resource for teachers with problems, be they personal or professional, in school or out. Teacher Support Line is being widely used to discuss stress, anxiety and depression, and conflicts with managers or colleagues, among other issues. All of Teacher Support Line's fully qualified counsellors have worked in or with the teaching profession.

According to Teacher Support Line, NQTs are contacting them with issues concerning stress and isolation, as well as concerns over poor induction, conflicts with induction tutors/mentors and financial problems.

Ringing a helpline such as Teacher Support Line is by no means an admission of failure. By seeking help and advice you are taking important steps to reaching solutions that will enable you to continue your career with less stress and increased satisfaction.

Teacher Support Line also has an e-mail counselling service. This is only appropriate for enquiries that do not relate to:

- abuse involving children;
- any situation requiring an urgent or rapid intervention;
- any situation that affects your ability to express yourself in written form.

If at all in doubt, call the Teacher Support Line.
Learn this number! 08000 562 561.
For more information, take a look at www.teachersupport.info.

Managing day to day

Focus 90 per cent of your time on solutions and only 10 per cent of your time on problems.

(Anthony J D'Angelo)

- Develop a flexible attitude to your work. Detachment can sometimes be necessary as the path of least resistance affords some freedom from stress.
- Adopt the 80 per cent philosophy. Drop your need for perfection; you can still get an 'A' grade with 80 per cent!
- Have at least one evening a week and one full day at the weekend off. Even if you are tempted to work, don't.

- Don't expect yourself to be on task 100 per cent of the time. Daydreaming is good for you.
- Be aware of times when you can still your mind throughout the day even if it is during assembly or in the toilet!
- Stay in the present. Avoid thinking about what you have to do in the future and what you've done in the past. Give all your attention to the task in hand – divided attention leads to tension.
- Set realistic goals for yourself.
- Prepare your room for the next day the night before.
- Take any opportunities to share the burden of your work. For example, a classroom assistant may offer to put up a wall display, or the SEN department may want to develop some differentiated work for a child.
- Identify the *value* of the tasks you have to perform. If you cannot discern the value of a task, speak to your induction tutor/mentor; perhaps it needn't be performed in the future.
- Break each project down into manageable chunks.
- Aim to inject more humour into your life. Laughter is a tremendous stress releaser.

ACTION Using an A4 sheet of paper, write down all the things you like to do, places you like to go and friends you like to see when you are not pressured by work. Keep the sheet in a place where you will see it frequently and be sure to make the commitment of doing at least one thing on the list every week. Even if this treat is as small as browsing round your favourite shop or buying your favourite magazine, be sure to do it so that you send self-nurturing signals to yourself.

ABOUT USING AFFIRMATIONS

An affirmation is an often-repeated phrase that focuses on something positive. Affirmations are an excellent way of managing negativity, but there are some important points to remember when constructing them:

- Always use positive statements. Say 'My work is enjoyable and manageable' rather than 'I am not stressed about my work.'
- Use present rather than future statements. 'I am calm and relaxed' is better than 'I will be calm and relaxed.'

- Visualize your ideal scenario while you use affirmations. Believe that you can create the situations you want to create.
- Repeat your affirmations often throughout the day. Research suggests that the mind needs to hear an affirmation at least six times before positive benefits can be achieved.

ABOUT REDUCING WORKLOAD

The DfES recently issued a list of common tasks that need not routinely be carried out by teachers and should, as soon as practicable, be transferred to support staff or ICT:

- collecting money;
- chasing absences;
- bulk photocopying;
- copy-typing;
- producing standard letters;
- producing class lists;
- record keeping and filing;
- classroom display;
- analysing attendance figures;
- processing exam results;
- collating pupil reports;
- administering work experience;
- administering examinations;
- invigilating examinations;
- administering teacher cover;
- ICT troubleshooting and minor repairs;
- commissioning new ICT equipment;
- ordering supplies and equipment;
- stocktaking;
- cataloguing, preparing, issuing and maintaining equipment and materials;
- minuting meetings;
- coordinating and submitting bids;
- seeking and giving personnel advice;
- managing pupil data;
- inputting pupil data.

For further information, visit www.teachernet.gov.uk/remodelling.

Maintenance tips

The long-term management of stress requires you (and those you work with) to be ever vigilant. Ignoring negative stress in schools is costly and short-sighted.

- In his book *Calm at Work* (1997), Paul Wilson writes that deciding to become calm is the first step in being calm. Analyse how much your attitude is responsible for the degree of negative stress you experience.
- Work with colleagues to encourage stress-reducing practices that can be adopted. Even the development of a forum for the discussion of negative stress would be helpful.
- Once you are in the habit of dealing with stress on a daily basis, you can resolve to learn from the experience rather than let negative stresses accumulate unaddressed.
- Keep an ongoing list of what triggers the symptoms of stress in you. This will probably need to be updated regularly as your proficiencies develop.
- Keep a running list of everything that calms and relaxes you: perhaps a book, a person or a place – anything that makes you feel good. You could even include photographs of yourself when you are relaxed and happy. Refer to the list whenever the ill effects of stress start to develop.
- Maintain a positive attitude about the work that you do. If talking to certain people results in you feeling down, avoid them.
- Pursue a hobby – something you have always wanted to do. If it increases physical activity, even better. Outside interests often serve to balance your working life.
- If massage, reflexology or some other relaxing experience works for you, book a session regularly.

Morale boosting

There can be few things more depressing than a staffroom full of teachers constantly bemoaning the state of their working conditions. Listening to all that does nothing for your morale and the way you view your career.

One way round such a situation is actively to aim to raise the morale of colleagues, providing, of course, that you have the energy! Although listening to the grievances of others is an important way to help, there comes a point when the negative cries of colleagues need to be balanced by some positive responses.

'Lifting' colleagues

> We don't see things as they are; we see them as we are.
>
> (Anais Nin)

The idea behind lifting colleagues is that everyone should benefit:

- Remembering the birthday of a fellow teacher can do wonders for morale. Alternatively you could take a treat in for colleagues on your birthday. This will change the pattern of the usual break time.
- You could set up a staff entertainments committee if your school doesn't have one already, which could arrange staff social events such as cinema or theatre trips, sporting competitions or just a visit to the local pub.
- Make one day of the week (perhaps Friday) a treat day. Take it in turns to bring something in for the benefit of all the staff, either as a school or as a department.
- Try to mark significant events such as the end of a half-term or term, or the end of an inspection.
- Perhaps have an ongoing quiz, board game or competition to lighten the atmosphere in the staffroom.
- Show an interest in the home lives of colleagues. Be vigilant of others and offer to listen to anxieties.

HEALTH AND LIFESTYLE

During the financial year 2000–01, 2,610 teachers took early retirement on the grounds of ill health. Some were in their 20s and 30s – shocking evidence that the job can take its toll.

In addition to this, an estimated 275,000 full-time or part-time teachers in England had some sick leave in 2000, which is approximately 56 per cent of the workforce. There were an estimated 2,660,000 days taken as sick leave, and on average a teacher taking sick leave was absent for 10 days during the year. The sick leave trend is on the up.

Good health is not a foregone conclusion for any of us, yet so often we can find excuses not to undertake health-improving pursuits. However, a little effort can reap great rewards in terms of increasing vitality and enjoyment of life. Teachers have the responsibility to give themselves a chance. Sit on early warning signs of health problems and you are nurturing a certain crisis.

The advice given here is intended to provide ideas on how health and lifestyle might be improved. Your healthcare practitioner should check out persistent health problems.

Diet and exercise

In order to operate, we have to feed and move our bodies. Without good food and exercise we cannot function at optimum levels. This has tremendous implications for work performance and stress levels, and consequently enjoyment of the job could be much diminished.

Eating for health

It's not the horse that draws the cart, but the oats.

(Russian proverb)

Erratic eating patterns and a deficient diet are increasingly being held responsible for many symptoms of ill health. There are several ways that teachers can use food to create health, providing these rules are followed:

- Always ensure you have at least 20 minutes in which to consume your lunch uninterrupted.
- Never eat while emotionally upset.

Despite the plethora of healthy eating books on the market, there are only three basic tenets of a good diet and health, which are easy to remember:

- Eat plenty of fresh, raw fruits and vegetables (at least five helpings a day).
- Avoid harmful substances such as sugar, caffeine, cocoa, alcohol, tobacco and recreational drugs.
- Moderation can be good enough. Remember the 80 per cent rule.

While you can increase your intake of fruits and vegetables immediately, it is important to wean yourself off harmful substances slowly. For example, if you consume caffeine in the form of tea, coffee, chocolate or fizzy drinks, reduce your intake by one cup a day, every day, until you are no longer reliant on the boost it gives you. By reducing gradually, you should avoid the withdrawal symptoms associated with addiction.

Replace caffeinated drinks with fresh, diluted fruit juices, filtered tap water or fruit/herb teas. Once you have cleared your body of caffeine you will not want to go back to being dependent on it.

A varied diet is important. Go for unprocessed wholefoods as often as possible and avoid eating combinations of white flour, sugar and fat.

ACTION Spend time at least one day a week preparing a really fantastic meal including plenty of fresh produce. Sit at a properly laid table, even if you are eating alone. You could invite some friends to share your meal but, if they are teachers, avoid school talk!

In his book *The Vitamin Bible* (1985), Earl Mindell suggests that teachers should take supplements of vitamin B-complex, vitamin C with bioflavonoids and good-quality multi-vitamin and mineral tablets, to help replenish the nutrients used up during the teaching day (refer to *The Vitamin Bible* for exact details). Always go for natural supplements, and buy them from your local health shop rather than supermarket.

It is relatively easy to ensure an intake of at least five fruits and vegetables a day. Try these suggestions:

- Buy them! This may sound obvious, but if you are not in the habit of buying fresh fruit and vegetables, it will be easy to sail past the section in the supermarket.
- Drink pure (diluted) fruit juices. Make sure, however, they don't contain hidden sugars and other additives.
- Add fruit to breakfast cereals and main-course dishes.
- Prepare a fresh salad to eat with your evening meal.
- Add salad vegetables to sandwiches.
- Make a batch of home-made soup and freeze it in portions. Eat it as a starter or main course.

This is not about being a food fanatic, but it is about treating foods that drain energy and vitality with caution.

Moving for energy

Any form of exercise is to be encouraged, as it undoubtedly boosts immunity and helps to relieve symptoms of depression and stress, but it doesn't have to be a chore. There are many ways of incorporating more movement into your working day:

- Everyone needs fresh air. Take a lunchtime walk around the school field or around the block and do some deep breathing as you go.
- Jog up stairs whenever possible.
- Walk short journeys instead of relying on the car. This is not always easy for a teacher, with books, boxes and bags to carry, but certainly possible on occasion.
- Give yourself some time each day to move freely. You might like to do this in private! Allow your body to sway, dance, shake etc – whatever it wants to do.
- Work into your diary a regular slot each week for an organized sporting activity, such as a class, or a game of tennis or badminton with a friend. These exercise slots will soon become sacrosanct!

Stretching is a wonderful way to tone muscles, increase suppleness and allow oxygen to flow freely around the body. Get into the habit of doing some simple stretching exercises in the morning, and throughout the day as appropriate. (See Appendix 9 for more information.)

ABOUT SNACKING AND HYPOGLYCAEMIA

When the brain is starved of glucose (which is carried in the blood) the body cannot function properly. Most people have experienced attacks of low blood sugar (or hypoglycaemia) and know how uncomfortable the associated feelings are such as sweating, shaking, feeling irritable and confused and suddenly, ravenously hungry. Usually these feelings can be relieved by eating, but if they aren't you must visit your healthcare practitioner. The best way to balance blood sugar levels is to eat little and often. Fortunately the teaching day lends itself to snacking in this way, but it is important to snack on the right foods.

According to the Institute for Optimum Nutrition, the best snack is one that consists of a carbohydrate plus a first-class protein (eg white meat, fish, dairy produce or tofu). This means eating, for example, a crispbread with cottage cheese, or raw vegetables with tuna pâté. This combination of carbohydrate and protein produces the optimum rate of sugar release into the bloodstream, which sustains even energy levels over time.

Disease prevention

People can have a very strange attitude towards illness and disease, or 'dis-ease'. Preventing ill health takes a low priority, yet when illness does strike we think it has done so unexpectedly, and feel victims of bad luck. Illness is simply evidence that your body is fighting to rebalance itself. Your body is your last line of defence and, before manifesting symptoms, it will have been sending signals that all is not well. Physical or mental disease is the loudest signal it can send so you owe it to yourself to listen.

A GP is usually the first port of call when illness strikes. Before you attend the surgery, you may have already taken time off work and tried various over-the-counter remedies. However, if you take a preventative approach, you may be able to stop your symptoms from taking hold. Fortunately there are now many widely accepted complementary therapies such as homoeopathy, acupuncture, massage and reflexology, which work by boosting immunity and vitality through taking a holistic approach. A complementary practitioner will look at all aspects of your life in the process of healing.

For ease of reference, the following section has been divided into physical health and mental health, although it is important to consider both, and not necessarily as separate entities.

Physical health

The best way to prevent physical 'dis-ease' is to boost your natural immunity to illness. When you consider the number of people a teacher interacts with every day and that each individual carries a different cocktail of germs, a healthy immune system is essential.

Frequent infections, colds, coughs, sore throats, allergies and even persistent tiredness are all signs of an immune system under pressure.

Become self-observant and listen to your body's needs. There are valid reasons for feeling tired; most cell repair takes place while we sleep. If we ignore tiredness, we are preventing this from taking place.

ABOUT TAKING TIME OFF SICK

It can sometimes be easier as a teacher to struggle through feelings of ill health rather than take time off and organize work for missed classes. Added to that is the burden of knowing that a colleague will probably lose valuable non-contact time in order to cover for you while you are at home. Struggling on to avoid the guilt so often associated with taking time off will not be positive in the long run. Inconvenient as it may seem, take a day sooner rather than a month later. Not surprisingly, recent research has shown that teachers (along with nurses, childminders and carers) have the highest rates of turning up to work when sick.

If you do need to take time off, follow your school's procedures for this closely. You will need to keep your headteacher informed and, if possible, anticipate how much time off you will need so that cover arrangements can be made (this is not always possible, so don't worry if you cannot be specific). You will need to get a doctor's certificate explaining your absence if you are ill for eight or more days. These certificates should be forwarded to your head-teacher immediately and he/she is obliged to treat them as confidential documents. You will need to refer to local arrangements if you are sick during the holidays. Look in your contract and the Burgundy Book, and talk to someone from your LEA's education personnel department and your union. *Always seek a second opinion on any instructions you are given from your school regarding sickness and holidays. You could inadvertently put your entitlement to holiday pay at stake.*

Other ways to boost your immune system include:

- Increase your intake of antioxidants, which help to boost your immunity. Vitamin A strengthens cells that keep viruses at bay, and vitamin C will fight any that do get through. Zinc helps immune cells to mature, and selenium helps them identify invaders. Eat more apples, oranges, red, green and yellow vegetables, carrots, potatoes, grains, seeds, nuts and cereals.
- Take an immunity-boosting supplement such as echinacea, aloe vera, garlic or bee pollen. Your local health-food stockist will help you identify which one is most suited to you.
- Keep your lungs healthy by exercising, singing or playing a wind instrument.

ABOUT CHOOSING A COMPLEMENTARY PRACTITIONER

We should take as much care over choosing complementary therapists as we do over choosing a conventional doctor. Follow these guidelines to avoid the 'therapy merry-go-round':

- Read about different therapies and make a list of the ones that sound interesting.
- Look for local practitioners in the *Yellow Pages* or on notice boards in health shops and health centres, or by asking friends and family for personal recommendations. Make contact with your chosen practitioner before making an appointment to establish whether you think he/she can help you.
- Ensure that the practitioner you have chosen is fully qualified and a member of a recognized, professional body with specific codes of practice. Does he/ she have insurance to cover his/her actions as a healthcare practitioner?
- Many complementary therapies are now available on the NHS. If money is restricted, ask your GP if you can be referred.

Remember that you are in control of any form of healthcare, be it allopathic or complementary.

ABOUT FIGHTING COLDS

Take rest; a field that has rested gives a beautiful crop.

(Ovid)

The staffroom that doesn't have at least one teacher crouched in a chair desperately trying to muster the energy to teach through a severe cold simply doesn't exist!

At the first sign of congestion:

- Take high doses of vitamin C (one gram three times a day). Vitamins A and B-complex will help too.
- Suck a zinc lozenge. Zinc is thought to reduce the time you are sick.
- Eat lightly and drink plenty of water, as this washes out toxins.
- Use eucalyptus essential oil to clear sinuses.

Mental health

A key word in the maintenance of good mental health is 'balance', more specifically balance between home commitments including family, personal needs such as social activities and self-pampering, leisure and rest, and the demands of work. Ironically, many new teachers find themselves in the catch-22 situation of not having time to create balance, yet suffering because of the resulting imbalance.

A big step towards regaining balance is to recognize what aspects of your life you can be in charge of, and retaining that control. For example, your timetable commitments are part of your contract, and you cannot arrive at school one day and say 'I really need some time to prepare for the science afternoon, so can someone else teach year 3 this morning?' However, you can arrange to set work requiring minimal assessment during weeks when you know your workload will be especially heavy. Remember that you have *choices* and *control*. Put *your* needs first.

When pressures are mounting and the control is slipping away, be assertive in asking for support and limiting the demands made on you. There is not a teacher in the profession who has not had to take stock at some stage, and this is much harder to do alone. Support can come from:

- other NQTs;
- your induction tutor/mentor;
- your head of year/school/department;
- friends and family.

Ignoring signs of overload can lead to anxiety, depression and stress.

ABOUT PANIC ATTACKS

These episodes, which may involve shortness of breath, palpitations, sweating and a feeling of impending doom, signify severe discontent and must be taken seriously. However, they are perfectly treatable and there are many techniques that can be employed to restore balance. Do visit your healthcare practitioner if you suffer a panic attack.

There are four particularly effective ways to improve mental health that even the most serene could usefully employ:

- Deal with your emotions. It might not be appropriate or constructive to shout at a class, however angry you feel, but that emotion must be discharged later on. Frustration and anger at pupils or colleagues can be vented on a pillow, or in a car parked in a secluded place (open the windows and yell it out). Do be sure to address the problem calmly when the initial anger has subsided. Seek counselling (Teacher Support Line: 08000 562 561) if it would help.

- Utilize your inbuilt remedies. Crying is an excellent way to release emotion, and research has shown that laughter can help to cure even the most serious of illnesses. Some staffrooms have a joke board, which encourages laughter and lifts tension, helping staff regain a positive perspective. Try watching comedy shows and films, or reading a few pages of a funny book each evening.

- Develop relaxation skills. Not only will all aspects of your life seem more manageable, but there will be noticeable improvements in your physical health too. When we are deeply relaxed our pulse and breathing rates slow down and blood pressure drops. However, few people are able to relax deeply without learning techniques from a book or a class. Information on local classes can be found in health centres, libraries and adult education programmes. You may prefer to learn yoga or t'ai chi, both of which incorporate movement with relaxation and meditation.

- Utilize the power of the mind to cultivate a positive attitude. There are always two ways to view any situation, positively and negatively; remember those choices. Affirmations can be very useful in helping to assert the positive and minimize the negative.

ACTION When a problem or anxiety is getting out of hand, write it down as a heading. Underneath, write answers to these questions:

- What is the core of this problem?
- What can I do about it?
- Can anyone help me out?
- What can he/she do about it?
- What are the best and worst scenarios?

This should help you see that the problem is not insurmountable.

Looking after yourself

> Things turn out best for the people who make the best out of the way things turn out.
>
> (Art Linkletter)

Most teachers are extremely conscientious when it comes to nurturing those in their care, but don't extend that generosity to themselves. It cannot be expressed strongly enough how important self-nurturing is for NQTs. Do not take yourself for granted. Rather, engage in meaningful self-care.

Day-to-day maintenance

> Live and work but do not forget to play, to have fun in life and to really enjoy it.
>
> (Eileen Caddy)

Making improvements to your health and lifestyle is best done gradually. Dramatic changes will probably lead to a reversion to the old way. Try adopting one item at a time from the list of day-to-day maintenance and then reap the rewards:

- Take care over breathing. Rapid, shallow breathing can lead to varying degrees of hyperventilation, the symptoms of which can be dizziness, irritability, tension in the abdomen and excessive sighing. Spend a few moments several times a day doing simple breathing exercises, for example: breathe in to a count of four, hold for two, breathe out to a count of four and pause for two. Repeat five times. This is not only calming, but energizing too.
- Develop awareness of your slack times and learn to anticipate them. Treat energy slumps with breathing exercises and appropriate snacks, and pace yourself.
- Pay attention to your posture. You should aim for a balance between tension and relaxation, with your back straight and shoulders down.
- Create good sleeping patterns rather than 'crashing-out' patterns. If you don't wake feeling rested, aim to get more hours of sleep *before* midnight.

- Talk about work frustrations with colleagues. Start a support circle for this purpose if there is no forum for this sort of discussion at your school.
- Pursue a hobby – something you really enjoy. Be it painting, ceramics, woodwork, sport, gardening or cookery, just let your creativity flow.
- Get used to saying 'I can't afford it!' – not the cruises and convertibles, but the multi-tasking and working without adequate breaks.

ABOUT VOICE PROTECTION

It will come as no surprise that teachers are among the most likely to be referred to a speech therapist for help to minimize permanent voice damage. Of course, that does not mean that you will necessarily suffer – susceptibility plays an important role – but being aware of how you can protect your voice is invaluable. Common throat disorders that teachers seem to suffer from are pharyngitis, laryngitis, vocal cord polyps, vocal cord nodules and contact ulcers (sores on the mucus membrane covering the cartilages to which the vocal cords are attached).

To preserve the good health of your voice and throat, try these ideas:

- Develop non-verbal cues for your class(es) to follow, such as standing in a particular place when you want to issue instructions or tapping a desk with a pen to get the attention of those around you.
- Avoid shouting in the classroom at all costs. It is terrible for your voice as well as disturbing to other classes around you.
- Consciously relax you neck and jaw as often as possible. Yawning is an excellent way of doing this. Aim to lower your shoulders as soon as they rise in tension.
- Drink plenty of water throughout the day. This helps to keep your throat lubricated and avoids the potentially scalding effects of hot tea and coffee.
- Avoid drinking spirits neat.
- Cut down on your dairy intake to reduce the formation of mucus.

ABOUT HEAD LICE AND NITS

Head lice are small insects that live on the human scalp. Just a few millimetres long, they are a light greyish brown in colour. They feed on human blood and lay their eggs (nits) on the hair shaft, securely glued on. Nits have a 7- to 10-day gestation period in the warmth from the head. When the new lice hatch, the cycle begins again.

Lice cannot jump or fly so they require head-to-head contact in order to walk from person to person. They also need warmth to survive so they cannot live on coats and scarves and other clothing or bedding.

Head lice are a community problem, but it seems that 80 per cent of those affected are aged between four and 14. Estimates suggest that in primary schools one child in 10 gets infected each year.

Routine head inspections are no longer carried out in schools. Responsibility for checking for lice lies firmly with a child's parents. If you see live lice on a child, you should notify the parents as soon as possible, and be particularly vigilant of children who appear to get frequent infestations. Your school may be adopting a whole-school approach with 'Bug Busting' days (for more information on the 'Bug Buster' kit, visit www.chc.org/bugbusting).

What to look out for

Children who scratch vigorously, especially behind the ears and the nape of the neck where the hair tends to be thicker and warmer.

Treatments

An occupational hazard, especially for teachers of the very young, is catching head lice:

- Using a nit comb, comb your hair, when wet, over a sheet of white paper. This may give you a clear indication of whether you have been infected, but it is not wholly fail-safe, so don't assume you are free from them if you find none in this way.
- There are specific insecticide treatments for head lice but these are thought to be pretty ineffective, as not only do the lice become resistant to the chemicals but the chemicals are thought to be potentially harmful to human health.
- One method of treatment that many swear by is to apply an excessive amount of conditioner to the hair after washing. Then, using a fine nit comb,

comb through the hair from the roots to the very tips in an organized way, checking the comb after each sweep. The conditioner makes it impossible for the lice and nits to cling to the hair. This treatment can be performed every other day for about two weeks for best results.

- Another method of encouraging lice to leave is to wash hair in a basin of water to which lavender oil, lemon juice or vinegar has been added, and then to comb through as described above. Repeat often. Using olive oil rather than water makes it easier for people with very curly hair to get a fine nit comb through.
- If you find any live lice in your hair, then every member of your household should be treated.
- There are some homoeopathic treatments available. A qualified practitioner will be able to advise. Likewise, a trip to your local health store may offer treatments that are alternatives to the insecticides available.

Finding that you are host to head lice is no indication of the cleanliness or condition of your hair. They are not at all fussy and simply need blood and warmth in order to survive.

CHAPTER 9

Above and beyond – your non-teaching commitments

EXTRA COMMITMENTS

From school plays, outings, clubs and gardens to PTAs, staff committees and looking after class pets, there is no end to the extra commitments you may be cajoled into making. It is also no coincidence that NQTs often get asked to do extra jobs; existing staff have been there and done that and now say 'Sorry, I don't have time to take anything else on.'

Knowing your natural limits

The best line to take with extra commitments is to avoid them, if possible, in your first year unless you really want the experience that the commitment will provide, or unless it will add to your relaxation, eg acting in the school play if drama is a recreation for you. You will have enough on your plate working through your induction year without adding to the demands on your time. Taking extras on can result in you working at a pace above your optimum, which could result in a reduction in your effectiveness.

If you are not sure whether you can manage an extra commitment, agree to do it on the condition that you can review it after a few weeks. Provide yourself with a get-out, and the extra work will not seem like such an added stress.

If you are asked to take on duties in your department or curriculum area, such as being an ICT coordinator or being responsible for SEN, talk to your induction tutor/mentor. There will probably be a clause in your contract giving your headteacher the ability to ask you to do what he/she deems reasonable, but it is not practical for you to take on such duties as an NQT.

Can you say 'no'?

Most teachers, when asked if they are assertive, will reply positively, simply because of the nature of their job. Yet, if they are asked the question 'Do you ever feel put upon?', they will still give a positive answer. So how does this add up? Perhaps some teachers are not as assertive as they think they are. In order to express yourself assertively, you have to be able to view yourself and your work positively. If you don't, you can hardly justify why others should listen to your assertions.

There are three main reasons why some teachers find it difficult to say 'no' to additional tasks they don't want to take on:

- Managers lead them to believe they are obliged to complete the extra tasks.
- They are insecure in their performance and think that performing the extra tasks will improve their feelings of self-worth.
- They want to create the impression that they are ready for anything.

These reasons are more destructive than positive. There is no doubt that it is the assertive (as opposed to aggressive, dominating or weak) individual who gains the most respect in the workplace. (See Appendix 9 for more information.)

Duties

You will probably be involved in the supervision of pupils at some stage in the school day, whether as a paid lunchtime duty (the supervision of pupils at lunchtime is not something you can be directed to do without receiving additional payment) or a break or end-of-day duty. Before doing your first such duty:

- Find out exactly what the procedure is. Ask questions such as:
  - 'Where do I have to patrol?'
  - 'How long for?'
  - 'What happens if I am detained with my class?'
  - 'Who will I be on duty with?'
  - 'Will I have the same duties each week?'
  - 'Do I need a whistle?'
  - 'What is the procedure in the event of accidents?'
- Work with a colleague if possible. This can make a potentially lonely time pass more quickly.
- Make sure you get the refreshment you need.

ABOUT BEING ASSERTIVE

An easy route to stress and anxiety is by committing to too many projects. This usually results in feelings of being overwhelmed and unable to cope:

- An important step in the development of assertiveness skills is to practise some positive self-recognition. If you allow yourself to acknowledge what you are good at, you will boost your feelings of self-worth.
- Use affirmations daily, based on your skills. This will help to remove the need for positive strokes through taking on additional work.
- Accept any positive recognition that others give you.

When you are in the position of needing to express yourself assertively, use these ideas:

- Use 'I' statements to express yourself positively, for example 'I would be interested in playing the part of the beast in "Beauty and the Beast" but I feel it would adversely affect the way I manage my workload at the moment.'
- Don't put yourself down. Say 'I don't feel that is appropriate for me at the moment' rather than 'I can't do that.'
- Think about how you are using your body when you are being assertive. Tone of voice, body language, eye contact etc all make a difference to the way your words are received.
- If you are anticipating a situation when you fear you will be 'put upon', use creative visualization to enable you to 'see' yourself behaving assertively. Focus on the best possible outcome for you.

Being assertive is not just about saying 'no'. It is also about making requests yourself. 'I need', 'I would like', 'Do you think I could have. . .?' are all phrases that NQTs will need to use throughout their first year of teaching, and probably beyond.

- Use the opportunity to get to know pupils on a more informal basis. It could be a time to chat about music, TV or holidays etc. You'll be surprised how useful such conversations can be.
- Try not to let anything get in the way of your duties. Other members of staff will soon get annoyed if they have to cover for you.

ABOUT 'BUFFER TIME'

'Buffer time' is directed time for the supervision of pupils. According to the NASUWT, at the beginning of a session this is 'no more than the time it takes the teacher to go to the classroom to receive the pupils when they are allowed into the school building. At the end of a session it is no more than the time it takes to dismiss pupils from the classroom.'

Be aware that you should not be asked to do duties at the end of the morning session and the start of the afternoon session.

If pre-session briefings are the habit in your school, these should only take place before the start of the morning session and should last no more than 10 minutes. Technically, they should be incorporated in buffer time.

Covering for absent staff

The dreaded cover timetable – many a teacher's face drops at the sight of it as it's posted on the staffroom notice board. Yet another free period gone and you have to spend it with someone else's year 11 on a Friday afternoon. Great!

While the general rule is that you still have to teach the class to the best of your ability (and you may be observed doing this in an OFSTED inspection, although this would be unusual), the absent teacher will usually have made arrangements for the lesson, especially if his/her absence was planned. The lesson plan should be achievable for a teacher not familiar with the subject and should rely more on individual work rather than being a teacher-led session. Use these points to help:

- Find out if there is a system for the posting of set work for cover lessons. Will instructions be in the relevant room or in the staffroom? Where are books left? Will paper be supplied or will you need to take some? What happens if no work is set? Answers to these questions can help to ease a potentially stressful situation.
- If you know you will be covering a certain class, try to get as much information as possible in advance.
- Be strict about behaviour but don't have very high expectations of what pupils may achieve. Think back to when you were at school and your attitude to lessons when your teacher was absent.
- If you manage to get some of your own work done during a cover lesson, treat it as a bonus. Strictly speaking, you should be teaching. If you don't

try to get anything done, you won't be annoyed when pupils' interruptions prevent you from achieving anything.

- If no work has been set, your skills of management will be put to their greatest test. There should be a head of department hovering to make sure that you are coping if you have not spoken before the lesson but, if not, send a pupil to his/her room for further instructions. In the meantime you will have to get the class in order and keep them occupied. Above all, keep calm and controlled.
- If the department has no contingency plans in the event of staff absence, you are on your own. For this reason it is worth having some general lessons planned that will challenge pupils and be a worthwhile use of their time. Perhaps base such lessons around a cross-curricular theme such as citizenship. Don't feel you have to teach a lesson of the subject you are covering if no work has been set.
- Take the opportunity to get to know pupils you don't teach. This can do great things for your reputation in the school. Also observe the pupils you do teach. Do they behave differently in another classroom?
- Feed back to the class teacher what happened in the lesson and any information you feel he/she should know. You could simply leave a note in his/her pigeon-hole if you don't get a chance to speak.

There has been recent union 'cover to contract' action in response to concerns over workload and cover arrangements. For further information on the latest situation regarding cover, contact your union or visit its Web site.

ABOUT SETTING COVER WORK YOURSELF

Aim to prepare some interesting lesson plans for cover teachers to follow with your classes in the event of your absence. You could have them ready in a file for the teacher to select on the day. This means that you don't have to think about what your classes can do when you have phoned in with a crippling migraine at 8 am! Tell colleagues in advance where your lesson plans are (perhaps keep them in a file in the staffroom) and if your room is kept tidy it will be easy for other teachers to find resources such as paper etc. Make your instructions easy to follow – put yourself in the reader's position – and include any photocopied sheets that may be needed (don't expect a colleague to do this, as he/she probably won't have time before the lesson begins).

ORGANIZING SCHOOL VISITS

Taking on the organization of a school visit is something that even the most experienced teachers find time-consuming and potentially troublesome. Your school should have clear guidelines for teachers to follow when organizing visits, and if you do find yourself at the helm take as much advice from colleagues as you can.

The DfES document *Health and Safety of Pupils on Educational Visits* (1998) states that: 'Pupils can derive a good deal of educational benefit from taking part in visits with their school. In particular, they have the opportunity to undergo experiences not available in the classroom. Visits help to develop a pupil's investigative skills and longer visits in particular encourage greater independence.'

Although, as a new teacher, you probably won't be landed with the task of organizing a school visit from scratch, and certainly should not be asked to lead a residential visit, you will almost certainly be involved in them at some level. Before organizing a school visit, make sure you read a copy of the above document, which is available on request from the DfES Publication Centre: 0845 602 2260. Your school may also have a copy. It contains all the information you need regarding the legality of different kinds of school visits as well as health and safety considerations for all on the visit. It also has an extensive list of useful contacts.

As well as the good practice guide, Health and Safety of Pupils on Educational Visits, a three-part supplement has recently been published by the DfES:

- *Standards for LEAs in Overseeing Educational Visits* is ultimately for LEAs, but there is plenty within of use and interest to teachers;
- *Standards for Adventure* is aimed at the teacher or youth worker who leads adventure holidays;
- *A Handbook for Group Leaders* is aimed at anyone who leads groups of people on educational visists. It sets out good practice in supervision, ongoing risk assessment and emergency procedures.

The supplement is available from the DfES order line, or to download from www.teachernet.gov.uk.

Checklist for planning a visit

The first stage of planning a visit is convincing your headteacher that the trip is worth doing, that it fits into the curriculum you are teaching and that it carries minimum risks. This is because your employer is still responsible for the health and safety of its employees (who carry a duty of care for pupils) when out on visits, as well as having to account for the way time is spent in their schools. Go no further than this at first because, if you don't get approval of the idea in principle as well as permission from your headteacher, the trip cannot go ahead.

When you present the idea to your headteacher (or head of department) have your justifications for the trip well rehearsed. It's a good idea to have a printed sheet ready to leave with the headteacher. On the sheet you should include:

- where you propose to take the children;
- whom you propose to take (including staff, supervisors and children);
- why the trip is necessary;
- what aspect of the curriculum you would be covering;
- how you would link it into work before and after the trip;
- how much you estimate the trip will cost.

Once you get the go-ahead to start the planning, use this checklist:

1. Find out if your school has guidelines for planning a visit (head of department, induction tutor/mentor or headteacher should be able to confirm this). If it has, use them; otherwise, use this checklist.
2. Carry out a risk assessment. The DfES document mentioned above suggests basing a risk assessment on the following considerations:
   - What are the hazards?
   - Who might be affected by them?
   - What safety measures need to be in place to reduce risks to an acceptable level?
   - Can the group leader put the safety measures in place?
   - What steps will be taken in an emergency?

   The document also states that: 'A risk assessment for a visit need not be complex but it should be comprehensive. . . Pupils must not be placed in situations which expose them to an unacceptable level of risk. Safety must always be the prime consideration. If the risks cannot be contained then the visit must not take place.'

   The document suggests that teachers consider these factors when assessing the risks:
   - the type of visit/activity and the level at which it is being undertaken;
   - the location, routes and modes of transport;

- the competence, experience and qualifications of supervisory staff;
- the ratios of teachers and supervisory staff;
- the group members' age, competence, fitness and temperament; and the suitability of the activity;
- the special educational or medical needs of pupils;
- the quality and suitability of available equipment;
- seasonal conditions, weather and timing;
- emergency procedures;
- how to cope when a pupil becomes unable or unwilling to continue;
- the need to monitor the risks throughout the visit.

Once you have completed your risk assessment, make sure all those involved in the trip (but not pupils) have a copy.

3. If possible, go on an exploratory visit to:
   - ensure at first hand that the venue is suitable to meet the aims and objectives of the school visit;
   - obtain names and addresses of other schools that have used the venue;
   - obtain advice from the manager;
   - assess potential areas and levels of risk;
   - ensure that the venue can cater for the needs of the staff and pupils in the group;
   - become familiar with the area before taking a group of young people there.

   If you can't go on an exploratory visit, get the necessary information from telephone calls. You also need to make sure you have identified good places to delegate as meeting points, especially for lost pupils.

4. Think about joining up with another teacher for the trip. Perhaps another year group would benefit from the visit, or you could link with pupils from another subject area.

5. Talk through the financial arrangements with your head of department or headteacher. Maintained schools cannot charge for visits that take place during school hours, but they can ask for voluntary contributions. There may be some money available from the school to subsidize the trip, in which case you will be able to adjust the figure you request in donation accordingly. Many schools overestimate the size of the donation to allow for some parents not being able to pay the full amount. This is perfectly acceptable under current law.

6. Make sure you know who will be responsible for first aid on the trip. You will have to have a first aid box with you (your school will provide this) and it is a good idea to find out where the nearest hospital will be.

7. Work out the best form of transport (which may not necessarily be the cheapest). If the group is small enough, a mini-bus may do, but usually a coach is the best option. Also consider walking (if appropriate) and going by train. All mini-buses and coaches that carry children between 3 and 15 years of age must be fitted with a seat belt for each child. Check this when looking. Work out what would be the best pick-up and drop-off points.

8. Decide on the exact timing of the day, including toilet and lunch breaks. Prepare one itinerary for pupils and one for adults.

9. Who would be the group's leader? It is important to appoint one person (usually the organizer) to whom all other staff and supervisors may refer.

10. Work out how many adults need to go on the trip. Your LEA may have set ratios; otherwise, the DfES document (cited earlier) has set the following as an example guideline for local (non-swimming) visits:
    - one adult for every six pupils in years 1 to 3 (under-fives reception classes should have a higher ratio);
    - one adult for every 10–15 pupils in school years 4 to 6;
    - one adult for every 15–20 pupils in school year 7 upwards.

    However, even if the group you are taking out is small enough to warrant only one adult, think of the implications if you are taken ill. Never go on a trip as the only adult. Parents, volunteers and non-teaching assistants may be used instead of teachers to boost the supervision ratio but, before you ask for such help, keep in mind that many schools like to have Criminal Records Bureau checks performed on all adults who will have access to pupils. Make sure you plan the roles of each adult attending the visit and convey those roles to them. Your plans for supervision should also take into account the sex and ability of the pupils.

11. Prepare a letter informing parents of the trip. Many schools have a standard format for this. Aim to give sufficient information for parents to make an informed decision on whether their child should attend, but not be swamped with detail. Make yourself available for parents to ask you questions if necessary. You will also need to mention what clothing (if different) children will need, what food should be provided by parents and whether any extra money should be taken (perhaps for spending in a gift or souvenir shop etc). It can be worth mentioning the standard of behaviour that is expected of pupils on the trip.

12. Think about whether you want to ban carbonated drinks, glass bottles, personal stereos etc.

13. Keep equal opportunities issues in mind, especially when you arrange subgroups.

14. If possible, involve pupils in the planning of work to be completed on the trip. This helps to ensure that they understand the relevance of the trip and can place it clearly in the context of the curriculum they are following. It also encourages them to complete the work.

15. Get a list of any children with medical needs. Their parents should supply information on any medication that their child needs as well as give their consent (in writing) for you to administer it. Some teachers like to take a list of each child, the names of their GPs and next of kin and emergency contact numbers. This is usually unnecessary, as most trips are in school hours and, in the event of any emergency, you would contact the school, where all this information is held, as soon as possible.

16. Sort out insurance in good time. Your headteacher will be able to do this for you. You may think it appropriate to make copies of the insurance schedule available to parents before the trip.

17. Discuss the standards of behaviour that you expect. It is particularly important that pupils realize how identifiable they are in school uniform.

18. Think about how travelling time might be used constructively. Perhaps give pupils a quiz to do based on what they might see on the journey.

19. Write a list of everything you will personally need on the day, from lunch to worksheets, waterproofs to registers.

20. Think about how pupils will complete their work on the day. Will they have time to do tasks? Will clipboards be necessary? Will they use exercise books, paper or worksheets with gaps to fill in?

21. Inform any colleagues who would have taught the pupils you are taking off site of the exact details of the trip. It can be extremely annoying if they have planned an exam or assessment for your group and half of them are not there.

22. Arrange work for a cover teacher to set for any classes you are unable to teach.

23. Inform catering staff of the numbers you will be taking off site. They will need to adjust the amount they cook for the day and plan any free lunches in advance.

24. Create a contingency plan for arriving back late. Who will you phone? Will he/she be able to contact parents?

25. Make sure there is someone who is able to deputize for you in the event of an emergency. If you are incapacitated for whatever reason, the trip should not necessarily be called off. You will have to keep the person informed of all the arrangements.

ABOUT COLLECTING MONEY FOR A TRIP

Your school should have arrangements in place for the collection of monies for a trip. Speak to your bursar about this. If you find you have some money left over you could perhaps allocate this for tips for any guides and drivers you have. Always seek advice from your headteacher when it comes to charging for a visit, as he/she will have to follow guidelines from the LEA and DfES.

ABOUT THE JOURNEY

The travelling time on a trip can be potentially problematic. Children may get travel-sick, become excitable or, worse, start misbehaving. Having a focus for the journey often helps to pre-empt any troubles and, if you can make this light-hearted, even better. A quiz with a prize for the winner is usually great for occupying the time and creating unity in the group through a common task. Try to invoke a sense of anticipation of the day.

Pitfalls to avoid

- Don't plan too much initially before getting firm approval from the powers that be.
- Once you have approval, pace your planning so that you don't have a last-minute rush. Remember that you will also have to perform all your other duties on top of organizing the trip. Try to avoid being the sole organizer of a trip. This would be a pretty unfair expectation to make of an NQT.
- Don't get saddled with the cost of an exploratory visit. You should be able to claim your expenses back. Speak to the bursar.
- Don't make arrangements over the phone without asking for written confirmation.

Summary (for planning a visit)

1. Get a copy of your school's guidelines.
2. Do a risk assessment.
3. Go on a preliminary visit.
4. Perhaps join up with another teacher/class.
5. Discuss finances with the headteacher.

6. Consider first aid arrangements.
7. Assess transport possibilities.
8. Create an itinerary.
9. Designate a leader.
10. Decide on supervision levels.
11. Inform parents of the details of the trip.
12. Think about banned items.
13. Remember equal opportunities.
14. Allow pupils to help you plan work.
15. Find out any medical needs.
16. Sort out insurance.
17. Discuss standards of behaviour.
18. Consider using travel time.
19. Create a list of personal things you will need.
20. Consider the practicalities of how pupils will work.
21. Inform colleagues of those you will be taking out if necessary.
22. Arrange cover work if necessary.
23. Inform catering staff about those you are taking out.
24. Create a plan for late arrival back.
25. Arrange a deputy for the trip in case of an emergency.

Checklist for the actual day

All your meticulous planning will pay off now as you enjoy a trouble-free trip. Use this list as guidance:

1. Start with a headcount. It's not sufficient simply to call a register.
2. Continue to count heads at regular intervals throughout the day.
3. Take a mobile phone (which should be provided by your school) and some spare cash (again, talk to the bursar) for emergencies.
4. Make sure that pupils are fully strapped in before the coach starts to move and that they stay strapped in throughout the journey. At least you won't have to contend with children trying to sit more than two to a seat!
5. Staff and helpers should be evenly spread throughout the group on the journey and through the day.
6. Ask helpers unknown to the children to wear name badges.
7. Make sure children know which adults are assigned to their group.
8. Designate a central point as a meeting place in the event of children getting lost.

9. If travelling by coach, make arrangements with the driver about where and when you will meet again. Make a note of the coach's registration number.
10. Note anything that works particularly well on the day.
11. Keep a record of behaviour, both good and bad. Pupils should receive feedback when they get back to school, and you will have to discuss this aspect of the trip with your headteacher when you get back.
12. Recap on the day on the journey back. You could also go over some of the work the pupils have done and explain what comes next.
13. Evaluate the day for the purposes of future trips. Is there anything you would change in the future, or anything you would never do again?

Pitfalls to avoid

- Don't forget a sick bucket/bag, a bottle of still mineral water for the vomiting child, plenty of tissues and some mints – he/she will want to be refreshed after throwing up!
- Don't think you can relax for a minute throughout the day. You will need to be more vigilant than usual.
- Don't be so concerned about how the day flows that you forget to enjoy it.

Summary (for the actual day)

1. Count heads regularly.
2. Take a phone and some money.
3. Strap pupils in on the journey.
4. Spread helpers throughout the group.
5. Give helpers name badges.
6. Explain groups to children.
7. Decide on a meeting point.
8. Arrange when and where to meet the driver.
9. Note what works well on the day.
10. Record good and bad behaviour.
11. Recap on the day on the journey.
12. Evaluate the day.

WRITING REPORTS

Whatever schools call them, there's no getting away from the fact that you will have to write thousands of these throughout your teaching career, despite the fact that government guidance states that teachers are only required to produce one report to parents per pupil per academic year. It's an onerous job; you will need to give accurate messages in an accessible form while under a great deal of time pressure.

Report writing

Do:

- Take care over presentation. Would you mind if your reports were published?
- Keep to internal deadlines. Your headteacher, head of department or head of year will probably want to read them before they leave the building.
- Set yourself mini-deadlines of 5–10 reports at a time.
- Consider writing drafts, or at least jotting down key words for inclusion.
- Start your comments positively and focus on progress.
- Avoid educational jargon (of which there is a plethora). A recent poll found that about a quarter of parents thought that the information given to them by their (state) school was 'full of jargon' (telephone poll of 2,000 parents of children attending state schools, commissioned by the DfES and conducted in late 2001). Remember that acronyms can be confusing.
- Offer constructive suggestions for improvement.

Don't:

- Allow a report out of your hands with errors and corrections. Start again if necessary.
- Forget that it is the written comments that parents tend to take most notice of, as opposed to test results and attainment levels.
- Attempt to do a whole class set in one go.
- Forget your accountability. Can you substantiate all you write?
- Express limits. It is better to focus on possibilities (as opposed to predictions).
- Waffle. Select apt, crisp language.
- Hide the negatives, but be aware that reports are not the place to spring nasty surprises on parents.

When considering the actual words you will use, take care over creating a stockpile of phrases to scatter throughout your reports, as it is essential that they should apply to a child's work and progress. 'Tries hard', 'Could try harder', 'Makes a good effort', 'Makes no effort', 'Talks too much' and 'Doesn't speak out' are all meaningless and reflect more on teaching style than any aspect of the child in question. (For example, why does the child make no effort? Because he/she is bored? Because the work is too easy? Be aware of how your comments could reveal shortcomings in teaching style.) As long as your comments are specific to the child and relate to the skills required of the subject, where appropriate, your reports will be valid and noted, and you will not lay yourself open to criticism from within or outside your school. Remember that your reports should be accessible in style to all parents, particularly bearing in mind those whose first language may not be English.

A quick search on the Internet will reveal the growing number of sites dedicated to report writing. Many schools, too, have created comment databases for teachers to use to ease the task. If you use such a database, remember the following:

- Each comment should be backed up with an example, either written in the report or spoken at the parents' evening.
- The language of such comment databases might not match the way in which you would naturally phrase things; therefore they are best used as inspiration to trigger your own thought processes.
- Each comment should add meaning and clarity to the report.

The following lists of positive and negative comments have been put together by staff at St Martin's School in Brentwood, Essex:

Positive comments

- Has proved to be an extremely committed pupil with genuine enthusiasm for the subject.
- Teaching . . . has been a privilege. His/her constant enthusiasm and willingness to learn have been a pleasure to watch.
- He/she is extremely conscientious, has set him/herself high standards and is achieving them.
- His/her work reflects consistent effort.
- Possesses the ability to apply quickly what he/she has learned.
- Is a very conscientious pupil who takes pride in all he/she does.
- Has shown the ability to achieve a great deal in this subject.
- Has maintained the highest standards this year.
- Has demonstrated outstanding commitment.
- Seems determined to succeed.
- Has grown in confidence.
- Has improved greatly.

- Has shown a very sound/firm grasp of this subject.
- Is finding the subject difficult but always tries very hard to make progress.
- Can apply him/herself most effectively.
- I have been pleased with. . .
- I have been encouraged by. . .
- A perceptive/inquisitive/thorough approach.
- A lively intellect.
- A sensitive and mature student.
- A very encouraging start.
- Has worked conscientiously/effectively/diligently/enthusiastically.
- Has made enthusiastic/pleasing/outstanding contributions to class discussion.
- Has made pleasing/generally pleasing/very pleasing progress.
- Is developing into a mature and conscientious/committed student.
- Is a conscientious and committed student who has undoubtedly worked very hard this year.
- Has evidently worked at his/her best to produce such good results.

Negative comments

- . . . . .'s poor presentation skills have impeded his/her progress.
- Although keen to do well . . . . . allows his/her concentration to lapse far too often.
- . . . . . seems to have lost some of his/her willingness. He/she is an able pupil and usually conscientious but this must be a sustained feature of his/her work if he/she is to fulfil his/her potential.
- . . . . .'s expectation that others will give the answers in class often leads to a loss of concentration.
- . . . . . only works under pressure.
- . . . . . needs to organize his/her work more efficiently.
- . . . . . lacks commitment.
- His/her performance is erratic.
- Homework often appears rushed, has not been checked for avoidable errors and consists of a bare minimum.
- Should adopt a far more mature attitude.
- . . . . . has a considerable weakness in. . . . .
- Some weaknesses remain.
- Should not allow him/herself to be so easily distracted.
- Needs to become more effectively involved in group work/class discussion/ etc etc.

- Needs to target/focus/marshal his/her energies/enthusiasm more appropriately/effectively/maturely.
- Lacks confidence but can make pleasing contributions.
- Can lack application at times.
- Has a tendency to be immature.
- Has shown a lack of regard for authority which has been profoundly disturbing in its intensity and scope.
- A lack of attention to detail has hampered his/her progress.
- Frequent absence has made genuine progress difficult.
- Has worked poorly.
- Needs to adopt a more rigorous approach.
- Can lack concentration.
- Can lack the application required at this level.
- Has struggled with some of the more difficult aspects of the course.
- Seems unable to cope with even the most basic concepts.
- Potential there, motivation sometimes lacking.
- A student whose boundless enthusiasm is channelled in any direction but mine.

PARENTAL CONSULTATIONS

Sometimes referred to as 'open evenings', 'appointment evenings' or 'parents' evenings', you will probably have to face several throughout the school year. They can be daunting, especially if you did not get a chance to attend one during your training but, with a little preparation, the event should present no problems.

Before the big day

- Don't save important concerns about a child until parental consultation time as you may be met with anger and defensiveness. Aim to communicate with parents sooner rather than later about behaviour or work problems.
- Prepare for the night by having pupils' books marked up to date, and records of attendance, homework, general participation in class etc to hand.
- Make sure you know who is coming to see you and what their relationship is to the child. Be prepared to see older siblings in some cases, and occasionally divorced or separated parents may want two appointments.
- Talk to colleagues about who is coming to see you to make sure you will not be meeting any parents known to be difficult or aggressive, either

towards staff members (relatively rare) or their children. You may want to ask a member of the senior management team to hover near you when you are talking to such a parent.

- Be prepared for a long evening. Make sure you have plenty of sustenance with you, especially if you won't have time to get home before the evening begins.
- Aim to have a free evening as far as marking and preparation are concerned. You won't feel like doing much by the time you get home.

On the night

- It is worth making the effort to look smarter than usual when meeting parents, especially for the first time.
- Have a name card on your table (these are usually provided by the school).
- Stand up when greeting parents. It may feel as though you are bobbing up and down all night, but staying seated can appear rude.
- Don't use educational jargon. Explain everything, as a parent may not want to ask for clarification. These evenings can be just as daunting for parents as well.
- Let parents know exactly what you expect of their child.
- Focus on the *progress* the child has made. He/she may be top of the class, but has he/she *improved*?
- Show parents evidence of the child's achievements. Let them look through books etc.
- Record what happens at each interview. You don't need to include much detail, but it will be useful for future reference especially when writing the next round of reports. You could have a form ready (see Table 9.1) to minimize work on the night.
- Don't slot extra consultations in that haven't been booked unless you have clear gaps.
- Be professional when other staff members or pupils are being discussed.
- Aim to give advice on how achievement can be improved. Make this advice easy to adopt and encourage the parent to pass the information on to the pupil.
- Do not get drawn into making predictions about a child's future performance. Parents may hold you to what you say.
- Try to focus immediately on the task in hand. Don't get sidetracked by general conversation; otherwise you'll get irretrievably behind.
- Take drink breaks whenever you need them. Most schools arrange for drinks to be brought to teachers.

Table 9.1 *Parent evening specimen form*

Parent	Pupil	Key points	Action	Target date
Mrs Barker (mother)	Kevin Barker 8DS	Civil War extension work	Give Kevin additional reading references and exercises if wanted	Start asap and review after a few weeks

- If you find yourself with some spare time during a parents' evening, ask a colleague if you can observe him/her in action.
- Don't worry if things don't go according to plan. It will be a learning process, and you, your induction tutor/mentor or a member of the senior management team can deal with every situation.

Being heard

- The best way to ensure that you are *heard* is to show you know how to *listen*. Demonstrate your attentiveness and empathy and the parent will be more likely to listen to what you have to say.
- Encourage parents to say what they want to say in order to keep the dialogue going. This is, after all, an opportunity for parents to speak as well as you.
- Think about your tone of voice. Always meet rising tension with calm. If a parent's voice rises, lower yours.
- Don't dilute what you want to say about a child to try to pacify a dominant parent. The key is to be truthful rather than blunt.
- Reiterate the fact that your main concern is the child and how he/she can develop his/her potential.

Facing a refusal to listen

Occasionally, adopting the above tips on being heard by a parent won't work and you may face a point-blank refusal to listen to your reasoning. Read the following section in advance to help should such a situation arise.

Dealing with difficult parents

Do:

- Be aware of prejudices that parents may be airing. It may be necessary to discuss what the parent has said to you with your headteacher.
- Be concise and consistent and have justifications for your views.
- Maintain eye contact as much as possible.
- Focus on achievement and behaviour, both good and bad.
- Explain that everyone has many facets to their character and that the child's behaviour and attitudes at school may not necessarily reflect the way he/she is at home.
- Try to motivate the parents into joining you in working for the child. Encouraging a partnership can often work.

Don't:

- Retract any statements you have made about a child simply because the parent won't accept them.
- Try to force the parent to see your point of view, but present your opinions and trust that they will be digested eventually.
- Focus on problems. Rather move towards solutions.
- Focus on personality.
- Forget that the parent may be feeling embarrassed by and disappointed with the child.
- Struggle on with a conversation that is not moving forward positively without offering the parent the opportunity to talk to a member of the senior management team.

Seeing parents at other times

It is wise to have an 'open-door' policy when it comes to seeing parents. If you encourage an ongoing dialogue with them, you are less likely to get into difficult situations on parents' consultation evenings:

- Let parents know the best way for them to get in touch with you if they want to discuss anything. Do you have a good time when they can ring you or a good day when they can call in after school? Make sure you keep such arrangements contained, and on your terms.

- If you have a need to talk to a parent on the telephone about his/her child, prepare a script, or some notes at least, and have to hand all the information you need.
- Parents are entitled to see their child's records but this is definitely a senior management matter. Pass the request on.

EXAMPLE The most difficult aspect of this year has been that, more times than not, my parents have perceived me as the 'enemy' and think that I really don't have their child's best interest in mind. Thankfully, I have an administration that is on top of their faculty and they know exactly what's going on in my room and support me 100 per cent. Otherwise, if I had not had the support, I think that I would've crumbled under the pressure. It's tough being young and without children of my own when I try to give guidance on particular situations. Not only do I have to be policeman, nurse, mother, entertainer, counsellor and teacher all in one, I am also forced to be a Dr Spock or James Dobson-type family counsellor who gives advice on child rearing!

(Katherine L Cole, USA)

ABOUT DOCUMENTING YOUR VIEWS

If a difference of opinion arises between you and a parent, it may be pertinent to document your views and why you hold them. This is so that you can refer to the conversation later, should you need to. You may also want to discuss what you have written with your mentor or a member of the senior management team. Place a copy in the child's records and keep a copy for yourself.

OTHER ADULTS IN YOUR CLASSROOM

The involvement of support teachers in classrooms of mainstream and special schools across the country has increased over recent years. Furthermore, there are projected increases in the number of classroom assistants supporting pupils and teachers. In primary schools in particular, many teachers would not be able to function efficiently without the input of adult helpers. The head of a school appoints most helpers, both paid and voluntary. It would be unusual for you to arrange your own helpers, as schools carry out CRB checks on most, if not all, adults with access to pupils.

If your school has a policy on dealing with adults in the classroom, use it. If not, these ideas will help:

- Make sure you know *why* the adult is helping you. Is the adult there for learning support for one pupil or as an extra pair of hands and eyes for you? Is he/she paid or voluntary?
- Inform your helpers of your classroom rules and routines and the *reasons* for them.
- Inform helpers of first aid procedures in your school and routines for fire practice. They'll also need to know about tea and coffee arrangements and where to put bags and coats etc, although your school's management team should arrange for them to receive some induction.
- Make sure your helpers understand the need for confidentiality. You don't want your pupils and lessons being discussed outside school.
- Back your helpers so pupils see you presenting a united front.
- A priced DfEE report, *The Management, Role and Training of Learning Support Assistants,* is available to order on 0845 602 2260.
- *Working with Teaching Assistants: A good practice guide* (DfEE 0148/2000) is available free of charge on 0845 602 2260.
- There is a Teaching Assistants portal on the Teachernet Web site: www.teachernet.gov.uk/teachingassistants.

Staying in charge

Having extra adults in your classroom does throw some children into confusion. They will need to know exactly who is in charge and won't necessarily understand the significance of teacher training, or that you are still in charge even if it is the headteacher who is providing some classroom support.

The best way round this is to involve helpers in discussion on their role. You need to define what your ideal working relationship is and continue to work on it. Questions to look at are:

- What do you expect helpers to do?
- What have they been employed to do?
- What do they want to do?
- How much power of reward and sanction do you want your helpers to have (check your school's policy on this)?

- Can helpers give pupils permission to go to the toilet or to leave the room for other reasons?
- Do you want helpers to carry any equipment or will you make sure they have access to all they may need while in your classroom?
- What do you want your helpers to tell you about their interactions with a child? If you have to spend too long on feedback, you simply lose gained time, yet you must be informed of all child protection issues at least.

Every now and then you should aim to give your helpers some positive feedback. Pinpoint what aspects of their work are particularly helpful to you and what seems to be working very well. This way, you should fall into a comfortable rhythm with your helpers, knowing how best to deploy them in your lessons.

Making your intentions clear

The only way to be clear in what you need your helpers to do is to know for yourself. What, exactly, are your learning intentions for your pupils? How can your helpers enable pupils to achieve them?

If you are fortunate enough to have regular helpers with whom you can build a good relationship, they will be able to follow your lessons as you go along, without too much need for planning discussions. If not, you will need to brief your helpers so they don't have to bluff in front of pupils. Don't expect them to be familiar automatically with the intricacies of the curriculum you teach.

An interesting exercise is to place yourself in the position of a support teacher in one of your lessons. Do you know what you are doing and why? Do you know where this work is coming from and where it is going? The need for communication between you and your support teachers is great and you may have to be 'creative' in looking for opportunities to meet.

Maximizing the use of classroom support

The most effective way of maximizing the use of other adults in your classroom is to raise the status of in-class support amongst the children you teach. This will ensure that pupils view your helpers as a valuable resource that they should make use of rather than an embarrassing reminder of their self-perceived 'inadequacies'.

You may also want to think about preparing an information sheet for helpers in your classes, or perhaps giving some brief training sessions on certain aspects of your work such as hearing children read etc. Mutual feedback is always valuable. If you don't have time to talk immediately after a lesson, ask your helpers to jot down any points they would like to raise and arrange a mutually convenient time to meet.

Support teachers can help you to mark your progress through your induction year in a way that your induction tutor/mentor cannot, simply because they will be witnessing your work on a daily or weekly basis for the full length of a lesson. They will see how your relationships with the pupils develop over time and how effectively you relax into your job in ordinary, unobserved circumstances. Support teachers can also give you valuable insight into how key pupils behave in the presence of other teachers, a perspective you couldn't possibly achieve alone.

Delegating tasks

Paid support staff will have guidelines to follow regarding their work in your lessons. However, volunteers who help in your classroom are often giving up valuable time and it is worth organizing some structured tasks so that they do not feel they are surplus to requirements or wasting time. Perhaps ask helpers if there is anything they want to get involved in, or if they have any particular skills that can be utilized.

Think about how they can save you time by doing work displays or mounting, general tidying, collating worksheets, preparing materials etc. However, avoid the trap of relying on volunteers too heavily. You don't want your lessons to collapse if you find they can't be there for any reason.

ABOUT DELEGATING TO HELPERS

Do not ask helpers to perform duties that should only be done by a qualified teacher, tempting as it may be, eg marking, curriculum planning, report writing etc. You are ultimately responsible for what goes on in your classroom. You could, however, keep a notebook of ongoing tasks in your classroom to which helpers could refer.

CHAPTER 10

Inspections – your chance to shine

A fact of teaching life is that you will be inspected, probably by your head-teacher, your head of department, your induction tutor/mentor, an adviser and anyone else involved in your induction period. In addition to this, you may be inspected by OFSTED during your first year of teaching.

Inspections can seem totally daunting experiences, requiring preparation beforehand and recovery afterwards. Yet they do have clear purposes. The OFSTED document, *Inspecting Schools: The framework (effective from January 2000)* (1999), states that:

> An inspection provides an independent, external view of the school and the standards it achieves. Inspectors tell the school what it does well, where it has weaknesses and why they have come to their conclusions. They also look at how much the school has improved since the last inspection and where it needs to improve further.
>
> In order to do this the inspectors must be able to report on:
>
> - the educational standards achieved in the school;
> - the quality of the education provided by the school;
> - whether the financial resources made available to the school are managed efficiently;
> - the spiritual, moral, social and cultural development of pupils at the school.

OFSTED

Unfortunately, the word 'OFSTED' is enough to strike fear into the hearts of many teachers but, as an NQT, you should remember that a little knowledge about the inspection process and the reasons for inspection could help to alleviate any concerns you may have. There have been changes made to the way OFSTED operates over the years since its inception and it is not always useful to listen to tales of inspections that took place several years ago.

This section has been designed to give you a solid background to any OFSTED inspection you may face with the intention that it should assist in your preparation and place inspections in a helpful context.

The Office for Standards in Education, officially the Office of Her Majesty's Chief Inspector of Schools in England, was set up in 1992. It is a non-ministerial government department and is independent from the DfES.

The reason for OFSTED's existence is to improve standards of achievement and quality of education through inspection and subsequent public reporting. Teams of inspectors led by a registered inspector carry out inspections. The size of the team varies according to the size and needs of the school.

On its Web site, www.ofsted.gov.uk, OFSTED summarizes the key aspects of its school inspection system in this way:

- all schools are inspected regularly, at least once every six years;
- schools get a minimum of 6, maximum of 10 weeks, notice of their inspection date;
- every inspection leads to a public report;
- inspections conducted by independent inspectors;
- inspection contracts won by competitive tendering;
- every team has one lay member;
- inspection carried out to a published national framework;
- parents involved by being invited to pre-inspection meeting and sent summary of final report;
- quality control for whole system in hands of independent government department – OFSTED.

In addition to inspecting maintained schools, OFSTED also reviews local education authorities, reports on LEA-funded youth services and the impact of government initiatives such as Education Action Zones, and inspects:

- initial teacher training courses;
- all 16–19 education and training in sixth form and further education colleges;
- all early years childcare and education, the private, voluntary and independent nursery sector;

- independent schools (including independent special schools);
- service children's education.

The registered inspector and contractor of an OFSTED team must ensure that inspections are of an extremely high quality. According to *Inspecting Schools: The framework*, he/she must make sure that:

- judgements about the school and what it needs to do to improve are fair and accurate;
- communication of inspection findings is clear and helpful to the school;
- evidence is secure and substantiates all inspection judgements;
- the conduct of the inspection is to a high professional standard.

The Framework also outlines a code of conduct for inspectors, stating that they should:

- evaluate the work of the school objectively, be impartial and have no previous connection with the school, its staff or governors which could undermine their objectivity;
- report honestly and fairly, ensuring that judgements accurately and reliably reflect what the school achieves and does;
- carry out their work with integrity, treating all those they meet with courtesy and sensitivity;
- do all they can to minimise stress, in particular by ensuring that no teacher is over-inspected and by not asking for paperwork to be specifically prepared for inspection;
- act with the best interests and the well-being of pupils and staff as priorities;
- maintain purposeful and productive dialogue with staff, and communicate judgements of teachers' and the school's work, clearly and frankly;
- respect the confidentiality of information, particularly about teachers and the judgements made about their individual teaching.

ABOUT SHORT INSPECTIONS

Short inspections were introduced with the revised framework for inspection in January 2000. They are designed for schools already deemed to be most effective and should be regarded more as a 'check-up' rather than a full-blown 'medical'. Short inspections are usually two or three days long and, often, fewer inspectors are involved, as not all teachers will be observed.

As with full inspections, short inspections also report on standards, achievements, efficiency of financial management and the spiritual, moral, social and cultural development of pupils, but they do not report in detail on each subject.

OFSTED uses a combination of four main factors when deciding whether a school should have a full or a short inspection. So, if your school had a good report from the last inspection, has evidence of improvement or of sustained high standards, is doing well when compared with other similar schools and compares well in performance in relation to national averages, there's a pretty high chance that just a short inspection will be necessary.

When a team of OFSTED inspectors visits your school, they will need to answer the question, 'How well is the school doing and why?' They will base their findings on evidence gathered under the following headings:

1. What sort of school is it?
2. How high are standards?
   - The school's results and achievements.
   - Pupils' attitudes, values and personal development.
3. How well are pupils or students taught?
4. How good are the curricular and other opportunities offered to pupils or students?
5. How well does the school care for its pupils or students?
6. How well does the school work in partnership with parents?
7. How well is the school led and managed?
8. What should the school do to improve further?
9. Other specified features (school data and indicators).
10. The standards and quality of teaching in areas of the curriculum, subjects and courses (full inspections only).

The final report following an OFSTED inspection will include details on the characteristics of the school including information about the pupils and the area it serves, and the aims and priorities of the school. It will also look at key indicators, which summarize the attainment of boys, girls and all pupils at the end of each key stage, and attendance, and will state the percentage of teaching observed that is:

- very good or better;
- satisfactory or better;
- less than satisfactory.

'Satisfactory' means that teaching is adequate and that strengths outweigh weaknesses.

The DfEE Circular 2/98, *Reducing the Bureaucratic Burden on Teachers*, highlights concerns that excessive time is spent preparing for OFSTED inspections. It recommends that schools facing inspection should concentrate on the essentials. Always keep this in mind when you are involved in an OFSTED inspection.

Regardless of the opinion of OFSTED that it is judge and jury of the teaching profession, it is here to stay, and the fact remains that many teachers and schools greatly value the information they receive from an inspection. Use the ideas in the following sections as support in the event of an inspection.

BEFORE THE INSPECTORS ARRIVE

Although the prospect of an OFSTED inspection may send your school into a frenzy of preparation tinged with more than a hint of anxiety, it is important to keep a perspective of your role in all this. As an NQT, you will be inspected on your teaching and the way you manage your job.

Inspectors are well aware of the potential trauma of an inspection. Don't think of them as ogres who are detached from life in schools.

- Your headteacher will be given the opportunity to hold a meeting where staff can meet the registered inspector. If you are asked to attend such a meeting, make sure you go because it will allay many of your anxieties. Don't forget that as an NQT you may be one of a few teachers in your school who has not already been through an OFSTED inspection. Prepare some questions before the meeting or talk to your headteacher about any fears you might have. He or she will be able tactfully to present your questions to the registered inspector. After the meeting, you should at least know how the lesson observation forms will be used and how your teaching will be evaluated.

- Avoid panic and stress by talking about your concerns. Lean on your induction tutor/mentor and try to contact NQTs in other schools who have been through an OFSTED inspection. The Internet can be excellent for networking, especially the staffroom forums of the Web sites of the education press (for example, www.eteach.com).
- Take heart from the fact that NQTs, being used to having their work observed, generally perform well in OFSTED inspections.
- Recognize that you may have a need for increased relaxation during the weeks leading up to the inspection.
- Spend time talking to pupils about the inspection. The high media profile of OFSTED inspections means that pupils can be well aware of what is going on.
- If there is a class or child you are particularly concerned about try talking to that class or child in advance. Express your concerns and visualize your best possible scenario. Is there anything you can do to ease the situation? Take care not to over-prime; an inspector will detect this with ease.
- Aim to be totally prepared for the inspection week so that you don't have to work on lesson plans too much while the inspectors are at your school. It helps to have copies of lesson plans for inspectors to pick up as they enter your room, or leave them on the seat you would like them to use (preferably next to some 'angels'!).
- Give the inspector any additional information he/she may find useful, for example if a child in the class is going through a particular difficulty such as bereavement.
- Script certain parts of each lesson so that you know exactly what you will say.
- Look at your pupils' exercise books and replace any that are too damaged by graffiti.

ABOUT INSPECTION AS AN NQT

- No allowances are made for the fact that you are an NQT. However, inspectors are told exactly how long each member of staff has been teaching and will not expect new entrants to the profession to be experts.
- You cannot be held responsible for what has happened in your school in the past.
- As someone in the first year of teaching, you are in an excellent position to develop your skills as a teacher using any conclusions from the inspection. Use the inspection as an indicator of progress made since qualifying.
- Get support from other NQTs. There are heaps of inspection jokes around to lighten your thoughts!
- Don't prepare excessively. If you do you will certainly pay afterwards in terms of post-OFSTED apathy and fatigue, which could undo your hard work. Keep a steady, realistic pace.

ACTION Consider these questions when you are facing an inspection:

- What was your immediate reaction to hearing about the impending inspection?
- What are your greatest fears about the inspection?
- Do you have any unanswered questions about the inspection?
- Do you want to focus on any aspect of your work before the inspection?

Discuss your answers with your induction tutor/mentor and other NQTs. Make sure you find answers to your concerns in good time.

DURING THE INSPECTION

The worst thing you can possibly do is worry about what you could have done.

(Lichtenberg)

- Don't change the way you teach; trying new things out for your audience is not a good idea. Don't worry that your lessons may seem unexciting. You should be given the opportunity to discuss with inspectors the *context* of the work you were observed doing and your rationale for it.

- One inspector compared inspection with the driving test. You know how to teach/drive, but you have to *show* the inspector/examiner that you do. There will be many aspects of your teaching/driving that you do subconsciously, but you must make sure that the inspector/examiner knows you are doing them. The best analogy for this is looking in the rear-view mirror during a driving test. If you don't physically move your head, the examiner may not realize you have performed this crucial task and fail you. *Show* or *tell* the inspector all aspects of your teaching, especially your attention to detail; make explicit the implicit.

- It will come as no surprise that drama teachers tend to do well in inspections. Being able to rise to the occasion with a little acting will certainly serve you well.

- If a lesson seems to fall apart, stop what you are doing and start another activity. You will then be able to demonstrate your flexibility and originality when it comes to problem solving.

- At least 60 per cent of inspectors' time will be spent in lesson observations. However, inspectors have a responsibility to monitor the amount of time that each teacher is inspected. OFSTED's Quality Guarantee to teachers (as explained in *The Framework*) states that:
  - 'normally you will be observed teaching for no more than half of any one day, and never more than three-quarters';
  - 'inspectors will not judge teaching unless they have observed a significant part of the lesson, normally for at least 30 minutes'.

- You should be given an indication of how the inspector feels your lessons are going. The days of no feedback until the very end of the inspection have thankfully long gone.

- If you have any anxieties about the way that the inspection of your teaching is going, talk to your headteacher. He/she will be meeting the registered inspector on a daily basis so will be able to raise your concerns. For example, you may feel that you are being inspected too frequently.

- Make sure you indulge in some quality relaxation during inspection week, perhaps some early nights or a massage – whatever enhances your sense of relaxation.

EXAMPLE When the task is done beforehand, then it is easy.

(Ch'an Master Yuantong)

Although Louise was exhausted from the anticipation of the inspection she actually found the week quite exhilarating. Being so thoroughly prepared meant that her lessons flowed more smoothly than usual and she even found herself feeling pleased when an inspector arrived at her door to observe a lesson.

- Try to enjoy the week! This may seem impossible, but you will be more prepared than usual and more clued up on the work of your school, so ride that wave as much as you can.

ABOUT OBSERVATIONS

According to *The Framework*, during the inspection the inspectors will observe lessons, look at pupils' work and talk to pupils. They will make notes on:

- what the lesson is about;
- what is being taught, how well it is taught and the impact of the teaching on pupils' learning;
- evidence and evaluation of the standards pupils reach, their learning and their application in lessons;
- pupils' attitude and behaviour.

The inspector observing your lesson will be filling in an observation form. He/she will make evaluations according to a seven-point scale ranging from excellent (1) to very poor (6–7). Inspectors may talk to pupils about their understanding of the work and whether what they are doing is normal practice. Any such discussions should be totally unobtrusive.

Feedback

You will be offered oral feedback on the quality of your teaching towards the end of the inspection. The aim of this feedback is to explain the strengths and weaknesses of your teaching *as indicated by the snapshot of your skills that the inspection provided.*

Inspections – your chance to shine 291

According to *The Framework*, inspectors will:

- report on what they have seen and share their evaluations;
- explain their evaluations through exemplification;
- respond to questions and ensure that evaluations are understood;
- help teachers to improve through clear identification of what does and does not work.

The most important thing to remember here is that inspectors will be commenting on what they have observed during the inspection. It is not a judgement on your teaching in the past or on your expected future progress in the profession. If possible, ask your induction tutor/mentor to attend such feedback – it can be easy to hear the negative, ignore the positive and feel that you have to change all aspects of your teaching. If someone else is listening to what is said, he/she can elicit the important points for discussion afterwards.

AFTER THE INSPECTION

Within six weeks of the inspection, a final report will be sent to the headteacher and governors of your school. They will then have 10 days to send the summary report to parents and make the report public in libraries. They may even want to contact the press (depending on the outcome, of course). It is at this point that the work really starts. An action plan for school improvement must be written in response to the inspection report and this usually involves all members of staff.

Think about these points when the inspection is over:

- Don't cling on to the grade you are given too firmly. In an independent survey of schools' views by Market and Opinion Research International (MORI) during the summer term 1998, just under half of the schools that responded most valued inspection as an independent diagnosis of strengths and weaknesses. *Few felt that the teaching grades were important.* The grade you are given, if you receive one, is not an absolute judgement.
- There is often a collapse of morale after the inspection regardless of the outcome. Keeping the momentum going until the end of term can be a chore, but this is the same in most schools. If you feel tired or 'flat', ease up on your planning and try to take some time out for relaxation.
- If you are very unhappy about the way you were treated during the inspection, there is now the opportunity to make a complaint. The complaints

I.M. MARSH LIBRARY LIVERPOOL L17 6BD
TEL. 0151 231 5216/5299

procedure is sent to all schools when they are advised of an imminent inspection. Your school should also have set up a forum for the airing of concerns related to the inspection. If your concerns have not been heard by the time the inspection has ended, contact your union for advice before complaining to OFSTED.

- Many schools mark the end of an inspection with some form of celebration. This is important, as you have collectively reached a milestone in a school's life and to ignore this fact can be a missed opportunity to give each other the proverbial pat on the back. You could also aim to treat yourself in some way when the dust has settled and your energy has returned.

OTHER OBSERVATIONS

As an NQT you will have other teachers observing your lessons as part of your induction. This can be daunting, but is mostly very constructive. However, in order for the observations to hold value for you, aim to:

- Spend time beforehand talking to your observer about the lesson you plan to teach, its place in the scheme of work and what it will lead on to.
- Give your observer all the necessary documents for the lesson, eg lesson plan (if applicable) and any worksheets or textbooks used.
- Decide where would be the best place for your observer to sit.
- Decide how much of the lesson will be observed.
- Decide when you can meet to discuss the lesson and hear the feedback.
- Listen to the feedback carefully and accept any tips that may be offered while justifying your actions when appropriate.

Utilizing the feedback

It can be tiresome when you have completed your training, to listen to yet another review of your teaching skills. However, think of these positive aspects: your observer may not have seen you teach before so will be looking at you through fresh eyes; and you will be observed in the context of your school, and therefore feedback should be specific to your job.

EXAMPLE I was due to be observed by my mentor and she was late for the lesson. I had introduced to the class what I had planned for them so when she finally turned up she had missed the crucial part. In her feedback she kept talking about what I could have done differently when, if she had looked at my scheme of work, she could have seen my rationale for doing what I did. I was really angry that I had spent so much time preparing for the observation in vain.

(NQT, Greenwich)

After each observation you should be given some constructive feedback. This should reflect on what happened in the lesson, what was learnt by the children and how effective your teaching appeared to be. There should be a dialogue. Don't feel you have to sit and listen to what your observer has to say without being able to interject and explain your actions and decisions.

You may want to amend your Career Entry Profile. This will help you to glean the most from the observations and to feel that you are not working alone by involving your induction tutor/mentor. Often, additional support and training are blocked by lack of money. If there isn't any money for you to go on courses etc, there needs to be some other form of affordable follow-up care, which can be written into your action plan. Try not to let any amendments be forgotten until the next observation, inspection or appraisal when it is likely that the same points will be picked up. If the appropriate support is not forthcoming, talk to your induction tutor/mentor.

CHAPTER II

ICT and CPD – your early development

COMPUTER-RELATED ICT AND THE NQT

This is quite a controversial area of teaching, with daunting expectations of ITT courses combining with the mixed bag of resources available in schools (some are still being described as 'information poor').

A starting point for NQTs must be the document outlining the requirements of the ITT National Curriculum for the use of ICT in subject teaching. A copy of this can be downloaded from the TTA Web site. It is a very comprehensive document covering all the expectations of NQTs regarding effective teaching and assessment methods, and knowledge and understanding of, and competence with, information and communications technology. Make sure you read this document; it not only outlines what you have to know but also makes some useful suggestions on the applications of ICT.

There could well be a gap in skills that NQTs must fill once in post, especially if the ITT provider passed responsibility for ICT training on to a hard-pressed teaching-practice school. Clearly it is going to take time to get everyone up to the expected standards, and key issues about the use of ICT in schools will have to be addressed (issues to do with equality of opportunity and financing to name a few). Nevertheless, ICT in schools is being given 'massive priority' and the emphasis is on an ICT culture in all schools, at all ages and in all subjects.

The TTA has produced exemplification materials relating to National Curriculum subjects in both the primary and secondary phases. Each booklet can be downloaded from the TTA Web site: www.canteach.gov.uk, or ordered on 0845 606 0323.

Online support

Internet support for teachers is growing literally every day, from individual teachers sharing their schemes of work and lesson plans to commercial organizations providing a rich selection of resources. And, of course, there's the government support too in the form of the National Grid for Learning (NGfL) at www.ngfl.gov.uk.

The National Grid for Learning

The NGfL is 'the gateway to educational resources on the Internet', provided by the DfES and the British Educational Communications and Technology Agency (BECTa). It is a network of educationally valuable content on the Web that aims to 'connect the learning society' and be a major part of the way teachers use the Internet for both teaching and preparation as well as being a resource for other members of the learning society. It would be well worth reading BECTa's information sheets on the NGfL (available to download from www.becta.org.uk/technology/infosheets/index.html).

The development of the 'Grid' is ongoing so the resource links already in existence will grow. The sites within the Grid are all safe and appropriate for teaching, as they are closely monitored by 'Web keepers'. Have a good look at the Virtual Teacher Centres (VTCs, found at http://vtc.ngfl.gov.uk), as they are designed to support your work as a teacher.

At the time of writing, the NGfL offers:

- learning resources;
- games and quizzes;
- lesson plans and worksheets;
- subscription services;
- reference material;
- libraries and archives;
- museums and galleries;
- government information;
- advice;
- learning opportunities;
- jobs;
- online purchasing.

Applications of ICT for NQTs

There are many possible applications of ICT here, and only two initial questions to ask of any application you may have for ICT in the course of your work: 'Will it improve the quality of education I deliver?' and 'Will it ease my workload?' Both are equally valid questions to ask.

Don't forget the other forms of ICT that have traditionally had a role to play in education, such as radio, TV and video. They can all add to the breadth of your lessons when used appropriately and are simply tools to aid the delivery of the skills you must teach. If your approach to ICT is imaginative and creative, you won't get bogged down in the technical.

Using ICT within your curriculum area

This is where subject-specific INSET will be invaluable. The key is to know the best situations in which to use ICT and when not to use it:

- When will it add to the quality of your teaching?
- When is ICT the *best* resource to use?
- Are there explicit links between the subject matter and the application of ICT in each circumstance?
- Is it possible for children to identify what they have learnt from the application of ICT in your lesson?

Use your links with NQTs in other schools to find out what software and CD ROMs they are using and what Web sites they make use of, as well as taking advice from your curriculum leader(s) and the adviser responsible for NQTs in your LEA (who will be able to talk to the relevant advisers/inspectors for your curriculum area). Any schemes of work that you follow should have ICT opportunities highlighted, especially where they may benefit the way you teach children with special educational needs.

With such a rapidly changing market, there will be new resources available on a daily basis and it's virtually impossible to keep your finger on every pulse, so lean on the support that's there.

Communication

This may at first appear to be of limited use to NQTs, but this is not the case.

E-mail

This is an excellent form of communication for teachers. You can keep in touch with former colleagues and your ITT provider and access your mail on your terms – much less demanding than the telephone!

Newsgroups

The use of newsgroups as a teacher's aide is now well recognized by enthusiasts. They are an excellent way of sharing ideas, gaining answers to questions that would previously have taken valuable time to research and linking with teachers overseas. It is a good idea to 'lurk' for a while to get an idea of the nature of the group before posting your own message. Don't be surprised by the good will out there. There are many people willing to spend time helping you problem-solve.

Newsgroups can help to guard against the isolation that some teachers experience. You can also use them to pass on skills that you have learnt and share your resources. You are in a profession that can only thrive in a culture of give and take. There is simply no need to keep reinventing the wheel.

One potential hazard of subscribing to newsgroups is the possibility of receiving spam – unwanted junk electronic mail. One way round this is to disguise your e-mail address so that the harvesting software used to extract live addresses from newsgroups is thwarted! Make it clear in any message you send how readers can alter your address so that messages can reach you if you want to receive private mail that isn't posted to the whole group.

Resource preparation

Gone are the days when a hastily cobbled worksheet will suffice. ICT is being used ingeniously by teachers around the country to produce excellent class-specific and even pupil-specific resources. There may be hard work involved initially, but with the time-saving properties of ICT the resources can be readily adapted with ease.

Word processing and desktop publishing

Use clipart to add graphics to worksheets. Vary the font and font size as appropriate and remember that, if you are using ICT to create acetates for overhead projectors, you will need to use large print.

When asking pupils to use word-processing skills, encourage them to take advantage of the creative/design aspects of the task. Whatever their subject, all documents should have at least some element of this in their production.

The Internet

Not only can this help with your own research and in teaching research skills to pupils (crucial in any subject), but some teachers are now taking advantage of their own free Web space from home connections and creating their own Web pages.

By creating your own Web site (or, at least, pages on your school's Web site), you are providing direct access for pupils and parents to the work of the classes you teach. You could use it to post extra snippets of work and puzzles etc and to display pupils' work. You could also include information for parents on the way you teach, homework policies, classroom rules etc.

Although the number of homes with Internet access is still relatively small, you could encourage pupils to use the site while at school and invite parents to browse it on parents' evenings or other occasions when they are in school.

Record keeping

Put an end to scrappy mark books filled with blobs of correction fluid! Use ICT to store records of pupils' attainment and of progress through schemes of work. However, you will probably still want to make use of a daily planner unless you have a computer for personal use in your classroom.

Be aware of how you can link databases and spreadsheets with word-processed documents. This can make report writing easier if you are keeping an ongoing record of achievement of each child in, for example, Word, as well as records of the group's marks in a spreadsheet.

One word of caution. Think about the content of information you keep on a computer that pupils may have access to. Your ICT coordinator will be able to give you advice on data protection/confidentiality considerations.

Databases

Databases are excellent for the storage of schemes of work and information on classes. They can help in the organization of most aspects of your work as a teacher and cut down on the amount of paper you need to accumulate.

Spreadsheets

Spreadsheets have applications for teachers of all subjects. They are particularly useful for keeping track of coursework, forecasting and 'what if' scenarios. Use them in conjunction with ongoing records of achievement and your task at report-writing time is easy!

Health and safety issues

It is important to be aware of health and safety with ICT. Much will, of course, be common sense; nevertheless, repetitive strain injury (RSI) and eyestrain in particular need to be guarded against. You also have a responsibility to ensure that ICT equipment is used safely:

- Make sure you are familiar with your school's policy on health and safety when using ICT.
- Think about workstation design and encourage pupils to make changes to their seating arrangements where possible.
- Teach good postures for sitting (forearms horizontal and parallel with thighs) and encourage children to be aware of the distance between the screen and their eyes.

The BECTa information sheet, 'Health and safety: the safe use of ICT in schools', will be particularly useful here.

Teachernet

The Schools Communications Unit within the DfES runs Teachernet: www. teachernet.gov.uk. There are six main areas of the Web site:

- Teaching and Learning (a gateway to educational resources available on the Internet);
- Management (giving school managers access to key online information);
- Professional Development (bringing together the relevant information on CPD);
- Research (for teachers interested in all aspects of research);
- Education Overview (access to key information of the government's strategy for education in England);
- Useful Sites (sorted alphabetically).

ABOUT PROTECTING YOUR COMPUTER

With so much conflicting information about the extent of the virus problem, it is important to take the risk of damage seriously. Despite the hundreds of thousands of viruses in existence only a few cause 98 per cent of the damage. Take preventative measures by installing anti-virus software on your own machine and restricting the amount of data you transfer from one machine to another. Only use machines allocated for teachers' use when working at school, back up all your work on paper and disk and only accept files from trusted sources. However, it is impossible to reduce the risks of infection completely if you are going to take advantage of the Internet, e-mailing and newsgroups. For information about hoax viruses and useful links, try www.symantec.com.

LOOKING AHEAD

> When teachers stop growing, so do their students.
>
> (Roland Barth)

As you reach the successful conclusion of your induction year you can look ahead to a career in which you will face many challenges, changes and triumphs. There are so many directions you could take and ways you can make a positive impact on the lives of your pupils in a society that now demands creativity and resourcefulness.

Early and continuing professional development

It is a requirement of the Standards for Qualified Teacher Status that teachers 'are motivated and able to take increasing responsibility for their own professional development'. This encompasses a pretty broad range of activities, but, in short, can be taken to mean that you will:

- identify the areas of practice you need to develop;
- set targets for your own improvement;
- convey your learning needs;
- work independently at developing your specialist skills;
- make full use of the possible sources of professional development that exist;
- seek help when appropriate;

- give and receive help, advice and constructive criticism;
- contribute to the development of others.

The early professional development of NQTs is of great importance to the General Teaching Council for England, the government and many other bodies with interests in education. For teachers to be successful educators there is broad acceptance that their training should not end with the induction period and that teachers are most likely to remain in the profession if their early professional development needs are met.

Although the quality of the early professional development that you receive following on from your induction is in part dependent upon the attitude that your school and employers take towards it, you still retain tremendous scope to impact your own development in a positive way.

The government is currently running a pilot programme of early professional development for teachers in their second and third years in the profession. The purpose is to build on the induction period and bolster the support available to teachers at this crucial phase. At the time of writing, there are 12 LEAs involved in the scheme (but keep an eye on www.teachernet.gov.uk/early_professional_development for updated information).

Although each LEA has devised its own plan for the early professional development of post-induction teachers, they are offering broadly similar kinds of support, including:

- school-based activities including action research;
- focus on classroom practice skills as well as management skills;
- peer mentoring/coaching partnerships;
- focused classroom observation;
- pupil tracking;
- subject self-review;
- data analysis;
- action planning.

Recognizing development opportunities

Professional development does not have to mean attending a one-day in-service training course. There are many opportunities for professional learning facing most teachers on a daily basis. These include:

- focused observations of colleagues at work;
- studying your own teaching through video;
- action research;

- distance learning;
- reading professional journals and texts;
- engaging in online discussions and other technology-mediated learning;
- self-directed study perhaps linked to academic awards;
- giving and receiving tutoring and mentoring;
- working with a study or learning team;
- attending 'masterclasses';
- team teaching;
- planning and assessing with colleagues;
- developing resources with colleagues;
- peer coaching;
- collaborative school cluster projects;
- job shadowing;
- researching existing effective practice;
- personal reflection;
- observations and placements in other schools.

The DfEE document *Learning and Teaching* (2001) revealed that when the government consulted on professional development, teachers repeatedly mentioned the following two points as having most impact on their classroom performance: 'opportunities to learn from and with other teachers, in their own or other schools' (by observing, through collaboration and through coaching and mentoring); and 'high quality focused training on specific skill areas, underpinned by excellent teaching materials and direct support to apply their learning back in the classroom'.

If there is a culture of support for professional development at your school then there will be no problem in identifying the opportunities that may face you. If not, a degree of ingenuity might be needed. Remember that a main goal of professional development is to improve classroom practice. The DfEE document *Learning and Teaching* cited research that showed that successful changes in teachers' practice are most likely when continuing professional development involves:

- a focus on specific teaching and learning problems;
- opportunities for teachers to understand the rationale behind new ideas and approaches, to see theory demonstrated in practice and to be exposed to new expertise;
- sustained opportunities to experiment with new ideas and approaches, so that teachers can work out their implications for their own subject, pupils, school and community;

- opportunities for teachers to put their own interpretation of new strategies and ideas to work, building on their existing knowledge and skills;
- coaching and feedback on their professional practice over a period of weeks and months.

ACTION Using knowledge of the style of learning that suits you best, combined with the experience of your induction period, consider the kinds of professional development that you have found most effective. Is there anything that you have not had the opportunity to experience that would further your development? Is there anything that you have learnt but not been able to apply in the context of your classroom? Where would you like your professional development to take you?

ABOUT INDIVIDUAL AND INSTITUTIONAL DEVELOPMENT

Any continuing professional development that you undertake will necessarily need to balance your needs as a learning and reflecting practitioner and the needs of the institution to which you belong. Development priorities should be informed by both to avoid conflict and tension arising.

Career development opportunities

Take a look at the professional development pages on TeacherNet (www. teachernet.gov.uk) and you'll see an extensive and up-to-date list of career development opportunities and links for teachers. These include:

- professional bursaries (for specific individual professional development needs);
- sabbaticals (for a significant period of development);
- Teacher's International Professional Development (for learning about and from overseas schools);
- Advanced Skills Teachers;
- award-bearing training (leading to a recognized postgraduate qualification);
- Best Practice Research Scholarships;
- Fast Track (for accelerated career development).

ABOUT THE CPD 'MINDSET'

The early stage of your career is a key time to harness a sound attitude towards professional development. There is the potential for development each and every day that you are in school, and the teacher who is adept at recognizing when these opportunities occur is the teacher who will ultimately be most effective and successful. Don't get hung up on a quest for perfection though; this is both unachievable and undesirable. Be aware, too, that your work/life balance should not be compromised. Giving thought to the motivations behind your professional development can help to conserve this. Finally, be honest to yourself about what it is that you do well. How can you assist colleagues in their development?

Planning for future directions

Although continuing professional development is largely your responsibility, your school should be ensuring that you have the opportunities to undertake appropriate, valuable development and that you are motivated in this. These questions may also help when planning for your future:

- Where do you instinctively want to go in your career?
- What existing skills do you want to develop? What new skills do you want to pursue?
- What funds are available to you?
- Can you identify distinct short-, medium- and long-term goals?
- Are you happy to be flexible in your goals (given that the experience and skills you gather may lead you in new directions)?
- Do you know where to get any information you may need?

Pacing your targets

As the induction period is so busy, it probably won't be until your second year at the earliest that you start to think about your own target setting for further development. When you do get round to this, pacing is crucial. Expect too much of yourself and your performance will suffer, not enough and you risk stagnation.

If possible, don't depend on future study for anything ('I must complete this MA in two years, as otherwise I won't be able to go for... by my deadline').

ABOUT PERFORMANCE MANAGEMENT

Your early and continuing professional development should not come solely under the heading of 'performance management', although the two are clearly linked in that they should both relate to pupil progress and improvements in professional practice.

The Performance Management System allows for each teacher post-induction to have an annual performance review by his/her line manager to discuss learning and development needs. At the review, one or more development objectives will be set. The DfES (www.teachernet.gov.uk/Standards_Framework/standard-index.cfm) suggests that the following sources can be drawn from when deciding on development objectives:

- feedback from colleagues, a mentor, your line manager or an OFSTED inspector;
- the particular expectations and responsibilities built into your current job, or other posts within your school;
- your career aspirations at this particular point in your career;
- views about how the nature of teaching is changing, or is likely to change over the next few years, and the new skills that this may require;
- research evidence about the characteristics of effective teachers;
- the national standards for teaching that exist, setting out the expectations for effective performance in different roles within a school.

This will keep harmful stress at bay and allow you to work at a pace most suitable for you. Above all, make sure that any further professional development you do above the INSET you are offered responds to issues raised by your induction and Career Entry Profile and serves to fuel your enthusiasm for your career.

There is little value in targets that are not achievable. They will only serve as a source of unnecessary stress and anxiety. When setting targets, try to strike the balance between sensibly stretching yourself and going full out for every experience you have not yet encountered. Be realistic.

For every professional goal you set yourself, set a personal goal too, however small that may be. Don't neglect your non-working life, as the costs are far too high.

Gathering evidence of skills and achievements

> Looking back and evaluating is important. Your own achievement is one of your best inspirations. When you realize you have achieved something, it is one of your most reliable sources of strength.
>
> (Rimpoche Nawang Gehlek)

The phrase 'lifelong learning' is one that all teachers are being encouraged to embrace. Linked to this is the fact that all professional experiences form a valid part of your development; it is possible to learn something positive from every event in your career.

Many schools have devised their own individual professional development record that teachers can fill in and add to throughout the year. These are intended to supplement the Career Entry Profile for NQTs. If your school does not have such a system of individual record keeping, use the framework in the following section to keep track of significant achievements and milestones. It will make any inspections and appraisals you experience significantly easier to prepare for. Acknowledgements for the following ideas must go to Bishop Luffa CE School in Chichester and Davison CE School in Worthing.

ABOUT THE PROCESS OF GATHERING EVIDENCE

The whole exercise of gathering evidence of your skills and achievements should not become a chore. It is a necessary part of moving through any profession and should therefore be considered as an aspect of the maintenance of your work. Aim to update your records on a regular basis (perhaps once a month) so that the time you spend on the task is minimized. Don't wait until the end of a term when your energy and enthusiasm are likely to be at their lowest

Individual professional development record

There only needs to be a maximum of three parts to this record, the final part of which could be replaced by the Career Entry Profile as appropriate. Create a file that you can add to easily and that can slip into your portfolio (see Chapter 2).

Start with a current CV including your name, all contact details, all your qualifications, both academic and otherwise, the institutions that awarded them and when. Also include your full employment history (not just in teaching) and brief outlines of previous job descriptions, quantifiable achievements and transferable skills.

The second section should include your professional development experiences, and how they have impacted your work and understanding. Such experiences need not simply be courses you have attended, but may include anything that has contributed to your professional skills and knowledge. Think about these suggestions:

- curriculum and departmental meetings;
- advice passed on from other staff members;
- INSET;
- lesson observations;
- visits from LEA advisers;
- secondments and exchanges;
- visits to other schools;
- conversations with teachers from other schools;
- job shadowing;
- ICT training;
- cross-curricular meetings, eg SEN and ICT.

The impact of such experiences could initiate changes in the way you work, the way you respond to colleagues and the way you perceive your own professional development. You could put your findings under three headings: date, event and impact.

How to record professional development

Date 3 July 2002
Event Observation of Bob Hill's ICT lesson with year 10
Impact By not attempting to have all 30 pupils on task 100 per cent of the time, Bob utilized the skills of the more able pupils to assist those who needed extra help. In this way, all pupils were able to maximize the learning potential from the lesson. The way the hour flowed showed me that children appreciate the opportunity to test what they have learnt.

If your school requires you to complete INSET reports, you could file them in this section too. Alternatively, report on INSET courses using the above format. By recognizing how much you can learn from a variety of sources, you can realize how much you are able to help others.

The final section should cover your professional targets. For teachers with a Career Entry Profile, this part is unnecessary but, for others, this is a good opportunity to draw together your personal goals and those that have been identified from assessments and performance management. You could use the format shown in Figure 11.1 for each goal.

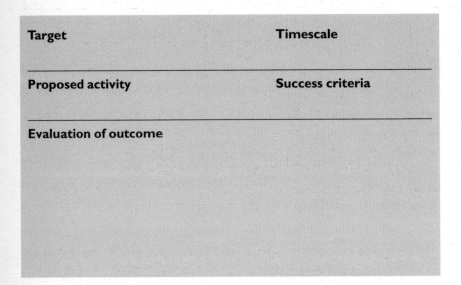

Target   **Timescale**

Proposed activity   **Success criteria**

Evaluation of outcome

Figure 11.1 *How to record your goals*

Changing posts within your school

Well is it known that ambition can creep as well as soar.

(Edmund Burke)

It can be possible (but not always advisable) for NQTs to move up the career ladder during the first year of teaching or in preparation for the second year. While it is important to consolidate, there are many opportunities for taking on responsibilities of varying degrees. For the greatest chance of success, always think about why you want to progress.

Possible areas for promotion

For those keen to develop their work in a particular subject area, the obvious choice is to work up the departmental ladder. This could mean taking a second- or third-in-command post in your subject area or, if your school is small enough, it could mean taking a head of department or subject coordinator post.

If you don't want to take on a different post, but would like to take on more responsibility, talk to your line manager about working on a specific project such as writing exam papers or the development of a scheme of work. This can be a gentler route into middle management.

Outside your subject area, there are many opportunities to enhance your responsibilities. All schools have a pastoral team, and there are usually posts of varying degrees of importance to be had, such as head of house, head of year or head of school. Again, if this is your chosen route of promotion, don't feel you have to achieve it in one step. Shadow the person who is already in post to see if there is an aspect of his/her job you would like to take on. Alternatively, there will be opportunities to coordinate many cross-curricular aspects of the school, such as special needs, ICT, literacy and numeracy, citizenship and personal and social education. The TTA has documents on the standards required of personnel in key middle-management positions that will give you a clear idea of what is involved in those areas in which you are interested. Visit www.canteach.gov.uk/community/standards/index.htm for further information.

ABOUT WANTING TO CONSOLIDATE

With the current trend in the teaching profession to progress, diversify and push for professional development early in your career, it can be easy to be swept along, assuming that onwards and upwards is where you really want to be. There is nothing wrong with consolidating your position for a few years before even thinking about the next step, rather than leaping into a promotion simply because 'you would be foolish not to'.

However, the Standards for Qualified Teacher Status do state that teachers must uphold the professional code of the General Teaching Council for England by demonstrating that 'They are able to improve their own teaching, by evaluating it, learning from the effective practice of others and from evidence. They are motivated and able to take increasing responsibility for their own professional development.'

MOVING TO ANOTHER SCHOOL

If you have decided to move to another school to continue your career, remember that you are in a more secure position now than you were as an NQT starting your first post. Consider what you have learnt in your first year, and the resources you have developed – all of this can be transferred to your new job.

Although your new school will have its own schemes of work, handbooks and ways of functioning, it is the movement of teachers around the country, along with the ideas that they bring, that prevents schools from stagnating. Remember to take these items with you to your new school:

- all the resources you have produced during your first year;
- copies of other resources you have used;
- all records of your professional development;
- copies of any handbooks you feel may be useful.

Don't be tempted to reinvent the wheel every time you join a new school!

ABOUT FACING NEW CHALLENGES

Although you have a whole year of teaching experience under your belt, it can be easy to feel like the 'youngster' again when you join a new school. There will be new ways of working and probably a new school day that you'll have to become familiar with, not to mention new classes to get to know. Don't expect that just because you don't have the excuse of being an NQT that you have to know everything. You should still be assigned a mentor and be given a thorough induction programme. See these new challenges as learning opportunities and don't expect to absorb everything at once.

AN EASTER APPRAISAL

One potentially negative aspect of working within the teaching profession is that moves between jobs tend to take place at set times through the year, and most often in time for the start of the new academic year in September. This can lead to teachers feeling trapped in a job for years at a time, if they don't take the opportunity to move at the appropriate times in the year. For this reason it is important to do regular personal appraisals of the way you feel about the profession and your job, to ensure that you give yourself the opportunity to move on if you want to.

ABOUT THE FAST TRACK

The Fast Track Teaching Programme is an accelerated development programme for teachers. In identifying the most talented teachers, it seeks to give intensive professional development to steer them to their full potential more quickly than might otherwise be possible.

Being on the Fast Track Programme means gaining a wide variety of experience in different settings, including schools that are in special measures or in challenging circumstances. By moving schools regularly (about every two years or so), the aim is that these teachers can become leaders more rapidly.

Teachers on the Fast Track get additional development opportunities and may make 'double jumps' up the pay scale with excellent performance. You do not need to be nominated by anyone in order to apply for the Fast Track. However, your application will need to be supported by a reference, which usually needs to be from your headteacher or performance management leader.

For further information on the Fast Track Programme, take a look at www.fasttrackteaching.gov.uk. You can also e-mail recruitmentteam@fast trackteaching.gov.uk or telephone 08000 562266.

During your first year of teaching, the best time to do one of these appraisals is during the Easter holidays. This gives you time to move on if that is what you want to do. In subsequent years of teaching, this appraisal can be done earlier in the year, allowing you longer to make changes.

Assessing your first two terms

This appraisal is for your eyes only. Don't spend more than an hour on it and treat it not as another aspect of your Career Entry Profile or a formal school appraisal but as your private opportunity to assess your position.

The following questions will help to focus your mind on your levels of satisfaction in your job:

- What have been the best events of my first two terms?
- What contributed to these events?
- What have been the worst events of my first two terms?
- What contributed to these events?
- What job satisfaction do I get?
- What would I like to change about my job?
- What factors make it difficult for me to achieve my duties?
- Does my current job allow me to move in the direction that I want my career to go?
- What other opportunities does my job offer me?
- What could I do to help me to achieve my objectives?
- What could my managers do to help me to achieve my objectives?
- Am I thriving on the demands of my job?

Is this the job for you?

It is quite usual for new teachers to go through a period of doubt about their chosen career. This can be compounded by feelings of exasperation at the length of time it takes to qualify and the amount of energy it takes to perform the functions of a teacher. Don't feel disheartened if you have these thoughts. It is virtually impossible to prepare for the emotional and physical investment you will put into your job, which is why it is so important to ask yourself at regular intervals 'Is this the job for me?' The answer may not necessarily be 'no'.

Unfortunately, nobody can help you answer this question. Family members, partners and friends may encourage you one way or the other, but only you will be able to understand the thrill you get from a teaching day going well (when others may say to you 'How can you bear to do all that preparation every evening?') or the exhaustion you feel when, after a disappointing day, you still have 60 books to mark (when others say 'You lucky thing – a job for life and all those long holidays!').

Put yourself first, use your personal appraisal and know that you are making the decision that inspires you most.

Options to choose

Still round the corner there may wait,
A new road or a secret gate.

(J R R Tolkien)

If you conclude that teaching is the career for you, your only considerations are your future professional consolidation and development. Use your personal appraisal and your Career Entry Profile to discuss with mentors and colleagues how you can progress.

However, if you feel you would like to move on from teaching, there are several steps you can take.

If teaching is not for you

Under no circumstances should you consider this decision to be weak or negative in any way. There are very few people who stay within the same career all their lives, and fewer still whom this will genuinely suit.

There are three options open to you at this point:

- Decide to stay on at your school for another year. After the upheavals of joining a new institution and completing the induction year, not to mention all the materials you have had to devise from scratch, the next year may be significantly easier. It may be possible to negotiate some changes that could ease your way, or ensure that you are teaching the same year groups, to minimize the time you will have to spend on resource development. Talk to your induction tutor/mentor or confidant about the best way to go about this.
- Reduce your teaching load to part-time to allow you time to pursue other career options.
- Start to make steps to leave. Take advantage of any careers counselling that may be on offer from your LEA and county careers service and utilize the information on careers in your local library. Be aware of your emotions while you are doing this. Don't slip into despondency or feelings of failure. As you close one door, another has to open.

If you do decide to leave the profession, but feel there may be a possibility of returning to it in the future, register yourself with the TTA's Keeping In Touch Programme (see Chapter 1 for further information).

Career satisfaction

For all its focus on improving your classroom performance and the achievement of your pupils, continuing and early professional development is not successful if it does not contribute significantly to your career satisfaction as well. If your need to thrive in your job is central to your plans for professional development, you can maximize the buzz you'll get from teaching and ensure that you'll reach the places you want to be.

Although external factors affect our career satisfaction – factors such as how well our managers reward/praise us for our work, and the opportunities that we may be given to link career satisfaction with professional development – we can take action, regardless of the circumstances in which we find ourselves, to ensure that we can work with vitality. These ideas may help:

- Adapt systems, within reason, to suit your way of working.
- Recognize the close connection between *professional* and *personal* development.
- Fully participate in any reviews of progress you may have.
- Link your work with your personality – are you spending most time on what suits you best?
- Recognize and celebrate (in some way) your achievements and progress.
- Spend time with like-minded colleagues, including those from other schools.
- Assist others in their professional development whenever appropriate.

PART V

Frequently asked questions

*'A teacher affects eternity; he can
never tell where his influence stops.'*
Henry Brooks Adams.

CHAPTER 12

Before getting a job

A teacher affects eternity; he can never tell where his influence stops.

(Henry Brooks Adams)

? *I have been asked to attend an interview and have been told that I may have to teach part of a lesson. Should I be given more detail before the day?*

It would be extremely poor practice if you arrived on the day and had not been told the age range you were going to be teaching, how many would be in the class and how long the lesson would be. You should certainly be given more detail before the day. The purpose of practical sessions in interviews is for members of the panel to assess how well you interact with pupils, whether you ask probing, stretching questions and if you can judge the ability of pupils and adjust your delivery accordingly. The usual format for this is for the interviewee to take a small group of pupils for approximately 20 minutes.

? *I have attended several interviews without success and feel sure that my nerves affect my performance. How can I remedy this?*

Preparation can help to relieve anxiety. Find out as much about the school as you can before the interview by looking at its Web site and OFSTED reports, and by closely analysing the information the school sends you. Pay attention to your diet for the few days prior to the interview and aim to avoid stimulants such as caffeine, chocolate, alcohol, sugar and nicotine, as these can make you feel 'hyped' and contribute to feelings of anxiety. Use positive self-talk so that negative thinking doesn't take hold. Affirmations such as 'I perform very well in interviews' or 'I answer the questions I am asked with ease' can work wonders, as can visualizing yourself being successful. Keep a bottle of Bach 'Rescue Remedy' or something similar (available at many wholefood outlets) in your pocket and take as directed; it can be extremely calming. A massage the day before an interview will also help to relax you.

If this doesn't work, ask your tutor from your ITT provider or a trusted friend or relative to take you through some mock interviews.

? *I have not managed to secure employment for September. Will this affect my career prospects?*

Not at all, providing you use the time gaining additional experience. Once your financial position is sorted out (you could get a temporary part-time job, or sign on), you could organize some voluntary work in a local school. If there is a 'small school' near you, voluntary work there would give you valuable insight into the alternatives available. You could also look into special schools. Add any additional experience you gain while job seeking to your CV and Career Entry Profile. When you do find a job and start mid-year, find out *at the interview* what the implications will be for your induction year – when will you be deemed to have started and completed your induction? Will you be given any additional support? Sometimes delays like this can be a blessing in disguise. You may not be in full-time employment, but what additional experience has it allowed you to get? You will probably find you will go for very different jobs as a result.

? *I have been offered a job but, as a mature entrant to the profession with 10 years' experience in industry, I am not happy with the salary I have been offered.*

As an NQT you are entitled to be placed at point M1 on the salary scale. However, your school has the discretion to reward you for previous experience that it deems to be relevant and, in principle, there is no restriction on where on the scale you can be placed up to point M6. Thereafter, and depending on satisfactory performance, you are entitled to automatic progression up the scale each year (up to point M6), providing you have worked in the previous year for at least 26 weeks as a teacher in employment. Progression beyond point M6 is performance-related, and not automatic. Your school will have a salaries policy that will cover the award of points for non-teaching experience and it really is at the discretion of your employers as to what points you will be awarded. However, your union will be able to offer advice on what you should be paid and may also offer to negotiate an improved salary on your behalf. This is probably your best option.

Having completed my training, I am not sure whether I want to enter the teaching profession. What are my options?

Having got this far, it would be a good idea to complete successfully an induction period. At least you won't have that ahead of you in future if you subsequently decide to teach. This would also give you a greater insight into the profession, as being a teacher in your own right is very different from being a student. Aim to get a job in a school other than where you did your training for a greater breadth of experience.

However, if you are *sure* that teaching is not for you, there would be little point in forcing yourself to pursue a path that is so obviously wrong. Take some careers guidance from your ITT provider for ideas on what could be your next step. Above all, view your decision *positively*. If you have cause for regret, perhaps it would be better to complete an induction period.

I have been offered a job but have another interview in a school in which I think I would rather work in a few days. What can I do?

This is a difficult situation. It is unlikely that the school that offered you a job will wait for you to be offered another and then weigh up the odds! You can ask for time to consider the first offer, or be totally honest and explain your dilemma. Unfortunately, the most likely outcome of this sort of situation involves taking an empty-handed leap of faith and rejecting the first offer in the hope that you will pass the second interview. With so much resting on the induction period, it is really important that you choose your first post wisely. Take heart in the fact that you have been successful at one interview.

I have been asked to undertake a significant amount of preparation during the summer holiday before my first term. Is this normal?

The expectations of newly qualified teachers regarding preparation before they begin their first term vary tremendously from school to school. A general 'rule' to follow is that at least 75 per cent of any holiday should be just that, pure holiday, *once you have started work*. You will probably not be paid for the holiday before your first term so if you need to earn money during that period you may not have time for schoolwork. However, you may feel more relaxed about starting your new job if you have done some preparation. The key is balance. If you feel uncomfortable about the demands that have been made of you before you are on the payroll, simply say that you have had to arrange other work commitments but will make sure you have read and digested all the necessary handbooks. You do need to think about the implications for your future workload if you are prepared to work for free!

? *I have accepted a job in my teaching practice school and will be teaching a class that I taught while I was training. I am concerned that pupils will not take me seriously as a 'proper teacher'.*

This is a common concern, but one that is not necessary. Pupils have remarkably short memories regarding such things and, once the summer holidays have passed, you will not be in their 'student' pigeon-hole! However, you will still need to spend time asserting your classroom rules and systems of reward and sanction so that they know how you work and what it will be like to have *you* as their teacher. Don't feel as though you have to do things in the same way as their previous teacher. This can be more tempting if you actually worked with their last teacher and you may even find yourself mimicking him/her subconsciously. Simply focus on asserting yourself.

? *I would like to do some supply teaching when I qualify as I am not sure where I want to work. Will this count towards my induction period.*

Supply work can complicate your induction period and it is best to avoid it in this important year if at all possible. However, if you do take on supply engagements, they need to be of a term or more in length to count towards your induction period *and you may only do this for a year and a term from the time you are awarded QTS*. Thereafter, all engagements must count towards induction.

Supply teachers should be treated as permanent employees for the purposes of induction. Advice to NQTs must therefore be to avoid supply teaching until the induction period has been satisfactorily completed if this is possible.

? *Do I need a DfES number in order to teach in England?*

No. The numbers are issued by the DfES Pensions Team to teachers paying into the pension scheme. You just need Qualified Teacher Status and to be registered with the General Teaching Council in order to teach in England.

CHAPTER 13

Once in your first post

? *My school doesn't seem to have an induction programme set up. Does this matter?*

Your induction into your new job and the profession generally is vitally important. You should be receiving extensive support and training to ensure that you pass your induction year. If you are not receiving a formal induction this will have implications for your future in the profession and you should contact your union representative and the named person at your LEA as soon as possible. It would also be a good idea to document your concerns for future reference. Talk to your induction tutor/mentor and your tutor from your initial teacher training provider for more ideas about improving your situation. Do not let this go on. Your school has a statutory responsibility to provide the support that will give you the best possible opportunity to pass your induction year.

? *I do not have a good relationship with my induction tutor/mentor. Does this matter?*

This is a problem for several reasons. Your aim should be to build good working relationships with all your colleagues. Also, an induction tutor/mentor is often the gatekeeper to additional INSET training and support and can make or break an NQT's experience of joining the teaching profession. With so much resting on the induction year, it simply isn't worth not having an excellent working relationship with your induction tutor/mentor. That said, if you really don't get on, perhaps your induction tutor/mentor does not have the skills (or time) necessary to perform the job to professional standards. Do talk to your induction tutor/mentor about your concerns, or, if that seems inappropriate, talk to a trusted colleague. If there are other NQTs at your school who share your induction tutor/mentor, talk to them about how they feel. It may be necessary to mention this to the person (usually a deputy headteacher) who has responsibilities for all NQTs. Again, do not let the situation go on indefinitely; it needs to be resolved as soon as possible.

? I have been assigned a mentor but not an induction tutor. Does this matter?

There is not any consistency in schools over the use of the terms 'induction tutor' and 'mentor'. Many use them interchangeably and, to a great extent, it really does not matter what name is given to the role. As an NQT, you are entitled to have a single person with responsibility for getting you through the induction period and for supporting you through your transition from training to employment. As long as you know who this person is, there should not be a problem. You may also have several colleagues who take on the role of professional 'buddy' or mentor. If you are still unsure whether your entitlements are being met, contact the named person with responsibilities for NQTs at your LEA.

? I have not been given a reduced timetable because my school cannot afford to give me this extra time. Is this OK?

Absolutely not! Your school will have been given additional funding (via the Standards Fund) specifically for the induction of NQTs. If there is none left, it has been badly mismanaged. If this is what you have been told, contact the named person at your LEA as soon as possible. Not having a reduced timetable has serious implications for your chances of successfully completing the induction period; if your school cannot give you induction time, how is it going to afford non-contact time for your induction tutor, who will need it to observe and support you? Remember, there are no second attempts at induction. This needs to be sorted out without delay.

? I want to move schools before the end of my induction period. Is this possible?

If you possibly can, get through the first year in the same school to give you a good chance of passing the induction period. Once this is completed successfully, you are free to move without risking complicating this important time. If there is no alternative but to move, your new school will have to pick up where your old school left off (providing you leave after one or two terms). Your original headteacher must retain all the documentation relating to your induction so that it can be passed on to your new headteacher.

? A pupil/parent has made a complaint about me. What should I do?

This is a relatively common occurrence so don't feel inadequate in any way, unless there really is cause for complaint about your actions. The usual explanation is a misunderstanding, and a skilful headteacher will be able to discern this and resolve the situation with no ill feeling. As soon as you are told of the complaint, take some time to jot down exactly what you perceive the situation to be. If possible, talk to your union about the complaint. You should be given the opportunity to relate your interpretation of events to an impartial listener.

If your headteacher does have cause to talk about your conduct, you're not the first new teacher and certainly won't be the last that this has happened to. There is a great deal to become familiar with in the first few years of teaching and you should treat such a pep talk as a learning experience – one that may even enable you to become a better teacher. If you feel disgruntled, talk to your headteacher – he/she should be able to explain the situation to your satisfaction. If not, talk to your union representative again.

? My head of department seems to be making unfair demands of me.

This is a common complaint and one that can be easily remedied.

First, keep a record of the expectations that have been made of you for future reference. It would also be a good idea to talk to other NQTs at your school to find out what their experiences are and, of course, talk to your induction tutor/mentor. This will help you to gain some perspective on the situation, as it can be easy to feel 'put upon'. Next, employ some skills of assertion! Explain to your head of department that you feel that if you take anything else on at the moment you will not be performing your tasks to adequate standards. You feel the need to consolidate what you have to do and focus on fewer tasks. If this doesn't help to relieve the pressure on you, talk to your induction tutor/

mentor or a trusted colleague to see if he/she will take up your case for you. Try your union as a last resort.

? *I teach many children with special educational needs and there does not seem to be adequate learning support in place for them. This is putting a great deal of pressure on me. What can I do?*

The first thing to do is identify exactly who has extra needs in your classes (this should have been done for you by your SENCO). Next, jot down some ideas on why support is needed in your lessons in particular. Do you rely on the use of a lot of equipment? Does your subject require heavy emphasis on writing and reading? You are expected to do a certain degree of differentiation in your lessons but, if this means you are writing additional schemes of work simply to accommodate the children with learning difficulties, you will soon burn yourself out. Talk to your SENCO about the problems. He/she will be able to give you some ideas on how to manage the extra needs in your classes and is also the person able to allocate additional non-teaching support to particular classes. Lean on your SEN department for help, differentiating materials etc. By raising this issue, you have shown your commitment to all the abilities in your classes and have opened up the possibilities of a more extensive working partnership with colleagues in the SEN department.

? *One particular child is making my lessons a misery. How can I deal with this?*

Whatever the age of the child, talking to him/her and explaining what it is about his/her behaviour (not personality) that you find unacceptable is always a good place to start. You need to establish clear expectations of the child and even clearer consequences for misbehaviour. Discuss with the child the rewards and sanctions you have in mind (and every opportunity for praise must be taken) and arrange a trial period of a week, after which you will have another talk. When you are getting to the point of hating a child, you need to take a step back and focus on finding solutions. It would be a good idea to talk to your induction tutor/mentor or head of department about your difficulties and the ways that you are attempting to resolve them. There may be established systems in your school for dealing with such situations that you can lean on. Never underestimate the effectiveness of being honest with children about their behaviour and your disappointment. You could also involve the child's parents by writing to them and outlining your expectations for improvements in the child's behaviour (clear this with your head of department or induction tutor/ mentor first). However, do something sooner rather than later, before you reach the point of just wanting the child to be removed from your lessons. Teachers who also teach or have taught the child will be a good source of support too.

? Am I within my rights to refuse to teach a child?

According to the DfES, there are no national guidelines on this. It is a local decision, so your LEA would deem whether a child is 'unteachable' and make other arrangements for his/her education. However, your induction tutor should ensure that you are given the support you need if you have a particularly difficult child so, if you get to the point of wanting to refuse to teach the child, there has been a failure of communication in your induction.

? While I was reprimanding one of my year 10 pupils, she became verbally aggressive and shoved past me on her way out of the room. I didn't make anything of it at the time, but I now feel that I should have. How can I prevent this from happening again?

Although you didn't follow up the incident at the time it is still important to record (to the best of your ability) what happened, what the contributing factors were and what, if anything, has happened since. Discuss the matter with your induction tutor/mentor, including any feelings you may have of anxiety for your safety. It would also be a good idea to discuss the incident with the girl in question (using some of the ideas in Chapter 6).

? I feel as though I am drowning under a sea of paperwork and have just been given a batch of reports to write. I simply don't have time to do everything. What can I do?

It can be very difficult to pace your work in your first year. Time management skills will develop as you get used to the rhythm of each term, but it is no failure to find yourself swamped from time to time. You will have to lean on others for a while. Ask your induction tutor/mentor if anyone can help you with marking and preparation to free up some time to focus on the reports. Some headteachers recognize the added pressures that report time brings and arrange for additional non-contact time. Ask your induction tutor/mentor if this is a possibility for you. At very busy times, you are perfectly justified in minimizing the amount of written work you ask classes to do and making sure that any homework you give will not require you to mark it outside lesson time. It is also worth remembering that at such times you may need to look after yourself a little more so that you don't fall ill when it all dies down.

? A group of children in my tutor group has been boasting about their drug-taking antics. What should I do with this knowledge?

While the children could well be bluffing, especially as they don't seem to want to hide what they are doing, you must take this seriously. Talk to your head of year about what you have heard and take any advice you are given. It may be that the parents will be contacted or some drugs-awareness counsellors brought in to focus on the issue. The key here is to share the knowledge you have with someone of higher authority than you.

? I have been asked to take on additional responsibilities and have only just completed my first two terms. I know I shouldn't take anything else on just yet, but don't want adversely to affect my career prospects. What can I do?

There are many issues here. Firstly, if your seniors have asked you to take on the work they clearly believe you can achieve it. However, if you want to focus on your induction year, you should not be put under undue pressure to take on extra responsibilities. Talk to your induction tutor/mentor about the situation, as he/she will probably have been consulted in the first place. Do also find out how much of a financial incentive is going to be provided. This shouldn't sway your decision, but it will give you insight into the way that your management team is working. As for fears for future career progression at the school, it would be perfectly reasonable to decline the offer of extra responsibilities in you first year and extremely unreasonable for this to affect your career prospects. If you express your desire to consolidate the vast amount you are learning in your first year for the sake of improving your teaching, and that you would be happy to consider the proposition again in the near future (perhaps six months' time), there should be no problem. If you feel that a tense atmosphere has been created, talk to your union representative. It may be necessary to document any conversations you have in case of a future need to refer to them.

I have been asked to take an assembly and I'm dreading it. I'm not a Christian and don't feel able to pretend for the sake of the assembly. Is there an alternative? Are there any online resources I can use to help me plan it?

Although collective worship in schools should be 'wholly or mainly of a broadly Christian character', only a majority (ie at least 51 per cent) of acts of worship in each term must meet that requirement, and secular assemblies can be held as well. In addition, you can include secular material promoting spiritual, moral, social and cultural development in any act of worship. Visit www.humanism.org.uk for further ideas. Other sites to peruse include www.amnesty.org.uk/student/index.shtml (Amnesty International's Web site) and www.oneworld.org/ (the Save the Children site). For a broadly Christian viewpoint, visit www.assemblies.org.uk (provided by the Society for the Promotion of Christian Knowledge).

I am coming to the end of my induction year and wonder if I should be looking to change schools to broaden my experience.

There is no law stating that teachers must keep moving from school to school as otherwise their experience will be severely limited, but it is worth thinking about the benefits of not teaching at the same school for years and years. A consolidation period of two or three years is perfectly acceptable and advisable in many cases, especially if you are happy in your school. Beyond that you may want to start thinking about promotion and additional responsibilities and, unless there are openings at your school, you will have to move on. Comfortable as it may seem to stay put, your next school may be a vast improvement on your first, and the simple fact that it is a different institution will mean that you will broaden your experiences. The decision is yours.

I would like to be able to lend materials and equipment freely to pupils, but so much is being stolen. What can I do?

The best approach is to have a formal system of lending things out. Use a book to record exactly who has what and when, and remember to note when the item is returned. This may seem complicated, but it will allow you to see who can be trusted and who needs reminding to return your property. It would be wonderful to be able to trust everyone but using a system like this helps to avoid disappointment.

The underlying issue of trust and responsibility needs to be addressed frequently with classes that don't always return the property that is loaned to them. This could be effectively covered in every subject under the banner of citizenship.

? *I keep hearing about creativity in schools but I don't really know what this means. How can I find out more?*

There is a lot being written now about this issue, particularly following the introduction of the revised National Curriculum, which, it is hoped, offers teachers greater flexibility in encouraging pupils to explore their creative potential. The bottom line regarding creativity in schools is based in preparing children for the workplace of the future with its global communications and rapid pace of technological change. Hand in hand with creativity come thinking skills, again given greater prominence in the revised curriculum. The current thinking is that creativity, thinking processes and thinking skills need to be taught explicitly. Some schools choose to do this within specific subjects while others infuse them in a cross-curricular approach.

Creativity in Education by Anna Craft *et al* (2001, published by Continuum) would be a good place to start further reading. There is also a forum for debating, investigating and exploring the nature of creativity in all and any educational contexts hosted at www.open.ac.uk/education-and-languages/creativity/index.html. *Teaching Children to Think* by Robert Fisher (published in 1995 by Stanley Thornes) is another useful read.

? *I'd like to teach my pupils some playground games to help them to develop cooperation outside the classroom. Where can I get ideas?*

The Internet is a good source of inspiration for playground games from around the world. Take a look at www.gameskidsplay.net for starters.

Now that citizenship has been introduced in schools, will I have to teach it even though I am a science teacher?

It is up to individual schools to decide how they organize the teaching and delivery of the programmes of study for citizenship. Many schools will not be marginalizing citizenship as a new subject but will look at the role that every subject and every teacher can play in this dimension of education. It is therefore highly likely that you will be involved in teaching citizenship matters as they relate to your area of expertise, just as you do with numeracy, literacy and ICT. Any subject associations that you belong to will undoubtedly have resources relating to citizenship and there are many specialist publications available now (see Appendix 8, 'Useful addresses' and Appendix 9, 'Further reading'). As with all elements of education that cross subject boundaries, it is best to become as involved as possible in order to enrich both your lessons and your relationships with the pupils you teach.

CHAPTER 14

On matters personal

? *I will be moving to a new area but have been unable to find suitable accommodation. Where can I go for help?*

Your first port of call should be the education personnel department of your LEA. They are familiar with the difficulties faced by NQTs moving to new areas and some even have county or borough accommodation available for rental. Another alternative is to speak to your regional union representative. Relocation packages are available in some circumstances from some LEAs.

? *After teaching in my school for nearly a term, I still feel like a newcomer. What can I do?*

It is likely that you will feel 'new' until another NQT joins your school. If this really bothers you, talk to your induction tutor/mentor about ways you can establish yourself more firmly in your position in the school. Another alternative is to enjoy the feeling – as soon as you get into your second year you'll be treated as part of the furniture and colleagues won't be able to remember if you've been at the school one year, two years or 10 years! What's more, neither will you!

? *I can't afford the deposit for my accommodation. What can I do?*

This is extremely common and it is no secret that teachers in their first few years struggle financially, as they try to juggle student loans with living and professional costs. Most banks are sympathetic to this plight and will arrange for a loan. Some particularly thoughtful LEAs will give an advance on salary for this purpose, but they are in the minority. Your LEA's education personnel department is a good place to start.

I've heard that there is help for newly qualified teachers for buying a property. How can I find out more?

There is a scheme called the Starter Home Initiative, which is run by the Office of the Deputy Prime Minister (ODPM). It has been designed to help key workers such as teachers, nurses and the police to buy homes in areas where high house prices are prohibitive. For further information, visit the ODPM Web site: www.housing.odpm.gov.uk.

My schoolwork has taken over my life and I don't seem to have a social life any more. How can I make changes?

This is actually more serious than it seems. All work and no play makes Jack extremely dull, not to mention Jack's lessons. It also has grave implications for mental and physical health. Sit down with your induction tutor/mentor and work out where you can ease up on your planning, preparation and marking. The first year of teaching is difficult and time-consuming, but you should be able to have at least one full day off at the weekend and at least one evening during the week. Not only that, but you should aim to limit the time you spend working in the evenings and stick to that limit. Long hours lead to increased stress levels, which lead to reduced performance and health problems. Get friends and family to keep an eye on you and aim to go on at least one social outing a week. You may also like to join a relaxation class, as this will mean you are not only 'off duty' but learning a valuable skill as well.

I am thinking of opting out of the teachers' pension scheme to help free up some money for bills. Is this wise?

Not under any circumstances. It is not the place of this book to offer financial advice, but it is generally accepted that teachers should pay in to the superannuation scheme as soon as they start in the profession and pay additional voluntary contributions (AVCs) as soon as possible after. Your union will be able to offer pension ideas and may be able to put you in touch with a financial adviser. Don't take advice from someone who is not an independent financial adviser – the world of pensions is extremely complex and there is a tremendous amount of misinformation floating around. Opting out of a pension scheme is usually interpreted as being misguided and short-termist, unless you know of a private scheme offering considerably better terms. That said, some teachers choose to opt out so that they can invest in an ethical pension. If this interests you, seek advice from an independent financial adviser specializing in ethical investments. You might also want to visit www.dfes.gov.uk/teachers_pensions and www.teacherspensions.co.uk (or telephone Capita Teachers' Pensions on 01325 745746).

? My headteacher has told me that my clothing is inappropriate. Do I have to accept it?

There are several issues here. First, you need to establish whether your clothing really is inappropriate or whether your headteacher simply doesn't like your style. Take some advice from the relevant union representative in your school. He/she will be familiar with the dress code of the school and will be able to help you discern whether or not your headteacher is being unreasonable. Secondly, how important is it to you that you wear clothes that upset your boss? Perhaps, in the interests of making a good impression, you should conform to your school's standards. Don't worry that your headteacher has had cause to correct you – that is part of the job after all!

? I seem to be catching every cough and cold that's around. What can I do?

The sheer number of people you are interacting with as a teacher means that your body has to fight off millions of germs every day. The fact that you are succumbing to so many of them indicates that your immune system is not as effective as it could be. Aim to boost immunity by taking care of your diet (emphasis on fresh fruit and vegetables), getting plenty of early nights, drinking fresh filtered water as opposed to caffeinated drinks and taking echinacea supplements, available from a good chemist or health-food shop. You should also aim to restrict your working time so that you can increase the amount of rest you get. Doing this over a period of a few weeks should see great improvements in your health and energy levels.

? *One of the colleagues I have to work with constantly undermines me, resulting in me feeling inadequate. How can I tackle this behaviour?*

It would be a good idea to talk to your induction tutor/mentor about this as it sounds as though this colleague is employing bullying tactics when he/she communicates with you. Explain what your concerns are and document any conversations you have with the colleague that result in you feeling inadequate. Make sure you refute all unfair claims made against you and contact Redress for further advice (see Appendix 9). It is important that you take steps to improve this situation as persistent criticism can seriously affect your performance and add unnecessarily to stress and anxiety levels.

? *I suspect I am being unfairly discriminated against. Is there anything I can do?*

The first thing you should do is document any situations that cause you to feel discriminated against. Write everything down so that when you talk to someone about it you have actual examples to refer to with dates and times. Next, read some of the Department of Trade and Industry factsheets about discrimination to help you determine whether or not that is what you are suffering. You may be interested in 'Disability discrimination in employment', 'Racial discrimination in employment' and 'Sex discrimination and equal pay', available to order from the DTI Web site: www.dti.gov.uk. Your union will also be able to give you advice on how to tackle your situation, as will your induction tutor/mentor. Try not to let this affect your work, although this can be unavoidable. By talking to colleagues you may gain some valuable support.

? *I am a smoker who has been told I can't smoke on the school premises any more. Is there anything I can do about this?*

No, your employer is acting within the law in disallowing smoking on school premises. If you need to smoke during the school day and your school does not have a smoking room, find somewhere off site where pupils won't observe you.

Appendix 1

STANDARDS FOR THE AWARD OF QUALIFIED TEACHER STATUS

1. Professional values and practice

Those awarded Qualified Teacher Status must understand and uphold the professional code of the General Teaching Council for England by demonstrating all of the following.

1.1 They have high expectations of all pupils; respect their social, cultural, linguistic, religious and ethnic backgrounds; and are committed to raising their educational achievement.

1.2 They treat pupils consistently, with respect and consideration, and are concerned for their development as learners.

1.3 They demonstrate and promote the positive values, attitudes and behaviour that they expect from their pupils.

1.4 They can communicate sensitively and effectively with parents and carers, recognising their roles in pupils' learning, and their rights, responsibilities and interests in this.

1.5 They can contribute to, and share responsibility in, the corporate life of schools.[1]

1.6 They understand the contribution that support staff and other professionals make to teaching and learning.

1.7 They are able to improve their own teaching, by evaluating it, learning from the effective practice of others and from evidence. They are motivated and able to take increasing responsibility for their own professional development.

1.8 They are aware of, and work within, the statutory frameworks relating to teachers' responsibilities.

2. Knowledge and understanding

Those awarded Qualified Teacher Status must demonstrate all of the following.

2.1 They have a secure knowledge and understanding of the subject(s)[2] they are trained to teach. For those qualifying to teach secondary pupils this knowledge and understanding should be at a standard equivalent to degree level.

In relation to specific phases, this includes:

a. For the Foundation Stage they know and understand the aims, principles, six areas of learning and early learning goals described in the QCA/DfEE Curriculum Guidance for the Foundation Stage and, for Reception children, the frameworks, methods and expectations set out in the National Numeracy and Literacy Strategies.

b. For Key Stage 1 and/or 2, they know and understand the curriculum for each of the National Curriculum core subjects and the frameworks, methods and expectations set out in the National Literacy and Numeracy Strategies. They have sufficient understanding of a range of work across the following subjects:
   - history or geography
   - physical education
   - ICT
   - art and design or design and technology
   - performing arts, and
   - Religious Education

to be able to teach them in the age range for which they are trained, with advice from an experienced colleague where necessary.

c. For Key Stage 3, they know and understand the relevant National Curriculum Programme(s) of study, and for those qualifying to teach one or more of the core subjects, the relevant frameworks, methods and expectations set out in the National Strategy for Key Stage 3. All those qualifying to teach a subject at Key Stage 3 know and understand the cross-curricular expectations of the National Curriculum and are familiar with the guidance set out in the National Strategy for Key Stage 3.

d. For Key Stage 4 and post 16, they are aware of the pathways for progression through the 14–19 phase in school, college and work-based settings. They are familiar with the Key Skills as specified by QCA and the national qualifications framework, and they know the progression within and from their own subject and the range of qualifications to which their subject contributes. They understand how courses are combined in students' curricula.

2.2 They know and understand the Values, Aims and Purposes and the General Teaching Requirements set out in the *National Curriculum Handbook*. As relevant to the age range they are trained to teach, they are familiar with the Programme of Study for Citizenship and the National Curriculum Framework for Personal, Social and Health Education.[3]

2.3 They are aware of expectations, typical curricula and teaching arrangements in the Key Stages or phases before and after the ones they are trained to teach.

2.4 They understand how pupils' learning can be affected by their physical, intellectual, linguistic, social, cultural and emotional development.

2.5 They know how to use ICT effectively, both to teach their subject and to support their wider professional role.

2.6 They understand their responsibilities under the *SEN Code of Practice*, and know how to seek advice from specialists on less common types of special educational needs.

2.7 They know a range of strategies to promote good behaviour and establish a purposeful learning environment.

2.8 They have passed the Qualified Teacher Status skills tests in numeracy and literacy and ICT.

3. Teaching

3.1 Planning, expectations and targets

Those awarded Qualified Teacher Status must demonstrate all of the following.

3.1.1 They set challenging teaching and learning objectives which are relevant to all pupils in their classes. They base these on their knowledge of:
   – the pupils
   – evidence of their past and current achievement
   – the expected standard for pupils of the relevant age range
   – the range and content of work relevant to pupils in that age range.

3.1.2 They use these teaching and learning objectives to plan lessons, and sequences of lessons, showing how they will assess pupils' learning. They take account of and support pupils' varying needs so that girls and boys from all ethnic groups can make good progress.

3.1.3 They select and prepare resources, and plan for their safe and effective organisation, taking account of pupils' interests and their language and cultural backgrounds, with the help of support staff where appropriate.

3.1.4 They take part in, and contribute to, teaching teams as appropriate to the school. Where applicable, they plan for the deployment of additional adults who support pupils' learning.

3.1.5 As relevant to the age range they are trained to teach, they are able to plan opportunities for pupils to learn in out-of-school contexts, such as school visits, museums, theatres, field work and employment-based settings, with the help of other staff where appropriate.

3.2 Monitoring and assessment

Those awarded Qualified Teacher Status must demonstrate all of the following.

3.2.1   They make appropriate use of a range of monitoring and assessment strategies to evaluate pupils' progress towards planned learning objectives, and use this information to improve their own planning and teaching.

3.2.2   They monitor and assess as they teach, giving immediate and constructive feedback to support pupils as they learn. They involve pupils in reflecting on, evaluating and improving their own performance.

3.2.3   They are able to assess pupils' progress, accurately using as relevant, the Early Learning Goals, National Curriculum level descriptions, criteria from national qualifications, the requirements of Awarding Bodies, National Curriculum and Foundation Stage assessment frameworks or objectives from the national strategies. They may have guidance from an experienced teacher where appropriate.

3.2.4   They identify and support more able pupils, those who are working below age-related expectations, those who are failing to achieve their potential in learning, and those who experience behavioural, emotional and social difficulties. They may have guidance from an experienced teacher where appropriate.

3.2.5   With the help of an experienced teacher, they can identify the levels of attainment of pupils learning English as an additional language. They begin to analyse the language demands and learning activities in order to provide cognitive challenge as well as language support.

3.2.6   They record pupils' progress and achievements systematically to provide evidence of the range of their work, progress and attainment over time. They use this to help pupils review their own progress and to inform planning.

3.2.7   They are able to use records as a basis for reporting on pupils' attainment and progress orally and in writing, concisely, informatively and accurately for parents, carers, and other professionals and pupils.

3.3 Teaching and class management

Those awarded Qualified Teacher Status must demonstrate all of the following.

3.3.1   They have high expectations of pupils and build successful relationships, centred on teaching and learning. They establish a purposeful learning environment where diversity is valued and where pupils feel secure and confident.

3.3.2   They can teach the required or expected knowledge, understanding and skills relevant to the curriculum for pupils in the age range for which they are trained.
      In relation to specific phases:
      a. those qualifying to teach Foundation Stage children teach all six areas of learning outlined in the *QCA/DfEE Curriculum Guidance for the Foundation Stage* and, for Reception children, the objectives in the National Literacy and Numeracy Strategy frameworks competently and independently;

  b. those qualifying to teach pupils in Key Stage 1 and/or 2 teach the core
     subjects (English including the National Literacy Strategy, mathematics
     through the National Numeracy Strategy, and science) competently and
     independently.

     They also teach, for either Key Stage 1 or Key Stage 2, a range of work
     across the following subjects:
     – history or geography
     – physical education
     – ICT
     – art and design or design and technology, and
     – performing arts
     independently with advice from an experienced colleague where appropriate;

  c. those qualifying to teach Key Stage 3 pupils teach their specialist subject(s)
     competently and independently using the National Curriculum Programmes
     of Study for Key Stage 3 and the relevant national frameworks and schemes
     of work. Those qualifying to teach the core subjects or ICT at Key Stage 3
     use the relevant frameworks, methods and expectations set out in the
     National Strategy for Key Stage 3. All those qualifying to teach a subject at
     Key Stage 3 must be able to use the cross-curricular elements, such as literacy
     and numeracy, set out in the National Strategy for Key Stage 3, in their
     teaching, as appropriate to their specialist subject;

  d. those qualifying to teach Key Stage 4 and post-16 pupils teach their specialist
     subject(s) competently and independently using as relevant to the subject
     and age range, the National Curriculum Programmes of Study and related
     schemes of work, or programmes specified for national qualifications.[4] They
     also provide opportunities for pupils to develop the key skills specified by
     QCA.

3.3.3 They teach clearly structured lessons or sequences of work which interest and
       motivate and which:
       – make learning objectives clear to pupils
       – employ interactive teaching methods and collaborative group work
       – promote active and independent learning that enables pupils to think for
         themselves and to plan and manage their own learning.

3.3.4 They differentiate their teaching to meet the needs of pupils, including the more
       able and those with special educational needs. They may have guidance from
       an experienced teacher where appropriate.

3.3.5 They are able to support those who are learning English as an additional
       language with the help of an experienced teacher where appropriate.

3.3.6 They take account of the varying interests, experiences and achievements of boys
       and girls, and pupils from different cultural and ethnic groups, to help pupils
       make good progress.

3.3.7 They organise and manage teaching and learning time effectively.

3.3.8   They organise and manage the physical teaching space, tools, materials, texts and other resources safely and effectively with the help of support staff where appropriate.

3.3.9   They set high expectations for pupils' behaviour and establish a clear framework for classroom discipline to anticipate and manage pupils' behaviour constructively and promote self-control and independence.

3.3.10   They use ICT effectively in their teaching.

3.3.11   They can take responsibility for teaching a class or classes over a sustained and substantial period of time. They are able to teach across the age and ability range for which they are trained.

3.3.12   They provide homework and other out-of-class work which consolidates and extends work carried out in the class and encourages pupils to learn independently.

3.3.13   They work collaboratively with specialist teachers and other colleagues and, with the help of an experienced teacher as appropriate, manage the work of teaching assistants or other adults to enhance pupils' learning.

3.3.14   They recognise and respond effectively to equal opportunities issues as they arise in the classroom, including by challenging stereotyped views, and by challenging bullying or harassment, following relevant policies and procedures.

Notes

[1] In this document, the term 'schools' includes Further Education and VI form colleges and Early Years settings where trainee teachers can demonstrate that they meet the Standards for Qualified Teacher Status.

[2] The Foundation Stage is organised into six areas of learning rather than into subjects. Throughout this document, references to 'subjects' include these areas of learning.

[3] For Key Stage 1 and/or 2 the National Curriculum Framework for Personal, Social and Health Education includes Citizenship.

[4] This could include work-related learning.

(TTA and DfES, 2002)

Appendix 2

STANDARDS FOR DETERMINING WHETHER AN NQT HAS SATISFACTORILY COMPLETED AN INDUCTION PERIOD

1. In order to recommend that a NQT has satisfactorily completed the induction period, the head teacher should be satisfied that the NQT has:
   a. continued to meet the Standards for the Award of QTS consistently in teaching at the school;
   b. met all the induction standards.

The Induction Standards

2. To meet the Induction Standards, the NQT should demonstrate that he or she:

Planning, teaching and class management

   a. sets clear targets for improvement of pupils' achievement, monitors pupils' progress towards those targets and uses appropriate teaching strategies in the light of this, including, where appropriate, in relation to literacy, numeracy and other school targets;
   b. plans effectively to ensure that pupils have the opportunity to meet their potential, notwithstanding differences of race and gender, and taking account of the needs of pupils who are:
      – underachieving;
      – very able;
      – not yet fluent in English.
      Making use of relevant information and specialist help where available;
   c. secures a good standard of pupil behaviour in the classroom through establishing appropriate rules and high expectations of discipline which pupils respect, acting to pre-empt and deal with inappropriate behaviour in the context of the behaviour policy of the school;

d. plans effectively, where applicable, to meet the needs of pupils with Special Educational Needs and, in collaboration with the SENCO, makes an appropriate contribution to the preparation, implementation, monitoring and review of Individual Education Plans;

e. takes account of ethnic and cultural diversity to enrich the curriculum and raise achievement.

Monitoring, assessment, recording, reporting and accountability

f. recognises the level that a pupil is achieving and makes accurate assessments, independently, against attainment targets, where applicable, and performance levels associated with other tests or qualifications relevant to the subject(s) or phase(s) taught;

g. liaises effectively with pupils' parents/carers through informative oral and written reports on pupils' progress and achievements, discussing appropriate targets, and encouraging them to support their children's learning, behaviour and progress.

Other professional requirements

h. where applicable, deploys support staff and other adults effectively in the classroom, involving them, where appropriate, in the planning and management of pupils' learning;

i. takes responsibility for implementing school policies and practices, including those dealing with bullying and racial harassment;

j. takes responsibility for their own professional development, setting objectives for improvements, and taking action to keep up-to-date with research and developments in pedagogy and in the subject(s) they teach.

National tests in numeracy

k. To complete induction successfully an NQT trained in England, qualifying on or after 1 May 2000 and before 1 May 2001, must have passed the national test for teacher training candidates in numeracy, before the completion of the induction period.

(DfES, 2001b: Annex A)

Appendix 3

CODE OF PROFESSIONAL VALUES AND PRACTICE FOR TEACHERS

General introduction: the high standards of the teaching profession

Teachers inspire and lead young people, helping them achieve their potential as fulfilled individuals and productive members of society. Their role is vital, unique and far-reaching.

This Code sets out the beliefs, values and attitudes that make up teacher professionalism. It shows that teachers use high levels of individual judgement and skill to meet the challenges of their profession.

It recognises that teachers work within a framework of legislation with many lines of accountability. The complicated and varied roles that teachers need to fulfil make teaching one of the most demanding and rewarding professions.

Many of those who enter the profession feel a strong sense of vocation in accepting the special challenge of teaching and its chances to improve the opportunities that young people have in life. First and foremost, teachers are competent classroom practitioners. The role of teachers is to achieve success for their pupils through a complex network of relationships. They need high levels of commitment, energy and enthusiasm. Like other professionals, teachers respond to a social situation that is continually changing.

To ensure the positive development of individual pupils, teachers work within a framework of equal opportunities and other relevant legislation, statutory guidance and school policies. Within this framework, teachers challenge stereotypes and oppose prejudice to safeguard equality of opportunity, respecting individuals regardless of gender, marital status, religion, colour, race, ethnicity, class, sexual orientation, disability and age.

We produced this Code after wide consultation, to confirm the values and high standards of professional practice by teachers. As such, it forms the basis of all the Council's advisory and regulatory work. We are carrying out work to develop the notes of guidance in the areas covered by this Code as well as a Code of Conduct for use in our regulatory role.

Professionalism in practice

Young people as pupils

Teachers have insight into the learning needs of young people. They use professional judgement to meet those needs and to choose the best ways of motivating pupils to achieve success. They use assessment to inform and guide their work.

Teachers have high expectations for all pupils, helping them progress regardless of their personal circumstances and different needs and backgrounds. They work to make sure that pupils develop intellectually and personally, and to safeguard pupils' general health, safety and well-being. Teachers demonstrate the characteristics they are trying to inspire in pupils, including a spirit of intellectual enquiry, tolerance, honesty, fairness, patience, a genuine concern for other people and an appreciation of different backgrounds.

Teacher colleagues

Teachers support their colleagues in achieving the highest professional standards. They are fully committed to sharing their own expertise and insights in the interests of the people they teach and are always open to learning from the effective practice of their colleagues. Teachers respect the rights of other people to equal opportunities and to dignity at work. They respect confidentiality where appropriate.

Other professionals, governors and interested people

Teachers recognise that the well-being and development of pupils often depend on working in partnership with different professionals, the school governing body, support staff and other interested people within and beyond the school. They respect the skills, expertise and contributions of these colleagues and partners and are concerned to build productive working relationships with them in the interests of pupils.

Parents and carers

Teachers respond sensitively to the differences in pupils' home backgrounds and circumstances and recognise the importance of working in partnership with parents and carers to understand and support their children's learning. They endeavour to communicate effectively and promote co-operation between the home and the school for the benefit of young people.

The school in context

Teachers support the place of the school in the community and appreciate the importance of their own professional status in society. They recognise that professionalism involves using judgement over appropriate standards of personal behaviour.

Learning and development

Teachers entering the teaching profession in England have been trained to a professional standard that has prepared them for the rigours and realities of the classroom. They understand that maintaining and developing their skills, knowledge and expertise is vital to achieving success. They take responsibility for their own continuing professional development, through the opportunities available to them, to make sure that pupils receive the best and most relevant education. Teachers continually reflect on their own practice, improve their skills and deepen their knowledge. They want to adapt their teaching appropriately to take account of new findings, ideas and technologies.

Conclusion

This Code is intended to help make sure that the professional work of teachers helps their pupils to develop themselves fully and reach their highest potential in life. It is intended to be an evolving document that will contribute to the definition of teacher professionalism and help in raising standards of achievement by pupils.

HOW TO USE THE CODE OF PROFESSIONAL VALUES AND PRACTICE

The General Teaching Council for England (GTC) recognises the challenges teachers face in carrying out their vitally important professional role. We expect the Code to provide a useful reference point and source of encouragement to teachers in England and elsewhere, whatever their circumstances and the demands upon them.

The Code is a core statement of professional values from which the GTC itself will draw inspiration in developing its work on behalf of the profession. At the same time, the GTC trusts that the Code will find practical uses within schools in the following suggested ways:

- as a discussion document
- as a reference point in creating policy
- as a benchmark of professional values
- as a source of useful guidance.

The GTC is preparing further guidance in these areas.

LEGAL STATUS OF THE CODE OF PROFESSIONAL VALUES AND PRACTICE FOR TEACHERS

The General Teaching Council for England (GTC) aims to speak up for teaching, support high standards of teacher professionalism and raise teacher status. This Code confirms and celebrates the high standards of teachers' professional practice in this country and describes the professional values that underpin that practice.

This Code says that it 'forms the basis of all the Council's advisory and regulatory work'. In practice, this means that it will inform and inspire all the council's advisory and policy development work.

Following the consultation with all registered teachers in May 2001, the GTC is developing notes of guidance for teachers on the main themes of the Code. This is to provide further legal and good practice advice to teachers. This work will be the subject of wide consultation with teachers and other partners to ensure its relevance and value.

How the Code relates to the disciplinary hearings

The GTC has particular responsibilities for hearing cases relating to teacher misconduct and competence. The GTC recognises that there is also a case to develop a Code of Conduct for use in this context. Such a Code is envisaged under section 5 of the Teaching and Higher Education Act 1998. The GTC will develop this document following significant practical experience of having undertaken its disciplinary work.

This Code of Professional Values and Practice is therefore not a set of standards against which teachers will be judged under the GTC's disciplinary powers nor is it appropriate for employers to use this code in their own disciplinary procedures.

(General Teaching Council for England, 2002a)

Appendix 4

CONTACT DETAILS OF LEAS IN ENGLAND

Barking and Dagenham
Education Department
London Borough of Barking and
Dagenham
Town Hall
Broadway
Barking
Essex IG11 7LU
Tel: (020) 8592 4500
Fax: (020) 8594 9837
www.barking-dagenham.gov.uk

Barnet
Education, Standards and Achievement
London Borough of Barnet
The Old Town Hall
1 Friern Barnet Lane
London N11 3DL
Tel: (020) 8359 2000
Fax: (020) 8259 3057
www.barnet.gov.uk

Barnsley
Education Services
Barnsley Metropolitan Borough Council
Berneslai Close
Barnsley
South Yorkshire S70 2HS
Tel: (01226) 770770
Fax: (01226) 773599
www.barnsley.gov.uk

Bath and North East Somerset
Education Department
Bath and North East Somerset Council
PO Box 25
Riverside
Temple Street
Keynsham
Bristol BS31 1DN
Tel: (01225) 394210
Fax: (01225) 394011
www.bathnes.gov.uk

Bedfordshire
Education Department
Bedfordshire County Council
County Hall
Cauldwell Street
Bedford MK42 9AP
Tel: (01234) 228144
Fax: (01234) 228619
www.bedfordshire.gov.uk

Bexley
Education and Leisure Services
London Borough of Bexley
Hill View
Hill View Drive
Welling
Kent DA16 3RY
Tel: (020) 8303 7777
Fax: (020) 8319 4302
www.bexley.gov.uk

Birmingham
Education Department
Birmingham City Council
Council House Extension
Margaret Street
Birmingham B3 3BU
Tel: (0121) 303 2872
Fax: (0121) 303 1318
www.birmingham.gov.uk

Blackburn with Darwen
Department of Education and Lifelong
Learning
Blackburn with Darwen Borough
Council
Town Hall
King William Street
Blackburn
Lancashire BB1 7DY
Tel: (01254) 585585
Fax: (01254) 698388
www.blackburn.gov.uk

Blackpool
Education and Cultural Services
Blackpool Borough Council
Progress House
Clifton Road
Blackpool FY4 4US
Tel: (01253) 476555
Fax: (01253) 476504
www.blackpool.gov.uk

Bolton
Education and Arts
Bolton Metropolitan Borough Council
PO Box 53
Paderborn House
Civic Centre
Bolton
Lancashire BL1 1JW
Tel: (0120) 433 3333
Fax: (0120) 436 5492
www.bolton.gov.uk

Bournemouth
Education Department
Bournemouth Borough Council
Dorset House
20–22 Christ Church Road
Bournemouth BH1 3NL
Tel: (01202) 456101
Fax: (01202) 456105
www.bournemouth.gov.uk

Bracknell Forest
Education Department
Bracknell Forest Council
Edward Elgar House
Skimped Hill Lane
Bracknell RG12 1LY
Tel: (01344) 424642
Fax: (01344) 354001
www.bracknell-forest.gov.uk

Bradford
Education and Schools Department
City of Bradford Metropolitan District
Council
Flockton House
Flockton Road
Bradford
West Yorkshire BD4 7RY
Tel: (01274) 751840
Fax: (01274) 740612
www.bradford.gov.uk

Brent
Education Department
London Borough of Brent
Chesterfield House
9 Park Lane
Wembley
Middlesex HA9 7RW
Tel: (020) 8937 3130
Fax: (020) 8937 3130
www.brent.gov.uk

Brighton and Hove
Education and Lifelong Learning
Brighton and Hove Council
King's House
Grand Avenue
Hove
East Sussex BN3 2SU
Tel: (01273) 293434
Fax: (01273) 293456
www.brighton-hove.gov.uk

Bristol, City of
Education and Lifelong Learning
Bristol City Council
PO Box 57
Council House
College Green
Bristol BS99 7EB
Tel: (0117) 903 7961
Fax: (0117) 903 7963
www.bristol-city.gov.uk

Bromley
Education Department
London Borough of Bromley
Civic Centre
Stockwell Close
Bromley BR1 3UH
Tel: (020) 8464 3333
Fax: (020) 8313 4049
www.bromley.gov.uk

Buckinghamshire
Education Department
Buckinghamshire County Council
County Hall
Aylesbury
Bucks HP20 1UZ
Tel: (01296) 395000
Fax: (01296) 383367
www.buckscc.gov.uk

Bury
Education Department
Bury Metropolitan Borough Council
Athenaeum House
Market Street
Bury
Lancashire BL9 0BN
Tel: (0161) 253 5000
Fax: (0161) 253 5653
www.bury.gov.uk

Calderdale
Education Department
Calderdale Metropolitan Borough
Council
Northgate House
Northgate
Halifax
West Yorkshire HX1 1UN
Tel: (01422) 357257
Fax: (01422) 392515
www.calderdale.gov.uk

Cambridgeshire
Education, Libraries and Heritage
Cambridgeshire County Council
Castle Court
Shire Hall
Castle Hill
Cambridge CB3 0AP
Tel: (01223) 717111
Fax: (01223) 717971
www.camcnty.gov.uk

Camden
Education Department
London Borough of Camden
Crowndale Centre
218–220 Eversholt Street
London NW1 1BD
Tel: (020) 7911 1525
Fax: (020) 7911 1536
www.camden.gov.uk

Cheshire
Education Department
Cheshire County Council
County Hall
Chester CH1 1SQ
Tel: (01244) 602301
Fax: (01244) 603821
www.cheshire.gov.uk

City of London
Education Department
Corporation of London
PO Box 270
Guildhall
London EC2P 2EJ
Tel: (020) 7332 1750
Fax: (020) 7332 1621
www.cityoflondon.gov.uk

Cornwall
Education Department
Cornwall County Council
County Hall
Treyew Road
Truro TR1 3AY
Tel: (01872) 322401
Fax: (01872) 323818
www.cornwall.gov.uk

Coventry
Department of Education and Lifelong
Learning
Coventry City Council
New Council Offices
Little Park Street
Coventry CV1 5RS
Tel: (024) 7683 3333
Fax: (024) 7683 1620
www.coventry.gov.uk

Croydon
Education Department
London Borough of Croydon
Taberner House
Park Lane
Croydon CR9 1TP
Tel: (020) 8686 4433
Fax: (020) 8760 0871
www.croydon.gov.uk

Cumbria
Education Department
Education Offices
Cumbria County Council
5 Portland Square
Carlisle CA1 1PU
Tel: (01228) 606060
Fax: (01228) 606896
www.cumbria.gov.uk

Darlington
Education Department
Darlington Borough Council
Town Hall
Darlington DL1 5QT
Tel: (01325) 380651
Fax: (01325) 380032
www.darlington.gov.uk

Derby, City of
Education Department
Derby City Council
Middleton House
27 St Mary's Gate
Derby DE1 3NN
Tel: (01332) 716854
Fax: (01332) 716870
www.derby.gov.uk

Derbyshire
Education Department
Derbyshire County Council
County Hall
Matlock
Derbyshire DE4 3AG
Tel: (01629) 585841
Fax: (01629) 585401
www.derbyshire.gov.uk

Devon
Department of Education, Arts and
Libraries
Devon County Council
County Hall
Exeter EX2 4QG
Tel: (01392) 382059
Fax: (01392) 382203
www.devon.gov.uk

Doncaster
Department of Education and Culture
Doncaster Metropolitan Borough
Council
PO Box 266
The Council House
Doncaster
South Yorkshire DN1 3AD
Tel: (01302) 737222
Fax: (01302) 737223
www.doncaster.gov.uk

Dorset
Education Department
Dorset County Council
County Hall
Colliton Park
Dorchester
Dorset DT1 1XJ
Tel: (01305) 224166
Fax: (01305) 225057
www.dorset-cc.gov.uk

Dudley
Department of Education and Lifelong
Learning
Dudley Metropolitan Borough Council
Westox House
1 Trinity Road
Dudley
West Midlands DY1 1JB
Tel: (01384) 818181
Fax: (01384) 814216
www.dudley.gov.uk

Durham
Education Department
Durham County Council
County Hall
Durham DH1 5UJ
Tel: (0191) 386 4411
Fax: (0191) 386 0487
www.durham.gov.uk

Ealing
Education Department
London Borough of Ealing
5th Floor, Perceval House
14–16 Uxbridge Road
Ealing W5 2HL
Tel: (020) 8579 2424
Fax: (020) 8280 1291
www.ealing.gov.uk

East Riding of Yorkshire
Department of Education, Leisure and
Libraries
East Riding of Yorkshire Council
County Hall
Beverley
East Riding of Yorkshire HU17 9BA
Tel: (01482) 887700
Fax: (01482) 884920
www.east-riding-of-yorkshire.gov.uk

East Sussex
Education Department
PO Box 4
County Hall
St Anne's Crescent
Lewes BN7 1UN
Tel: (01273) 481000
Fax: (01273) 481261
www.eastsussexcc.gov.uk

Enfield
Education Department
London Borough of Enfield
PO Box 56
Civic Centre
Silver Street
Enfield EN1 3XQ
Tel: (020) 8366 6565
Fax: (020) 8982 7375
www.enfield.gov.uk

Essex
Learning Services
Essex County Council
PO Box 47
Chelmsford CM2 6WN
Tel: (01245) 492211
Fax: (01245) 492759
www.essexcc.gov.uk

Gateshead
Education Department
Gateshead Metropolitan Borough
Council
Civic Centre
Regent Street
Gateshead
Tyne and Wear NE8 1HH
Tel: (0191) 477 1011
Fax: (0191) 490 1168
www.gateshead.gov.uk

Gloucestershire
Education Services
Gloucestershire County Council
Shire Hall
Gloucester GL1 2TP
Tel: (01452) 425302
Fax: (01452) 426420
www.gloscc.gov.uk

Greenwich
Education Department
London Borough of Greenwich
9th Floor, Riverside House
Beresford House
London SE18 6DF
Tel: (020) 8854 8888
Fax: (020) 8855 2427
www.greenwich.gov.uk

Hackney
London Borough of Hackney Education
Directorate
Edith Cavell Building
Enfield Road
London N1 5BA
Tel: (020) 8356 5000
Fax: (020) 8356 7295
www.hackney.gov.uk

Halton
Education Department
Halton Borough Council
Grosvenor House
Halton Lea
Runcorn
Cheshire WA7 2WD
Tel: (0151) 424 2061
Fax: (0151) 471 7321
www.halton.gov.uk

Hammersmith and Fulham
Education Department
Cambridge House
Cambridge Grove
Hammersmith
London W6 0LE
Tel: (020) 8748 3020
Fax: (020) 8576 5686
www.lbhf.gov.uk

Hampshire
Education Department
Hampshire County Council
The Castle
Winchester
Hampshire SO23 8UG
Tel: (01962) 841841
Fax: (01962) 842355
www.hants.gov.uk

Haringey
Education Department
Civic Centre
High Road
London N22 8LE
Tel: (020) 8489 2648
Fax: (020) 8862 2906
www.haringey.gov.uk

Harrow
Education Department
London Borough of Harrow
PO Box 22
Civic Centre
Harrow
Middlesex HA1 2UW
Tel: (020) 8863 5611
Fax: (020) 8427 0810
www.harrow.gov.uk

Hartlepool
Education and Community Services
Hartlepool Borough Council
Civic Centre
Victoria Road
Hartlepool
Cleveland TS24 8AY
Tel: (01429) 266522
Fax: (01429) 523777
www.hartlepool.gov.uk

Havering
Department of Children and Lifelong
Learning
London Borough of Havering
Town Hall
Main Road
Romford RM1 3BC
Tel: (01708) 434343
Fax: (01708) 433850
www.havering.gov.uk

Herefordshire
Department of Education
County of Herefordshire Council
PO Box 185
Blackfriars Street
Hereford HR4 9ZR
Tel: (01432) 260000
Fax: (01432) 264348
www.herefordshire.gov.uk

Hertfordshire
Education Department
Hertfordshire County Council
County Hall
Hertford SG13 8DF
Tel: (01992) 555555
Fax: (01992) 588674
www.hertscc.gov.uk

Hillingdon
Youth and Leisure Services
London Borough of Hillingdon
4 East 01
Civic Centre
High Street
Uxbridge
Middlesex UB8 1UW
Tel: (01895) 250529
Fax: (01895) 250831
www.hillingdon.gov.uk

Hounslow
Education Department
London Borough of Hounslow
Civic Centre
Lampton Road
Hounslow
Middlesex TW3 4DN
Tel: (020) 8583 2000
Fax: (020) 8862 5249
www.hounslow.gov.uk

Isle of Wight
Education Department
Isle of Wight Council
County Hall
Newport
Isle of Wight PO30 1UD
Tel: (01983) 821000
Fax: (01983) 826099
www.iwight.gov.uk

Isles of Scilly
Education Department
Council of the Isles of Scilly
Town Hall
St Mary's
Isles of Scilly TR21 0LW
Tel: (01720) 422537
Fax: (01720) 422202
No Web site, but see Cornwall for some
details

Islington
Education Department
London Borough of Islington
Laycock Street
London N1 1TH
Tel: (020) 7527 5566
Fax: (020) 7457 5555
www.islington.gov.uk

Kensington and Chelsea
Department of Education, Libraries and
Arts
Royal Borough of Kensington and
Chelsea
Town Hall
Hornton Street
London W8 7NX
Tel: (020) 7361 3334
Fax: (020) 7361 3481
www.rbkc.gov.uk

Kent
Department of Education and Libraries
Kent County Council
Sessions House
County Hall
Maidstone
Kent ME14 1XQ
Tel: (01622) 671411
Fax: (01622) 694091
www.kent.gov.uk

Kingston-upon-Hull, City of
Department of Learning Services
Kingston-upon-Hull City Council
Essex House
Manor Street
Kingston-upon-Hull
HU1 1YD
Tel: (01482) 610610
Fax: (01482) 613407
www.hullcc.gov.uk

Kingston upon Thames
Department of Education and Leisure
Royal Borough of Kingston upon
Thames
Guildhall
High Street
Kingston upon Thames
Surrey KT1 1EU
Tel: (020) 8546 2121
Fax: (020) 8547 5296
www.kingston.gov.uk

Kirklees
Education Department
Kirklees Metropolitan Council
Oldgate
Huddersfield HD1 6QW
Tel: (01484) 221000
Fax: (01484) 225264
www.kirkleesmc.gov.uk

Knowsley
Education and Lifelong Learning
Knowsley Metropolitan Borough
Council
Huyton Hey Road
Huyton
Merseyside L36 5YH
Tel: (0151) 443 3276
Fax: (0151) 443 5627
www.knowsley.gov.uk

Lambeth
Education Department
London Borough of Lambeth
International House
Canterbury Crescent
London SW9 7QE
Tel: (020) 7926 1000
Fax: (020) 7926 2296
www.lambeth.gov.uk

Lancashire
Department of Education and Cultural
Services
Lancashire County Council
PO Box 61
County Hall
Preston PR1 8RJ
Tel: (01772) 254868
Fax: (01772) 261630
www.lancashire.gov.uk

Leeds
Education Department
Leeds City Council
3rd Floor East, Civic Hall,
Calverley Street
Leeds LS1 1UR
Tel: (0113) 247 5590
Fax: (0113) 395 0219
www.leeds.gov.uk

Leicester City
Education Department
Leicester City Council
Marlborough House
38 Welford Road
Leicester LE2 7AA
Tel: (0116) 252 7700
Fax: (0116) 233 9922
www.leicester.gov.uk/city/

Leicestershire
Education Department
Leicestershire County Council
County Hall
Glenfield
Leicester LE3 8RF
Tel: (0116) 232 3232
Fax: (0116) 265 6634
www.leics.gov.uk

Lewisham
Directorate for Education and Culture
London Borough of Lewisham
3rd Floor, Laurence House
Catford
London SE6 4RU
Tel: (020) 8314 8527
Fax: (020) 8314 3039
www.lewisham.gov.uk

Lincolnshire
Education and Cultural Services
Lincolnshire County Council
County Offices
Newland
Lincoln LN1 1YQ
Tel: (01522) 552222
Fax: (01522) 553257
www.lincolnshire.gov.uk

Liverpool
Education and Lifelong Learning
Service
Liverpool City Council
Education Offices
4th Floor
4 Renshaw Street
Liverpool L1 4AD
Tel: (0151) 233 2822
Fax: (0151) 233 3029
www.liverpool.gov.uk

Luton
Education Department
Luton Borough Council
Unity House
111 Stuart Street
Luton
Bedfordshire LU1 5NP
Tel: (01582) 548001
Fax: (01582) 548454
www.luton.gov.uk

Manchester
Education Department
Education Offices
Manchester City Council
Crown Square
Manchester M60 3BB
Tel: (0161) 234 7125
Fax: (0161) 234 7007
www.manchester.gov.uk

Medway
Department of Education and Leisure
Medway Council
Civic Centre
Strood
Rochester
Kent ME2 4AU
Tel: (01634) 306000
Fax: (01634) 890120
www.medway.gov.uk

Merton
Department of Education, Leisure and
Libraries
London Borough of Merton
Merton Civic Centre
London Road
Morden
Surrey SM4 5DX
Tel: (020) 8543 2222
Fax: (020) 8545 3443
www.merton.gov.uk

Middlesbrough
Education and Leisure
Middlesbrough Borough Council
PO Box 69
First Floor
Vancouver House
Gurney Street
Middlesbrough TS1 1EL
Tel: (01642) 245432
Fax: (01642) 264175
www.middlesbrough.gov.uk

Milton Keynes
Department of Learning and
Development
Milton Keynes Council
Saxon Court
502 Avebury Boulevard
Milton Keynes MK9 3HS
Tel: (01908) 691691
Fax: (01908) 253289
www.mkweb.co.uk

Newcastle upon Tyne
Department of Education and Libraries
Newcastle upon Tyne City Council
Civic Centre
Barras Bridge
Newcastle upon Tyne NE1 8PU
Tel: (0191) 232 8520
Fax: (0191) 211 4983
www.newcastle.gov.uk

Newham
Education Department
London Borough of Newham
Broadway House
322 High Street
Stratford
London E15 1AJ
Tel: (020) 8555 5552
Fax: (020) 8503 0014
www.newham.gov.uk

Norfolk
Education Department
Norfolk County Council
County Hall
Martineau Lane
Norwich NR1 2DL
Tel: (01603) 222301
Fax: (01603) 222119
www.norfolk.gov.uk

North East Lincolnshire
Department of Education
North East Lincolnshire Council
Eleanor Street
Grimsby DN32 9DU
Tel: (01472) 313131
Fax: (01472) 323020
www.nelincs.gov.uk

North Lincolnshire
Educational and Personal Development
North Lincolnshire Council
PO Box 35
Hewson House
Station Road
Brigg DN20 8XJ
Tel: (01724) 297241
Fax: (01724) 297242
www.northlincs.gov.uk

North Somerset
Education Department
North Somerset Council
PO Box 51
Town Hall
Weston-super-Mare BS23 1ZZ
Tel: (01934) 888888
Fax: (01934) 888834
www.n-somerset.gov.uk

North Tyneside
Education Department
North Tyneside Council
Wallsend Town Hall
High Street East
Wallsend
Tyne and Wear NE28 7RR
Tel: (0191) 200 5151
Fax: (0191) 200 6090
www.northtyneside.gov.uk

North Yorkshire
Education Department
North Yorkshire County Council
County Hall
Northallerton
North Yorkshire DL7 8AE
Tel: (01609) 780780
Fax: (01609) 778611
www.northyorks.gov.uk

Northamptonshire
Education and Community Learning
Northamptonshire County Council
PO Box 216
John Dryden House
8–10 The Lakes
Northampton NN4 7DD
Tel: (01604) 236236
Fax: (01604) 236188
www.northants-ecl.gov.uk

Northumberland
Education Department
Northumberland County Council
County Hall
Morpeth
Northumberland NE16 2EF
Tel: (01670) 533000
Fax: (01670) 533750
www.northumberland.gov.uk

Nottingham, City of
Education Department
The Sandfield Centre
Sandfield Road
Lenton
Nottingham NG7 1QH
Tel: (0115) 915 5555
Fax: (0115) 915 0603
www.nottinghamcity.gov.uk

Nottinghamshire
Education Department
Nottinghamshire County Council
County Hall
West Bridgford
Nottingham NG2 7QP
Tel: (0115) 915 0600
Fax: (0115) 915 0603
www.nottscc.gov.uk

Oldham
Education and Cultural Services
Oldham Metropolitan Borough Council
PO Box 40
Civic Centre
West Street
Oldham OL1 1XJ
Tel: (0161) 911 4260
Fax: (0161) 911 3221
www.oldham.gov.uk

Oxfordshire
Education Department
Oxfordshire County Council
Macclesfield House
New Road
Oxford OX1 1NA
Tel: (01865) 815449
Fax: (01865) 791637
www.oxfordshire.gov.uk

Peterborough, City of
Department of Education
Peterborough City Council
Bayard Place
Broadway
Peterborough PE1 1FB
Tel: (01733) 563141
Fax: (01733) 748111
www.peterborough.gov.uk

Plymouth, City of
Lifelong Learning
City of Plymouth Council
Civic Centre
Armada Way
Plymouth PL1 2AA
Tel: (01752) 307400
Fax: (01752) 307403
www.plymouth.gov.uk

Poole
Education Department
Borough of Poole
Civic Centre
Poole
Dorset BH15 2RU
Tel: (01202) 633202
Fax: (01202) 633706
www.poole.gov.uk

Portsmouth
Education Department
Portsmouth City Council
Civic Offices
Guildhall Square
Portsmouth
Tel: (023) 9282 2251
Fax: (023) 9283 4571
www.portsmouthcc.gov.uk

Reading
Education and Community Services
Reading Borough Council
Civic Centre
Reading RG1 7TD
Tel: (0118) 939 0900
Fax: (0118) 958 9770
www.reading.gov.uk

Redbridge
Education and Lifelong Learning
London Borough of Redbridge
Lynton House
255–259 High Road
Ilford
Essex IG1 1NY
Tel: (020) 8478 3020
Fax: (020) 8478 9044
www.redbridge.gov.uk

Redcar and Cleveland
Education Department
Redcar and Cleveland Borough Council
PO Box 83
Council Offices
Kirkleatham Street
Redcar TS10 1YA
Tel: (01642) 444121
Fax: (01642) 444122
www.redcar-cleveland.gov.uk

Richmond upon Thames
Education Department
London Borough of Richmond upon
Thames
Regal House
London Road
Twickenham TW1 3QB
Tel: (020) 8891 1411
Fax: (020) 8891 7507
www.richmond.gov.uk

Rochdale
Education Department
Rochdale Metropolitan Borough
Council
PO Box 70
Municipal Offices
Smith Street
Rochdale OL16 1YD
Tel: (01706) 647474
Fax: (01706) 658560
www.rochdale.gov.uk

Rotherham
Education, Culture and Leisure Services
Rotherham Metropolitan Borough
Council
Norfolk House
Walker Place
Rotherham S65 1AS
Tel: (01709) 382121
Fax: (01709) 372056
www.rotherham.gov.uk

Rutland
Department of Education and Youth
Rutland County Council
Catmose
Oakham
Rutland LE15 6HP
Tel: (01572) 758481
Fax: (01572) 757713
www.rutnet.co.uk

Salford
Education and Leisure Department
Salford City Council
Chapel Street
Salford M3 5LT
Tel: (0161) 778 0123
Fax: (0161) 835 1561
www.salford.gov.uk

Sandwell
Department of Education and
Community Services
Sandwell Metropolitan Borough
Council
PO Box 41
Shaftesbury House
402 High Street
West Bromwich B70 9LT
Tel: (0121) 525 7366
Fax: (0121) 553 1528
www.sandwell.gov.uk

Sefton
Education Department
Sefton Metropolitan Borough Council
Town Hall
Bootle
Merseyside L20 7AE
Tel: (0151) 922 4040
Fax: (0151) 934 3239
www.sefton.gov.uk

Sheffield
Department of Education
Sheffield City Council
PO Box 67
Leopold Street
Sheffield S1 1RJ
Tel: (0114) 273 5722
Fax: (0114) 273 6279
www.sheffield.gov.uk

Shropshire
Education Services
Shropshire County Council
The Shirehall
Abbey Foregate
Shrewsbury SY2 6ND
Tel: (01743) 251000
Fax: (01743) 254415
www.shropshire-cc.gov.uk

Slough
Education Department
Slough Borough Council
Town Hall
Bath Road
Slough SL1 3UQ
Tel: (01753) 875700
Fax: (01753) 692499
www.slough.gov.uk

Solihull
Department of Education, Libraries and
Arts
Metropolitan Borough of Solihull
PO Box 20
Council House
Solihull
West Midlands B91 3QU
Tel: (0121) 704 6000
Fax: (0121) 704 6669
www.solihull.gov.uk

Somerset
Education Department
Somerset County Council
County Hall
Taunton
Somerset TA1 4DY
Tel: (01823) 355772
Fax: (01823) 355332
www.somerset.gov.uk

South Gloucestershire
Education Department
South Gloucestershire Council
Bowling Hill
Chipping Sodbury BS37 6JX
Tel: (01454) 863253
Fax: (01454) 863263
www.southglos.gov.uk

South Tyneside
Education Department
South Tyneside Metropolitan Borough
Council
Town Hall and Civic Offices
Westoe Road
South Shields
Tyne and Wear NE33 2RL
Tel: (0191) 427 1717
Fax: (0191) 427 0584
www.s-tyneside-mbc.gov.uk

Southampton
Lifelong Learning and Leisure
Department
Southampton City Council
First Floor, Civic Centre
Southampton SO14 7LY
Tel: (01703) 223855
Fax: (01703) 833221
www.southampton.gov.uk

Southend-on-Sea
Department of Education and Lifelong
Learning
Southend-on-Sea Borough Council
PO Box 6
Civic Centre
Victoria Avenue
Southend-on-Sea SS2 6ER
Tel: (01702) 215000
Fax: (01702) 432273
www.southend.gov.uk

Southwark
Department of Education and Lifelong
Learning
London Borough of Southwark
John Smith House
144–152 Walworth Road
London SE17 1JL
Tel: (020) 7525 5050
Fax: (020) 7525 5025
www.southwark.gov.uk

St Helens
Community Education and Leisure
Services Department
St Helens Metropolitan Borough
Council
The Rivington Centre
Rivington Road
St Helens
Merseyside WA10 4ND
Tel: (01744) 456000
Fax: (01744) 455319
www.sthelens.gov.uk

Staffordshire
Education Department
Staffordshire County Council
County Buildings
Tipping Street
Stafford ST16 2DH
Tel: (01785) 223121
Fax: (01785) 278639
www.stafford.gov.uk

Stockport
Education Department
Stockport Metropolitan Borough
Council
Stopford House
Piccadilly
Stockport SK1 3XE
Tel: (0161) 474 3808
Fax: (0161) 953 0012
www.stockportmbc.gov.uk

Stockton-on-Tees
Education Department
Stockton-on-Tees Borough Council
PO Box 228
Municipal Buildings
Church Road
Stockton-on-Tees TS18 1XE
Tel: (01642) 393939
Fax: (01642) 393479
www.stockton-bc.gov.uk

Stoke-on-Trent
Education Department
Civic Centre
Floor 2
Glebe Street
Stoke-on-Trent ST4 1HH
Tel: (01782) 232014
Fax: (01782) 236102
www.stoke.gov.uk

Suffolk
Education Department
Suffolk County Council
St Andrew House
County Hall
St Helens Street
Ipswich IP4 1LJ
Tel: (01473) 584800
Fax: (01473) 584624
www.suffolkcc.gov.uk

Sunderland
Education and Community Services
Sunderland City Council
PO Box 101
Civic Centre
Sunderland SR2 7DN
Tel: (0191) 553 1000
Fax: (0191) 553 1410
www.sunderland.gov.uk

Surrey
Education Department
Surrey County Council
County Hall
Penrhyn Road
Kingston upon Thames KT1 2DJ
Tel: 0845 600 9009
Fax: (020) 8541 9004
www.surreycc.gov.uk

Sutton
London Borough of Sutton
Learning for Life
The Grove
Carshalton
Surrey SM5 3AL
Tel: (020) 8770 5000
Fax: (020) 8770 6545
www.sutton.gov.uk

Swindon
Education and Community
Department
Swindon Borough Council
Sanford House
Sanford Street
Swindon SN1 1QH
Tel: (01793) 463068
Fax: (01793) 488597
www.swindon.gov.uk

Tameside
Education Department
Tameside Metropolitan Borough
Council
Council Offices
Wellington Road
Ashton-under-Lyne OL6 6DL
Tel: (0161) 342 8355
Fax: (0161) 342 3260
www.tameside.gov.uk

Telford and Wrekin
Education and Training Department
Telford and Wrekin Council
PO Box 440
Civic Offices
Telford TF3 4LD
Tel: (01952) 202100
Fax: (01952) 293946
www.telford.gov.uk

Thurrock
Education Department
Thurrock Borough Council
Civic Offices
New Road
Grays
Essex RM17 6GF
Tel: (01375) 652652
Fax: (01375) 652792
www.thurrock.gov.uk

Torbay
Education Services
Torbay Borough Council
Oldway Mansion
Paignton
Devon TQ3 2TE
Tel: (01803) 208200
Fax: (01803) 208225
www.torbay.gov.uk

Tower Hamlets
Education Department
London Borough of Tower Hamlets
Mulberry Place
5 Clove Crescent
London E14 2BG
Tel: (020) 7364 5000
Fax: (020) 7364 4296
www.towerhamlets.gov.uk

Trafford
Lifelong Learning Department
Trafford Metropolitan Borough Council
PO Box 40
Trafford Town Hall
Talbot Road
Stretford M32 0EL
Tel: (0161) 912 3251
Fax: (0161) 912 3075
www.trafford.gov.uk

Wakefield
Education Department
Wakefield Metropolitan District
Council
County Hall
Wakefield WF1 2QL
Tel: (01924) 306090
Fax: (01924) 305632
www.wakefield.gov.uk

Walsall
Education Department
Walsall Metropolitan Borough Council
Civic Centre
Darwell Street
Walsall
West Midlands WS1 1DQ
Tel: (01922) 650000
Fax: (01922) 722322
www.walsall.gov.uk

Waltham Forest
London Borough of Waltham forest
Lifelong Learning Services
Walthamstow Town Hall
Forest Road
London E17 4JF
Tel: (020) 8496 4578
Fax: (020) 8496 4558
www.lbwf.gov.uk

Wandsworth
Education Department
London Borough of Wandsworth
Town Hall
Wandsworth High Street
London SW18 2PU
Tel: (020) 8871 8013
Fax: (020) 8871 8011
www.wandsworth.gov.uk

Warrington
Education Department
Warrington Borough Council
New Town House
Buttermarket Street
Warrington WA1 2NJ
Tel: (01925) 442901
Fax: (01925) 442929
www.warrington.gov.uk

Warwickshire
Education Department
Warwickshire County Council
PO Box 24
22 Northgate Street
Warwick CV34 4SR
Tel: (01926) 410410
Fax: (01926) 412746
www.warwickshire.gov.uk

West Berkshire
Education Department
West Berkshire Council
Avonbank House
West Street
Newbury RG14 1BZ
Tel: (01635) 519722
Fax: (01635) 519725
www.westberks.gov.uk

West Sussex
Education Department
West Sussex County Council
County Hall
West Street
Chichester
West Sussex PO19 1RF
Tel: (01243) 777100
Fax: (01243) 777229
www.westsussex.gov.uk

Westminster
Education Department
Westminster City Council
PO Box 240
Westminster City Hall
64 Victoria Street
London SW1E 6QP
Tel: (020) 7641 2177
Fax: (020) 7641 3406
www.westminster.gov.uk

Wigan
Education Offices
Wigan Borough Council
Gateway House
Standishgate
Wigan WN1 1AE
Tel: (01942) 244991
Fax: (01942) 828811
www.wiganmbc.gov.uk

Wiltshire
Education Department
Wiltshire County Council
County Hall
Bythesea Road
Trowbridge
Wiltshire BA14 8JB
Tel: (01225) 713751
Fax: (01225) 713982
www.wiltshire.gov.uk

Windsor and Maidenhead, Royal Borough of
Education Department
Royal Borough of Windsor and
Maidenhead
Town Hall
St Ives Road
Maidenhead SL6 1RF
Tel: (01628) 798888
Fax: (01628) 796408
www.rbwm.gov.uk

Wirral
Education Department
Metropolitan Borough of Wirral
Hamilton Building
Conway Street
Birkenhead L41 4FD
Tel: (0151) 666 4288
Fax: (0151) 666 4338
www.wirral.gov.uk

Wokingham
Education Department
Wokingham District Council
PO Box 156
Shute End
Wokingham RG40 1WN
Tel: (0118) 974 6000
Fax: (0118) 974 6103
www.wokingham.gov.uk

Wolverhampton
Education Department
Wolverhampton Metropolitan Borough
Council
Civic Centre
St Peter's Square
Wolverhampton WV1 1RR
Tel: (01902) 556556
Fax: (01902) 554218
www.wolverhampton.gov.uk

Worcestershire
Education Services
Worcestershire County Council
County Hall
Spetchley Road
Worcester WR5 2NP
Tel: (01905) 763763
Fax: (01905) 766156
www.worcestershire.gov.uk

York, City of
Education Department
City of York Council
PO Box 404
10–12 George Hudson Street
York YO1 6ZG
Tel: (01904) 613161
Fax: (01904) 554249
www.york.gov.uk

Appendix 5

CONTACT DETAILS OF LEAS IN WALES

Blaenau Gwent County Borough Council
Municipal Offices
Civic Centre
Ebbw Vale NP23 6XB
Tel: (01495) 350555
www.blaenau-gwent.gov.uk

Bridgend County Borough Council
Civic Offices
Angel Street
Bridgend CF31 1LX
Tel: (01656) 643643
www.bridgend.gov.uk

Caerphilly County Borough Council
Caerphilly Road
Ystrad Mynach
Hengoed CF82 7EP
Tel: (01443) 815588
www.caerphilly.gov.uk

Cardiff County Council
Marland House
Central Square
Cardiff CF10 1EP
Tel: (029) 2087 2087
www.cardiff.gov.uk

Carmarthenshire County Council
County Hall
Carmarthen
Carmarthenshire SA31 1JP
Tel: (01267) 234567
www.carmarthenshire.gov.uk

Ceredigion County Council
County Offices
Marine Terrace
Aberystwyth SY23 2DE
Tel: (01970) 633610
www.ceredigion.gov.uk

Conwy County Borough Council
Government Building
Dinerth Road
Colwyn Bay LL28 4UL
Tel: (01492) 542500
www.conwy.gov.uk

Denbighshire County Council
Council Offices
Wynnstay Road
Ruthin LL15 1YN
Tel: (01824) 706000
www.denbighshire.gov.uk

Flintshire County Council
County Hall
Mold CH7 6ND
Tel: (01352) 704023
www.flintshire.gov.uk

Gwynedd Council
Council Offices
Shirehall Street
Caernarfon
Gwynedd LL53 1SH
Tel: (01286) 679262
www.gwynedd.gov.uk

Isle of Anglesey County Council
Council Offices
Llanefni
Anglesey LL77 7TW
Tel: (01248) 750057
www.anglesey.gov.uk

Merthyr Tydfil County Borough Council
Civic Centre
Castle Street
Merthyr Tydfil CF47 8AN
Tel: (01685) 725000
www.merthyr.gov.uk

Monmouthshire County Council
County Hall
Cwmbran NP44 2XH
Tel: (01633) 644644
www.monmouthshire.gov.uk

Neath Port Talbot County Borough Council
Port Talbot Civic Centre
Port Talbot SA13 1PJ
Tel: (01639) 763333
www.neath-porttalbot.gov.uk

Newport County Borough Council
Civic Centre
Newport
South Wales NP20 4UR
Tel: (01633) 244491
www.newport.gov.uk

Pembrokeshire County Council
County Hall
Haverfordwest
Pembrokeshire SA61 1TP
Tel: (01437) 764551
www.pembrokeshire.gov.uk

Powys County Council
County Hall
Llandrindod Wells
Powys LD1 5LG
Tel: (01597) 826000
www.powys.gov.uk

Rhondda-Cynon-Taff County Borough Council
Education Department
Grawen Street
Porth CF39 0BU
Tel: (01443) 687666
www.rhondda-cynon-taff.gov.uk

Swansea, City and County of
County Hall
Oystermouth Road
Swansea SA1 3SN
Tel: (01792) 636000
www.swansea.gov.uk

Torfaen County Borough Council
County Hall
Floor 4
Cwmbran NP44 3LY
Tel: (01495) 762200
www.torfaen.gov.uk

Vale of Glamorgan Council
Civic Offices
Holton Road
Barry CF63 4RU
Tel: (01446) 700111
www.valeofglamorgan.gov.uk

Wrexham County Borough Council
Ty Henblas
Queens Square
Wrexham LL13 8AZ
Tel: (01978) 297401
www.wrexham.gov.uk

Appendix 6

EDUCATION AUTHORITIES IN SCOTLAND

Aberdeen City Council
St Nicholas House
Broad Street
Aberdeen AB10 1FT
Tel: (01224) 522000
www.aberdeencity.gov.uk

Aberdeenshire Council
Woodhill Road
Aberdeen AB16 5GB
Tel: 0845 606 7000
www.aberdeenshire.gov.uk

Angus Council
The Cross
Forfar
Angus DD8 1BX
Tel: (01307) 461460
www.angus.gov.uk

Argyll and Bute Council
Argyll House
Alexandra Parade
Dunoon
Argyll PA23 8AJ
Tel: (01369) 704000
www.argyll-bute.gov.uk

Clackmannanshire Council
Lime Tree House
Alloa FK10 1EX
Tel: (01259) 452514
www.clacks.gov.uk

Dumfries and Galloway Council
30 Edinburgh Road
Dumfries DG1 1NW
Tel: (01387) 260427
www.dumgal.gov.uk

Dundee City Council
Floor 8
Tayside House
Crichton Street
Dundee DD1 3RZ
Tel: (01382) 433111
www.dundeecity.gov.uk

East Ayrshire Council
Council Headquarters
Kilmarnock KA3 7BU
Tel: (01563) 576000
www.east-ayrshire.gov.uk

East Dunbartonshire Council
Tom Johnston House
Civic Way
Kirkintilloch G66 4TJ
Tel: (0141) 578 8000
www.e-dunbarton.org.uk

East Lothian Council
John Muir House
Haddington
East Lothian EH41 3HA
Tel: (01620) 827827
www.eastlothian.gov.uk

East Renfrewshire Council
Eastwood Park
Rouken Glen Road
Giffnock
East Renfrewshire G46 6UG
Tel: (0141) 577 3404
www.eastrenfrewshire.gov.uk

Edinburgh, City of
City of Edinburgh Council
Wellington Court
10 Waterloo Place
Edinburgh EH1 3EG
Tel: (0131) 469 3000
www.edinburgh.gov.uk

Falkirk Council
McLaren House
Marchmont Avenue
Polmont FK2 0NZ
Tel: (01324) 506600
www.falkirk.gov.uk

Fife Council
Fife House
North Street
Glenrothes KY7 5LT
Tel: (01592) 414141
www.fife.gov.uk

Glasgow City Council
Nye Bevan House
20 India Street
Glasgow G2 4PF
Tel: (0141) 287 2000
www.glasgow.gov.uk

Highland Council
The Highland Council
Glenurquhart Road
Inverness IV3 5NX
Tel: (01463) 702000
www.highland.gov.uk

Inverclyde Council
105 Dalrymple Street
Greenock PA15 1HT
Tel: (01475) 712824
www.inverclyde.gov.uk

Midlothian Council
Midlothian House
Buccleuch Street
Dalkeith EH22 1DN
Tel: (0131) 270 7500
www.midlothian.gov.uk

Moray Council
Council Office
High Street
Elgin
Moray IV30 1BX
Tel: (01343) 543451
www.moray.gov.uk

North Ayrshire Council
Cunninghame House
Irvine KA12 8EE
Tel: (01294) 324100
www.north-ayrshire.gov.uk

North Lanarkshire Council
Municipal Buildings
Kildonan Street
Coatbridge ML5 3BT
Tel: (01236) 812222
www.northlan.gov.uk

Orkney Islands Council
Council Offices
School Place
Kirkwall
Orkney KW15 1NY
Tel: (01856) 873535
www.orkney.gov.uk

Perth and Kinross Council
2 High Street
Perth PH1 5PH
Tel: (01738) 475000
www.pkc.gov.uk

Renfrewshire Council
Council Headquarters
North Building
Cotton Street
Paisley PA1 1BU
Tel: (0141) 842 5000
www.refrewshire.gov.uk

Scottish Borders Council
Council Headquarters
Newtown Street
Boswells
Melrose TD6 0SA
Tel: (01835) 824000
www.scotborders.gov.uk

Shetland Islands Council
Hayfield House
Hayfield Lane
Lerwick
Shetland ZE1 0QD
Tel: (01595) 744000
www.shetland.gov.uk

South Ayrshire Council
County Buildings
Wellington Square
Ayr KA7 1DR
Tel: (01292) 612000
www.south-ayrshire.gov.uk

South Lanarkshire Council
Council Offices
Almada Street
Hamilton ML3 0AE
Tel: (01698) 454545
www.southlanarkshire.gov.uk

Stirling Council
Viewforth
Stirling FK8 2ET
Tel: (01786) 443322
www.stirling.gov.uk

West Dunbartonshire Council
Garshake Road
Dumbarton G82 1HG
Tel: (01389) 737000
www.west-dunbarton.gov.uk

West Lothian Council
Lindsay House
South Bridge Street
Bathgate EH48 1TS
Tel: (01506) 776000
www.wlonline.gov.uk

Western Isles Council
Comhairle nan Eilean Siar
Sandwick Road
Stornoway
Isle of Lewis HS1 2BW
Tel: (01851) 703773
www.w-isles.gov.uk

Appendix 7

EDUCATION AND LIBRARY BOARDS IN NORTHERN IRELAND

Belfast Education and Library Board
40 Academy Street
Belfast BT1 2NQ
Tel: (028) 9056 4000
www.belb.org.uk

North Eastern Education and Library Board
County Hall
182 Galgorm Road
Ballymena
County Antrim BT42 1HN
Tel: (028) 2565 3333
www.nelb.org.uk

South Eastern Education and Library Board
Grahamsbridge Road
Dundonald
Belfast BT16 2HS
Tel: (028) 9056 6200
www.seelb.org.uk/

Southern Education and Library Board
3 Charlemont Place
The Mall
Armagh BT61 9AX
Tel: (028) 3751 2200
www.selb.org/

Western Education and Library Board
1 Hospital Road
Omagh
County Tyrone BT79 0AW
Tel: (028) 8241 1411
www.welbni.org/

Council for Catholic Maintained Schools
160 High Street
Holywood
County Down BT18 9HT
Tel: (028) 9042 6972

Appendix 8

USEFUL ADDRESSES

If you know of an organization that should be included in these pages, please e-mail your suggestion to: eh@elizabethholmes.co.uk

Job seeking

See also the contact details of LEAs or equivalent in the UK for the maintained sector. The Web site www.easea.co.uk/secure/findit.asp allows you to search for an educational establishment in the UK.

British Council
Overseas Appointment Section
Bridgewater House
58 Whitworth Street
Manchester M1 6BB
Tel: (0161) 957 7383
www.britishcouncil.org

Gabbitas Educational Consultants
Carrington House
126–130 Regent Street
London W1B 5EE
Tel: (020) 7734 0161
e-mail: admin@gabbitas.co.uk
www.gabbitas.co.uk

Independent Schools Council
Grosvenor Gardens House
35–37 Grosvenor Gardens
London SW1W 0BS
Tel: (020) 7798 1590
Fax: (020) 7798 1591
e-mail: isc@iscis.uk.net
www.iscis.uk.net

Voluntary Services Overseas (VSO)
317 Putney Bridge Road
London SW15 2PN
Tel: (020) 8780 7200
e-mail: enquiry@vso.org.uk
www.vso.org.uk

Year Out Group
Queensfield
28 Kings Road
Easterton
Wiltshire SN10 4PX
Tel: 07980 395789
e-mail: info@yearoutgroup.org
www.yearoutgroup.org

Professional associations (unions, the TUC and Redress)

Association of Teachers and Lecturers (ATL)
7 Northumberland Street
London WC2N 5RD
Tel: (020) 7930 6441
e-mail: info@atl.org.uk
www.askatl.org.uk

National Association of School Masters/Union of Women Teachers (NASUWT)
Hillscourt Education Centre
Rose Hill
Rednal
Birmingham B45 8RS
Tel: (0121) 453 6150
e-mail: membership@mail.nasuwt.org.uk
www.teachersunion.org.uk

National Union of Teachers (NUT)
Hamilton House
Mabledon Place
London WC1H 9BD
Tel: (020) 7388 6191
www.teachers.org.uk

Professional Association of Teachers (PAT)
2 St James' Court
Friar Gate
Derby DE1 1BT
Tel: (01332) 372337
e-mail: hq@pat.org.uk
www.pat.org.uk

Redress: The Bullied Teachers' Support Network
Bramble House
Mason Drive
Hook
Near Goole
East Riding of Yorkshire DN14 5NE
Tel: (01405) 764432

Trades Union Congress (TUC)
Congress House
Great Russell Street
London WC1B 3LS
Tel: (020) 7636 4030
www.tuc.org.uk

Government departments, assemblies and agencies

Commission for Racial Equality
Elliot House
10–12 Allington Street
London SW1E 5EH
Tel: (020) 7828 7022
e-mail: info@cre.gov.uk
www.cre.gov.uk

Department for Education and Skills (DfES)
Sanctuary Buildings
Great Smith Street
Westminster
London SW1P 3BT
Tel: 0870 000 2288
Publication order line: 0845 602 2260
www.dfes.gov.uk

Department of Education for Northern Ireland (DENI)
Rathgael House
43 Balloo Road
Bangor
Co Down BT19 7PR
Tel: (028) 9127 9279
e-mail: mail@deni.gov.uk
www.deni.gov.uk

Department of Trade and Industry
1 Victoria Street
London SW1H 0ET
Tel: (020) 7215 5000
e-mail: enquiries@dti.gsi.gov.uk
www.dti.gov.uk
Publication Unit: (020) 7215 6024
e-mail: pubs.unit@dti.gsi.gov.uk

**National Assembly of Wales
Education Department**
Cathays Park
Cardiff CF10 3NQ
Tel: (029) 2082 5111
www.wales.gov.uk

**Office for Standards in Education
(OFSTED)**
Alexandra House
33 Kingsway
London WC2B 6SE
Tel: (020) 7421 6744
Publications enquiries: (020) 7421
6675
www.ofsted.gov.uk

**Scottish Executive Education
Department**
Victoria Quay
Edinburgh EH6 600
Tel: (0131) 556 8400
www.scotland.gov.uk

Teacher Training Agency
Portland House
Stag Place
London SW1E 5TT
Tel: (020) 7925 3700
Teaching information line (English
speakers): 0845 6000 991
Teaching information line (Welsh
speakers): 0845 6000 992
Publication order line: 0845 606 0323
e-mail: publications@ttalit.co.uk
www.canteach.gov.uk

Subject associations

These associations offer a wealth of specialist information, resources, links and
publications. NQTs usually benefit from
savings on the cost of membership in their
first year.

Art and design
**The National Society for Education
in Art and Design**
The Gatehouse
Corsham Court
Corsham
Wiltshire SN13 0BZ
Tel: (01249) 714825
e-mail: anniegall@nsead.org
www.nsead.org

Business studies
**Economics and Business Education
Association**
1a Keymer Road
Hassocks
West Sussex BN6 8AD
Tel: (01273) 846033
www.ebea.org.uk

Citizenship
Citizenship Foundation
Ferroners House
Shaftesbury Place
Aldersgate Street
London EC2Y 8AA
Tel: (020) 7367 0500
e-mail: info@citfou.org.uk
www.citfou.org.uk

Institute for Citizenship
62 Marylebone High Street
London W1U 5HZ
Tel: (020) 7935 4777
e-mail: info@citizen.org.uk
www.citizen.org.uk

Design and technology
Design and Technology Association
16 Wellesbourne House
Walton Road
Wellesbourne
Warwickshire CV35 9JB
Tel: (01789) 470007
e-mail: data@data.org.uk
www.data.org.uk

Nuffield Primary Design and Technology
Nuffield Curriculum Project Centre
28 Bedford Square
London WC1B 3JS
Tel: (020) 7436 4412
e-mail: Primarydandt@nuffield
foundation.org
www.primarydandt.org/home/

English
National Association for the Teaching of English
50 Broadfield Road
Sheffield S8 0XJ
Tel: (0114) 255 5419
e-mail: nate.hq@btconnect.com
www.nate.org.uk

Geography
Geographical Association
160 Solly Street
Sheffield S1 4BF
Tel: (0114) 296 0088
e-mail: ga@geography.org.uk
www.geography.org.uk

Royal Geographical Society with The Institute of British Geographers
1 Kensington Gore
London SW7 2AR
Tel: (020) 7591 3000
e-mail: info@rgs.org
www.rgs.org

Geology
The Geological Society
Burlington House
Piccadilly
London W1J 0JU
Tel: (020) 7434 9944
e-mail: enquiries@geolsoc.org.uk
www.geolsoc.org.uk

History
The Historical Association
59A Kennington Park Road
London SE11 4JH
Tel: (020) 7735 3901
e-mail: enquiry@history.org.uk
www.history.org.uk

ICT
Association for ICT in Education
138 Inchmery Road
Catford
London SE6 1DF
www.acitt.digitalbrain.com

MAPE – Supporting Effective Use of ICT in Primary Education
Cilgeraint Farm
St Anns
Nr Bethesda
Gwynedd LL57 4AX
Tel: (01248) 602655
e-mail: Val.siviter@mape.org.uk
www.mape.org.uk

Mathematics
Association of Teachers of Mathematics
7 Shaftesbury Street
Derby
DE23 8YB
Tel: (01332) 346599
e-mail: atm@atm.org.uk
www.atm.org.uk

Mathematical Association
259 London Road
Leicester LE2 3BE
Tel: (0116) 221 0013
e-mail: office@m-a.org
www.m-a.org.uk

Modern foreign languages

Association for Language Learning
150 Railway Terrace
Rugby CV21 3HN
Tel: (01788) 546443
e-mail: info@all-languages.org.uk
www.languagelearn.co.uk

Centre for Language Teaching and Research
20 Bedfordbury
London WC2N 4LB
Tel: (020) 7379 5101
www.cilt.org.uk

Music

Association of British Orchestras
Enterprise House
59–65 Upper Ground
London SE1 9PQ
Tel: (020) 7261 1555
e-mail: info@abo.org.uk
www.abo.org.uk

Schools Music Association
71 Margaret Road
New Barnet
Hertfordshire EN4 9NT
Tel: (020) 8440 6919
www.schoolsmusic.org.uk

PE

The Physical Education Association of the United Kingdom
Ling House
Building 25
London Road
Reading RG1 5AQ
Tel: (0118) 931 6240
e-mail: enquiries@pea.uk.com
www.pea.uk.com

Primary education

National Association for Primary Education
University of Leicester
Moulton College
Moulton
Northampton NN3 7RR
Tel: (01604) 647646
e-mail: nationaloffice@nape.org.uk
www.nape.org.uk

RE

Christian Education
1020 Bristol Road
Selly Oak
Birmingham B29 6LB
Tel: (0121) 472 4242
e-mail: enquiries@christianeducation.org.uk
www.christianeducation.org.uk

Science

The Association for Science Education
College Lane
Hatfield
Hertfordshire AL10 0AA
Tel: (01707) 283000
www.ase.org.uk

Social sciences

Association for the Teaching of the Social Sciences
PO Box 6079
Leicester LE2 4DW
e-mail: txl@le.ac.uk
www.le.ac.uk

Special educational needs

Association of Workers for Children with Emotional and Behavioural Difficulties
Charlton Court
East Sutton
Maidstone ME17 3DQ
Tel: (01622) 843104
e-mail: awcebd@mistral.co.uk
www.awcebd.co.uk

British Association of Teachers of the Deaf
21 The Haystacks
High Wycombe
Buckinghamshire HP13 6PY
Tel: (01494) 464190
e-mail: secretary@batod.org.uk
www.batod.org.uk

British Dyslexia Association
98 London Road
Reading RG1 5AU
Tel: (0118) 966 2677
e-mail: admin@dyslexiahelp-demon.co.uk
www.bda-dyslexia.org.uk

National Association for Special Educational Needs
NASEN House
4/5 Amber Business Village
Amber Close
Amington
Tamworth B77 4RP
Tel: (01827) 311500
e-mail: welcome@nasen.org.uk
www.nasen.org.uk

Tutoring

National Association for Pastoral Care in Education
c/o Institute of Education
University of Warwick
Coventry CV4 7AL
Tel: (024) 7652 3810
e-mail: napce@warwick.ac.uk
www.warwick.ac.uk/wie/napce

Organizations concerned with emotional literacy and/or alternative education

Advisory Centre for Education (ACE)
1C Aberdeen Studios
22 Highbury Grove
London N5 2DQ
Tel: (020) 7354 8318
www.ace-ed.org.uk

Antidote: Campaign for Emotional Literacy
5th Floor
45 Beech Street
London EC2Y 8AD
Tel: (020) 7588 5151
www.antidote.org.uk

Human Scale Education
Unit 8, Fairseat Farm
Chew Stoke
Bristol BS40 8XF
Tel: (01275) 332516
e-mail: Info@hse.org.uk
www.hse.org.uk

Re:membering Education
66 Beaconsfield Villas
Brighton BN1 6HE
Tel: (01273) 239311
e-mail: remember@mcmail.com
www.remember.mcmail.com

Self-esteem Network
32 Carisbrooke Road
London E17 7EF
Tel: (020) 8521 6977
e-mail: alexander@mcrl.poptel.org.uk

Miscellaneous

Age Exchange (for work in all areas of reminiscence)
The Reminiscence Centre
11 Blackheath Village
London SE3 9LA
Tel: (020) 8318 9105
e-mail: administrator@age-exchange.org.uk
www.age-exchange.org.uk

Andrea Adams Trust (workplace bullying)
Maritime House
Basin Road North
Portslade BN14 4WA
Tel: (01273) 704900
e-mail: mail@andreaadamstrust.org
www.andreaadamstrust.org

Association for Teacher Education in Europe
Rue de la Concorde 60
B-1050 Brussels
e-mail: atee@euronet.be
www.atee.org

Behaviour UK
JDJA Education Ltd
PO Box 4067
Poole BH13 7YR
Tel: 0870 077 7177
e-mail: info@behaviouruk.com
www.behaviouruk.com

British Educational Communications and Technology Agency (BECTa)
Milburn Hill Road
Science Park
Coventry CV4 7JJ
Tel: (024) 7641 6994
e-mail: becta@becta.org.uk
www.becta.org.uk

Centre for School Standards (National Literacy and Numeracy Strategies)
60 Queens Road
Reading RG1 4BS
Tel: (0118) 902 1001
www.standards.dfes.gov.uk/literacy/
www.standards.dfes.gov.uk/numeracy/

Community Service Volunteers
237 Pentonville Road
London N1 9NJ
Tel: (020) 7278 6601
e-mail: information@csv.org.uk
www.csv.org.uk

Don't Suffer in Silence.com (bullying)
Schools Inclusion Division
DfES
Sanctuary Buildings
Great Smith Street
London SW1P 3BT
Tel: 0870 000 2288
www.dfes.gov.uk/bullying/

Employers' Organisation
Layden House
76–86 Turnmill Street
London EC1M 5LG
Tel: (020) 7296 6781
www.lg-employers.gov.uk

Equal Opportunities Commission
Arndale House
Arndale Centre
Manchester M4 3EQ
Tel: 0845 601 5901
e-mail: info@eoc.org.uk
www.eoc.org.uk

European Association of Teachers
8 Staplegrove
Shoeburyness
Essex SS3 8AQ
Tel: 01702 586622
www.aede.org

General Teaching Council for England
344–354 Gray's Inn Road
London WC1X 8BP
Tel: 0870 001 0308
e-mail: info@gtce.org.uk
www.gtce.org.uk

General Teaching Council for Scotland
Clerwood House
96 Clermiston Road
Edinburgh EH12 6UT
Tel: (0131) 314 6000
e-mail: gtcs@gtcs.org.uk
www.gtcs.org.uk

General Teaching Council for Wales
4th Floor, Southgate House
Wood Street
Cardiff CF10 1EW
Tel: (029) 2055 0350
e-mail: information@gtcw.org.uk
www.gtcw.org.uk

National Association for the Education of Sick Children
The Satellite School
Regus House
Herald Way
Pegasus Business Park
Castle Donington DE74 2TZ
Tel: (01332) 638586
www.sickchildren.org.uk

National Confederation of Parent Teacher Associations
18 St Johns Hill
Sevenoaks
Kent TN13 3NP
Tel: (01732) 748850
e-mail: info@ncpta.org.uk
www.ncpta.org.uk

National Foundation for Educational Research
The Mere
Upton Park
Slough
Berkshire SL1 2DQ
Tel: (01753) 574123
e-mail: enquiries@nfer.ac.uk
www.nfer.ac.uk

National Society for the Prevention of Cruelty to Children
National Centre
42 Curtain Road
London EC2A 3NH
Tel: (020) 7825 2500
www.nspcc.org.uk

Royal Society for the Prevention of Accidents
Rospa House
Edgbaston Park
353 Bristol Road
Birmingham B5 7ST
Tel: (0121) 248 2000
e-mail: help@ rospa.co.uk
www.rospa.co.uk

Teacher Support Line
Hamilton House
Mabledon Place
London WC1H 9BE
Tel: (020) 7554 5200
For free counselling: 08000 562 561
Teacher Support Cymru: 0800 085 5088
e-mail: customers@teachersupport.info
www.teachersupport.info

TTA Keeping In Touch Programme
PO Box 3049
Chelmsford CM1 3YT
Tel: 0845 6000 993
e-mail: helpline@kit-tta.co.uk
www.canteach.gov.uk

Appendix 9

FURTHER READING

A browse through a good bookshop or the URLs listed in this book will undoubtedly open up more possibilities for further reading. The books chosen here are good starting points to trigger your own thoughts and lines of enquiry. Do also order the relevant publications from your union (most have extensive catalogues of books, booklets and reports).

Personal issues

Stress management

Grant Viagas, B (2001) *Stress: Restoring balance to our lives*, The Women's Press, London

Hare, B (1996) *Be Assertive*, Vermilion, London

Hindle, T (1998) *Manage your Time*, Dorling Kindersley, London

Lindenfield, G and Vandenburg, M (2000) *Positive Under Pressure*, Thorsons, London

Olivier, S (2002) *500 of the Most Important Stress-Busting Tips You'll Ever Need*, Cico Books, London

Peiffer, V (1997) *Principles of Stress Management*, Thorsons, London

Rechtschaffen, S (1997) *Time Shifting*, Doubleday Books, London

Wilson, P (1998) *Calm at Work*, Penguin, London

Well-being

Alexander, J (2000) *The Energy Secret*, Thorsons, London

Baker, P (2002) *Real Health for Men*, Vega, London

Chaitow, L (1998) *Natural Alternatives to Antibiotics*, Thorsons, London

Goleman, D (1996) *The Meditative Mind*, Thorsons, London

Golten, R (1999) *The Owner's Guide to the Body*, Thorsons, London

Grant Viagas, B (2001) *Sleep: A natural guide*, The Women's Press, London

Mindell, E (1999) *Earl Mindell's Vitamin Bible for the 21st Century*, Warner Books, London

Workplace bullying

Adams, A (1992) *Bullying at Work: How to confront and overcome it*, Virago, London

Field, T (1996) *Bully in Sight*, Success Unlimited, Didcot

Teaching issues

Multiple intelligences

Buzan, T (2001) *The Power of Spiritual Intelligence*, Thorsons, London

Gardner, H (1993) *Frames of Mind*, Basic Books, New York

Gardner, H (2000) *Intelligence Reframed: Multiple intelligences for the 21st century*, Basic Books, New York

Goleman, D (1996) *Emotional Intelligence*, Bloomsbury, London

Goleman, D (1998) *Working with Emotional Intelligence*, Bloomsbury, London

Hannaford, C (1995) *Smart Moves: Why learning is not all in your head*, Great Ocean Publishers, Arlington, VA

Silver, H F, Strong, R W and Perini, M J (2000) *So Each May Learn: Integrating learning styles and multiple intelligence*, Association for Supervision and Curriculum Development, Virginia

Citizenship

Bailey, R (2000) *Teaching Values and Citizenship across the Curriculum*, Kogan Page, London

Potter, J (2002) *Citizenship and Community Learning*, Kogan Page, London

Creativity

Buzan, T (2001) *The Power of Creative Intelligence*, Thorsons, London

Cropley, A (2001) *Creativity in Education and Learning*, Kogan Page, London

Epstein, R (2000) *The Big Book of Creativity Games*, McGraw-Hill, New York

Petty, G (1997) *How to be Better at Creativity*, Kogan Page, London

Behaviour management

Faupel, A, Herrick, E and Sharp, P (1998) *Anger Management*, David Fulton, London

Hook, P and Vass, A (2000) *Confident Classroom Leadership*, David Fulton, London

Watkins, C (1998) *Managing Classroom Behaviour: A bit like air traffic control*, ATL (this is available from the Association of Teachers and Lecturers despatch section (020 7782 1584); there is a charge for non-members)

The Web site of Trinity and All Saints College, University of Leeds (www.tasc.ac.uk/) has an extensive list of phase-specific and cross-phase books on classroom management and control.

Teaching and schools

Bentley, T (1998) *Learning Beyond the Classroom*, RoutledgeFalmer, London

Craft, A *et al* (2001) *Creativity in Education*, Continuum, London

Fisher, R (1995) *Teaching Children to Think*, Stanley Thornes, Cheltenham

Fontana, D and Slack, I (2002) *Teaching Meditation to Children*, Thorsons, London

Green, C (1999) *Educational Days Out: A handbook for teachers planning a school trip*, Kogan Page, London

McCarthy, K (1998) *Learning by Heart: The role of emotional education in raising school achievement* (coordinated by Re:membering Education; a downloadable version is available at www.remember@mcmail.com/papersandresearch/lbh.html)

Smith, L and Vickers, A (1995) *Supply Teachers*, Bright Ideas series, Scholastic, Leamington Spa

The National Foundation for Education Research publishes a newsletter. To be added to the mailing list, tel: (01753) 574123 or e-mail: enquiries@nfer.ac.uk.

Prim-Ed Publishing has a good selection of photocopiable resources, merit stickers and CD ROMs etc for primary-aged classes; available from Prim-Ed Publishing UK, 4th Floor, Tower Court, Foleshill, Enterprise Park, Courtaulds Way, Coventry CV6 5NX (tel: 0870 013 1208; e-mail: sales@prim-ed.com; Web site: www.prim-ed.com).

National Curriculum

The National Curriculum Handbook for Primary Teachers in England, Stationery Office, London

The National Curriculum Handbook for Secondary Teachers in England, Stationery Office, London

National Curriculum documents are available to download from www.nc.uk.net.

Tutoring

Hartley-Brewer, E (2000) *Self-Esteem for Boys: 100 tips*, Vermilion, London

Hartley-Brewer, E (2000) *Self-Esteem for Girls: 100 tips*, Vermilion, London

Marland, M and Rogers, R (1997) *The Art of the Tutor*, David Fulton, London

Marr, N and Field, T (2001) *Bullycide: Death at playtime*, Success Unlimited, Didcot

Smallwood Publishing Group has a good selection of books for teachers on emotional literacy, self-esteem and other issues related to tutoring; available from The Old Bakery, Charlton House, Dour Street, Dover, Kent CT16 1ED (tel: 01304 226800; e-mail: k.smallwood@smallwood.co.uk; Web site: www.smallwood.co.uk).

DfES publications

Have a look at the DfES Web site (www.dfes.gov.uk) for a full list of available publications. The following list is good to start with. DfES publications are available from the Publication Centre (tel: 0845 602 2260), and the following guidance is also available to download from the DfES Web site:

- 2/98, *Reducing the Bureaucratic Burden on Teachers* – the latest School Teachers' Pay and Conditions of Employment Document;
- 582/2001, *The Induction Period for Newly Qualified Teachers*;
- 0148/2000, *Working with Teaching Assistants: A good practice guide*;
- *Health and Safety of Pupils on Educational Visits* (DfEE, 1998);
- *Supporting Pupils with Medical Needs* (DfEE, 1996);
- *Guidance on First Aid for Schools* (DfEE, 1998);
- *National Healthy School Standard* (DfES, 2001).

Education White Papers and Green Papers can be downloaded from www.dfes.gov.uk/publications/key.shtml. It is also worth browsing www.teachernet.gov.uk/publications.

TTA publications

Publications from the TTA can be ordered on 0845 6060323, or downloaded from www.canteach.gov.uk. These may be of particular interest:

- *Sex and Relationship Education Guidance Notes*;
- *Using ICT to Meet Teaching Objectives* (series by subject and phase);
- *Supporting Induction: Overview*;
- *Supporting Induction: Support and monitoring of newly qualified teachers*;
- *Supporting Induction: Assessment of the newly qualified teacher*;
- *Supporting Induction: Quality assurance of the induction arrangements*;
- *The Role of the Induction Tutor*.

OFSTED publications

Have a look at the OFSTED Web site, www.ofsted.gov.uk/public/index.htm, for a full list of available free and priced publications. OFSTED publications are available from the order line: 07002 637833 (e-mail: freepublications@ofsted.gov.uk). The following is a start:

Equal Opportunities Commission and OFSTED (1996) *The Gender Divide: Performance differences between boys and girls at school*, HMSO, London

OFSTED (1999) *Inspecting Schools: The framework*, OFSTED, London

OFSTED (1999) *Handbook for Inspecting Primary and Nursery Schools*, Stationery Office, London

OFSTED (1999) *Handbook for Inspecting Secondary Schools*, Stationery Office, London

OFSTED (1999) *Handbook for Inspecting Special Schools and Pupil Referral Units*, Stationery Office, London

Weston, P (1999) *Homework: Learning from practice*, Stationery Office, London

Appendix 10

ACRONYM BUSTER

ACCAC	Awdurdod Cymwysterau Cwricwlwm Asesu Cymru (Qualifications, Curriculum and Assessment Authority for Wales)
ACE	Arts Council of England
ACW	Arts Council of Wales
ADD	Attention Deficit Disorder
ADHD	Attention Deficit Hyperactivity Disorder
AST	Advanced Skills Teacher
BSP	Behaviour Support Plan
C School	County School
CAA	Computer-Assisted Assessment
CAL	Computer-Assisted Learning
CATs	Cognitive Ability Tests
CEG	Careers Education and Guidance
CEP	Career Entry Profile
CPD	Continuing Professional Development
CRE	Commission for Racial Equality
CTC	City Technology Colleges
D&T	Design and Technology
DfES	Department for Education and Skills (formerly known as the Department for Education and Employment)
DHFETE	Department of Higher and Further Education Training and Employment (Northern Ireland)
EA	External Assessor
EAL	English as an Additional Language
EAZ	Education Action Zone
EBD	Emotional and Behavioural Difficulties
EDP	Educational Development Plan
EFL	English as a Foreign Language
EiC	Excellence in Cities

ELWa	Education and Learning Wales
EMTAG	Ethnic Minority and Traveller Achievement Grant
ESL	English as a Second Language
ESO	Education Supervision Order
ESOL	English as a Second or Other Language
Estyn	Her Majesty's Inspectorate for Education and Training in Wales
ESW	Education Social Worker
EY	Early Years
FEI	Further Education Institution
FHE	Further and Higher Education
FSM	Free School Meals
FTE	Full-Time Equivalent
GEST	Grants for Education, Support and Training (from the National Assembly for Wales)
GRTP	Graduate and Registered Teacher Programmes
GTCE	General Teaching Council for England
GTCS	General Teaching Council for Scotland
GTCW	General Teaching Council for Wales
HEADLAMP	Headteachers' Leadership and Management Programme
HEI	Higher Education Institution
HI	Hearing Impaired
HMI	Her Majesty's Inspectors
HoD	Head of Department
HoS	Head of School
HoY	Head of Year
HSC	Health and Safety Commission
HSE	Health and Safety Executive
IAP	Individual Action Plan
ICT	Information and Communications Technology
IEP	Individual Education Plan
IiP	Investors in People
IiYP	Investors in Young People
INSET	In-Service Education and Training
ITE	Initial Teacher Education
ITT	Initial Teacher Training
JMI	Junior, Middle and Infant
KS	Key Stage
LEA	Local Education Authority
LPSH	Leadership Programme for Serving Headteachers
LSU	Learning Support Unit
MFL	Modern Foreign Language
MLD	Moderate Learning Difficulties

NafW	National Assembly for Wales
NATED	National Assembly Training and Education Department
NC	National Curriculum
NFER	National Foundation for Educational Research
NGfL	National Grid for Learning
NHDP	National Headship Development Programme
NLS	National Literacy Strategy
NNP	National Numeracy Project
NNS	National Numeracy Strategy
NOF	New Opportunities Fund
NoR	Number on Roll
NPQH	National Professional Qualification for Headship
NQT	Newly Qualified Teacher
NRA	National Record of Achievement
NTA	Non-Teaching Assistant
OFSTED	Office for Standards in Education
OTT	Overseas-Trained Teacher
PANDA	Performance and Assessment Report
PHIP	Professional Headship Induction Programme
PI	Performance Indicators
PM	Performance Management
PMLD	Profound and Multiple Learning Difficulties
PoS	Programme of Study
PRP	Performance-Related Pay
PRU	Pupil Referral Unit
PSE	Personal and Social Education
PSHE	Personal, Social and Health Education
PSLD	Physical and Severe Learning Difficulties
PSP	Pastoral Support Programme
PT	Part Time
PTR	Pupil Teacher Ratio
QCA	Qualifications and Curriculum Authority
QTS	Qualified Teacher Status
RI/RgI	Registered Inspector
RoA	Record of Achievement
SAC	Scottish Arts Council
SACRE	Standing Advisory Council for Religious Education
SAO	School Attendance Order
SCD	Severe Communication Difficulties
SDP	School Development Plan
SEN	Special Educational Needs
SENCO	Special Educational Needs Coordinator

SLD	Severe Learning Difficulties
SLT	Senior Leadership Team
SMT	Senior Management Team
SNA	Special Needs Assistant
SOC	School Organization Committee
SRE	Sex and Relationship Education
SSE	School Self-Evaluation
STA	Specialist Teacher Assistants
STRB	School Teachers Review Body
TA	Teaching Assistant
TTA	Teacher Training Agency
TUC	Trades Union Congress
UK NARIC	National Academic Recognition Information Centre for the United Kingdom
VA	Voluntary-Aided
VC	Voluntary-Controlled
VI	Visually Impaired
VLE	Virtual Learning Environment

References

Ballard, J (1982) *Circlebook*, Irvington Inc, New York

Department for Education and Employment (DfEE) (1998) *Section 550A of the Education Act 1996: The use of force to control or restrain pupils*, Circular 10/98, DfEE, London

DfEE (1999) *Meet the Challenge*, Standards and Effectiveness Unit, DfEE, London

DfEE (2001) *Learning and Teaching: A strategy for professional development*, DfEE, London

Department for Education and Skills (DfES) (2001a) *School Teachers' Pay and Conditions of Employment 2001, Revised Guidance*, DfES, London

DfES (2001b) *The Induction Period for Newly Qualified Teachers*, DfES, London

Equal Opportunities Commission and Office for Standards in Education (OFSTED) (1996) *The Gender Divide*, Stationery Office, London

General Teaching Council for England (2002a) *Code of Professional Values and Practice for Teachers*, www.gtce.org.uk

General Teaching Council for England (2002b) *The Professional Learning Framework*, www.gtce.org.uk

Goleman, D (1998) *Working with Emotional Intelligence*, Bloomsbury, London

Hannaford, C (1995) *Smart Moves: Why learning is not all in your head*, Great Ocean Publishers, Arlington, VA

Mindell, E (1985) *The Vitamin Bible*, 2nd edn, Arlington Books, London

OFSTED (1999) *Inspecting Schools: The framework (effective from January 2000)*, OFSTED, London

Rechtschaffen, S (1996) *Time Shifting*, Rider Books, London

Teacher Training Agency (TTA) and DfES (2002) *Standards for the Award of Qualified Teacher Status*, TTA/DfES, London

Weston, P (1999) *Homework: Learning from practice*, Stationery Office, London

Wilson, P (1997) *Calm at Work*, Penguin Books, London

Index